Modern Hebrew Poetry

Modern Hebrew Poetry

A BILINGUAL ANTHOLOGY

Edited and translated by Ruth Finer Mintz

UNIVERSITY OF CALIFORNIA PRESS

BERKELEY AND LOS ANGELES

שירה עברית חדשה

אנתולוגיה דו-לשונית

מתורגמת וערוכה בידי רות פיינר מינץ

הוצאת האוניברסיטה של קליפורניה

ברקלי ולוס אנג׳לס

University of California Press
Berkeley and Los Angeles, California

University of California Press, Ltd.
London, England

© 1966 by The Regents of the University of California

The Hebrew texts of the poems are copyrighted © 1966 by Acum, Ltd., Israel
Library of Congress Catalog Card Number: 65-19246

Designed by Harvey Satenstein

Printed in the United States of America

Reissued 1982
ISBN 0-520-04781-8

4 5 6 7 8 9

ליאל
לרנה, לאביבה ושלום

for Yale
and for Rena, Aviva, and Shalom

To find no contradiction in the union of old and new;
to contemplate the Ancient of Days and all His works
with feelings as fresh as if all had then sprang forth
at the first creative fiat; characterizes the mind that
feels the riddle of the world, and may help to unravel it.

Samuel Taylor Coleridge
Biographia Literaria

Out of the dead letters welled forth songs of life.
"And If the Angel Should Ask"
Hayyim Nahman Bialik

Laugh, laugh at all the dreams
I the dreamer say to you
That I believe in man
Because I still believe in you.
"Credo"
Saul Tchernichovsky

PREFACE

The twentieth century has seen the destruction of the Jewish communities and cultural centers in Europe. It has also witnessed the reconstruction of national life and the contemporary renaissance of the Hebrew language in Israel. The tension of this struggle from Europe to Israel, in a pull of death and life, is forcefully expressed in the Hebrew poetry that again fashioned a vital idiom and flourished during this period. The individual eye and the personal voice of the modern Hebrew poet were marked by a particular sensibility to the spirit of this time. In the expression of both the individual and the group will to live, the modern Hebrew poet has been an animating force in reshaping the Hebrew language for its contemporary function.

My initial interest in the aesthetic impact of modern Hebrew poetry has been continually reinforced by experiences and insights which it communicated to me and which I wished to share. This, then, is a personal selection of poems which I have translated into English. I did not undertake a definitive presentation of modern Hebrew poetry, but rather an introduction to its general perspectives and its individual perceptions and forms. In a critical sense, however, I do believe that each poem is representative of a basic aspect of each poet's work.

I should like to call attention to the fact that I have not included any of the Hebrew poetry written in the United States during this time. I believe this poetry merits its own separate consideration.

With regard to translation, I have sought to be accurate rather than literal, to maintain the integrity of the poem as a whole, and to keep the vividness of imagery as well as its associative implication. Because Hebrew poetry is not written for the eye alone, I attempted, through the barriers that divide an inflected language from an analytic language, to respect the personal ear and rhythm of the poet or to find appropriate cadences. While I have used rhyme in many places, I have also been satisfied with assonances that echoed the connective function of the sound pattern. In some poems I found it necessary to abandon rhyme. I have worked to keep both the ideas and the emotional tension of the poem, and where I fell short of my aims in this respect, I omitted poems that I would have liked to include in this volume.

It has been a sustaining thought that my translations might interest those who are concerned for poetry and with poetry to venture into an old and new province within the domain of world literature—that of Hebrew poetry.

To the poets represented in this volume I express my appreciation for their generous permission to appear in my translation. To the heirs of the deceased poets I add my thanks. To ACUM Limited (Société d'Auteurs, Compositeurs et Editeurs de Musique en Israel; Membre de la "CISAC"), Israel, I am obliged for their extremely generous cooperation in granting permission for this use of Hebrew texts under their copyright, © 1966 Acum Ltd., Israel.

I also wish to acknowledge the kind cooperation of the following journals which first published versions of a number of the translations included here: *Inferno* (San Francisco), *Poetry* (Chicago), *Focus* (Jerusalem), and *Israel Argosy* (Jerusalem).

I wish to express my appreciation to Professor Shimon Halkin of the Hebrew University, Jerusalem, for encouraging me to go on with my translations. His teaching has contributed much to my understanding of Hebrew poetry. I wish also to thank Professor Wolf Leslau of the Department of Near Eastern and African Languages at the University of California, Los Angeles, for suggesting that I submit this manuscript. And I am bound to express my obligations to Dr. Arnold Band, Professor of Modern Hebrew Literature at the University of California, Los Angeles, for his careful reading of these poems. His guidance on problems involved in their translation has added immeasurably to their final form. The Introduction has been kindly read by Professors Isaac E. Barzilay, of Columbia University; Judah Goldin, of Yale University; and Wolf Leslau, of the University of California, Los Angeles; and also by Professors Hugh G. Dick and John J. Espey of the English Department of the University of California, Los Angeles. I have benefited from all their comments. Acknowledgement of indebtedness, however, in no way transfers the responsibility, which I am glad to accept.

I am doubly indebted to my husband Yale, whose continued interest has made possible the free time for this work and whose advice on technical matters has been invaluable. I must also commend my children for their patience generously sustained for the sake of this volume, and mention Rena in particular for her help in discovering the original locations of Biblical and Talmudic references hidden in the poems. I am grateful also to Shlomo Tussman for his help in reading the Hebrew proof, and to Nettie Lipton and my daughter Aviva for reading the English proof.

Finally, I wish to note with appreciation the interest and help of R. Y. Zachary, Editor of the Los Angeles Office of the University of California Press, and to add a word of thanks to Geoffrey Ashton, also of that office. And I am grateful to Bettina Klaus for her secretarial care of this manuscript.

Los Angeles   R. F. M.

CONTENTS

ת ו כ ן

xi

III THE MODERNISTS

III   המודרניזם העברי

INTRODUCTION

Modern Hebrew poetry grew out of the period of the Hebrew Renaissance whose pre-Palestinian development spanned the years between 1880 and 1920. It was distinguished from the poetry of the Enlightenment or Haskalah Period (1750–1880) by a more flexible style, characterized by more immediate imagery, and by an individual and personal tone. After 1920 it mirrored the transition of Hebrew from a refined literary tongue to that of an active, spoken language, echoing the cadences of a developing vernacular speech.

Born in a period of great doubt and pessimism, modern Hebrew poetry faced the disintegration of ghetto life in Eastern Europe and alienation from Jewish values in Western Europe. For all its rationalism and universal aspirations, modern Hebrew literature was rooted in the forms of an age-old religious civilization. Although it championed the Europeanization of Jewish life against the opposition of the most adamant orthodox elements, both Rabbinic and Hassidic, it was concerned with harmonizing secular ideology with the spirit of tradition in order to assure the continuity of Jewish identity and creativity in a modern world.

While the philosophical and publicist aspects of modern Hebrew literature came, in time, to actively embrace Zionism, poetry remained only passively Zionist. The first modern poets had not been active in political or social movements. Some considered themselves socialists, but most thought of themselves as lovers of Zion, even when they did not advocate a direct return to Palestine. Until 1920 their primary concern was Hebrew letters, which remained for them the lifeblood of the Jewish people. When, however, they saw that Jewish life in Eastern Europe was doomed, they had little faith in its creative existence anywhere except in Palestine. At the end of World War I, the Hebrew poets began to arrive in Palestine as part of the third wave of immigration.

Modern Hebrew poetry is humanistic in intention, although it is not entirely secular in character. It is personal rather than parochial but responds to the social stimulation of immediate atmosphere and world environment. It struggles to comprehend the whole three thousand years of Jewish history as they relate to contemporary Jewish life.

Schoolchildren in Israel today read "The Song of Deborah" and "The Song of the Sea," which are among the earliest poems recorded in the Hebrew Bible and were written down in approximately the eleventh century Before the Common Era (B.C.E.). These songs are studied not as archaic texts or primarily classical forms but rather as lyric and epic sources of a living language. For students who begin to read the Bible in the second grade, it is a contemporary book, both literature and history. Though biblical idiom is familiar, the language, however, is already strange, for Hebrew is the only language that is at once classical and modern. The difference between the Hebrew of the Bible and modern Hebrew is small compared with the difference between classical and modern Greek even though the Hebrew language has changed constantly during the more than three thousand years of its existence. These changes have created literary styles and new genres which have nurtured an ongoing and changing poetic tradition.

From its earliest beginning Hebrew poetry extended its unique creative scope and native individual forms through an awareness of the literary genres of the larger environments of which it was a part. Biblical forms and newly developed Hebraic forms were later merged by modern Hebrew poets with those of European poetry. However, without a knowledge of the Bible it is still hardly possible to read modern Hebrew poetry with a complete awareness of its associations in language, imagery, and themes.

Forceful brevity was characteristic of biblical poetry. It was accentual and unrhymed, but distinguished from prose by a marked rhythm and parallel structure, and its vocabulary was sharply imagistic. The Bible evolved as a collection of writings characterized by the moral view and the socioreligious purpose that pervaded the entire body of work, but which could, of course, also be read as a body of connected but independent works. To define basically Semitic styles in terms of Indo-European forms is at best an interesting exercise; nonetheless, one finds forms that can be fairly called the ode, the song, the idyl, the elegy, the meditation, the epithalamium, the hymn, and the threnody. The prophetic books have lyrical elements in a context of prose, but frequently consist of poetry of dramatic symbolism.

Following the return of the Jews from Babylonian exile in the sixth century B.C.E., Mishnaic Hebrew, a new prose style, first broadened the base of the Hebrew language to include a secular vocabulary concerned specifically with occupations, habits, and problems of daily life. Mishnaic Hebrew was a development of biblical Hebrew, richly colored by the colloquial Aramaic that was the international language in the Middle East during this time. Although classical Hebrew dominated poetic writings, the body of literature that Mishnaic Hebrew fostered (Mishnah, Talmud, Midrash, Liturgy, and Mystic Writings) later nourished the developing poetic styles.

The long period of codifying biblical law ended in 200 C.E., and the final form in which it was edited was called the *Mishnah* (review). For the next two to three hundred years this served as a focus of intense study both in Jerusalem and in Babylon, which had again become a large center of Jewish population.

Talmud was Mishnah with commentary. The Jerusalem Talmud was rich in legal, ethical, and legendary writings but it was the wider scope of the Babylonian Talmud that encompassed the communal and social life of the various Jewish communities for many centuries. As a source of Jewish law it recorded what was known of medicine, astronomy, agriculture, history, and geography. Finally edited in 500 C.E., the Babylonian Talmud, like the Jerusalem Talmud, was composed of two basic, related elements: the body of the derived law called *Halakhah*, and the body of legend called *Aggadah*.

Aggadah extended back to biblical times and was saturated with the Palestine environment. It had many facets in both content and form. Principles of faith, moral instructions, words of comfort, and a vision of the ideal world of the future were its concerns. Rich in literary forms, it included parable and allegory, personification and metaphor, lyric and song, lament and prayer, satire and polemic, idyllic story and dramatic colloquy. Word play, acrostic and number symbolism were also to be found in the variety of its aspects. Large portions of the Talmud are Aggadaic, although there is little Aggadah in the Mishnah. Scattered throughout the Talmud, Aggadah mingled indiscriminately with Halakhah. The whole of Aggadah can, in a way, be regarded as a popular mythology of the Jewish Universe, and all strata of society come under its magical yet critical appraisal.

Midrash, originally a form of oral exposition of biblical text, also combined the critical technique of textual analysis with the skill of creative imagination. Teachers used this method to shape the illustrative parables and poetic interpretations bringing new insights to the Jewish conceptions of the nature of man, the world, and their relationship to each other and to God. Midrashic literature, which consists almost entirely of Aggadah, grew over a period of a thousand years in countries of various religions and cultures and shows traces of the influences of different periods and localities; thus, Platonic, Stoic, and Pythagorean ideas are reflected as well as popular superstitions and beliefs from Babylon. Included in Midrashic literature were other Rabbinic books containing biblical interpretations in the spirit of Aggadah. All of

Midrash was a source of rich imagery and highly charged language. Of particular relevance to poetry was the *Pirke de-Rabbi Eliezer,* which concerned itself with the period from the creation of the world to the wandering of the Israelites in the Wilderness. The arrangement and preservation in written form of Midrash began probably as early as the period of Tannaim, the teachers of the Mishnah; however, there is no extant Aggadaic work edited before the fourth century C.E. About the end of the tenth century the work of editing and arranging the Midrashim came to an end. Jacob Ibn Haviv collected the Aggadaic portions of the Talmud in his *Ein Yaakov*, which remained popular reading until modern times. As a folk source Midrash enriched all of Hebrew poetry. The first major modern Hebrew poet, Hayyim Nahman Bialik, worked to successfully reëdit these texts for contemporary readers.

While the Bible remained the primary text of instruction for young children and the Talmud remained the text of erudite scholarship, after the fifth century C.E. Hebrew became a literary language spoken only by the learned. The mass of Jews, however, still used Hebrew three times daily in their prayer service. Preserved segments of early prayers recorded in Talmud and Midrash later became the core of the liturgy.

In its earliest post-biblical form, lyric poetry, essentially the expression of individual feeling, was devotional. This new genre, called *Piyyut*, emerged in Palestine between the fifth and seventh centuries C.E. It is interesting to note the aesthetic impact of the poetry of Yanai and Kalir as it appears in contemporary liturgy. The forms used by Kalir were related to the Byzantine poetry of his own time. These Byzantine hymns had been based on prevalent Greco-Roman melody types, but they had also borrowed liberally from the Psalms and Canticles, and freely included Hebrew melodies.

From the ninth to the twelfth century, Hebrew poets were composing Piyyut in Babylon, North Africa, Spain, Italy,

Provence, northern France, and Germany. In the provinces of northern Europe where continual disasters threatened Jewish life, Piyyut formed threnody and dirge, penitential hymn, and martyrology, but in the Mediterranean countries it expressed exalted elegy, songs of praise, celebration of season, and festival. In Provence and Germany, Piyyut was marked in form and musical setting by the troubadors and minnesingers, but in southern countries it showed the influence of Arab prosody. Stimulated by new poetic usages and philosophic imagery, some of the noblest Piyyutim were composed in twelfth-century Spain and sixteenth-century Palestine. In these countries, as in eighth-century Babylon, this poetry was enriched by Jewish mysticism.

The daring imagery of Piyyut had already extended convention. Piyyut succeeded in creating a new poetic language whose new usuages did not always please linguists and whose imagery and daring anthropomorphism did not always suit orthodox pietists. The body of genuine lyric expression it created was an example of a new trend within traditional framework. Originally written as a personal medium of expression, its significant influence lay in the fact that it did not remain in the exclusive province of literature, but was drawn into the familiar and functional areas of common usage through its place in the liturgies of the various Jewish communities.

Apocalyptic and esoteric writings had been part of Jewish tradition since earliest biblical times. Midrash and Aggadah were rich with related fragments; but a broadening and deepening of this interest in mysticism took place in Moslem Spain, where all major areas of inquiry were broadened and the general environment favored education. Literature and philosophy flourished as did mathematics and the sciences. Here too classical Cabbala was further developed. For the Cabbalists, Halakhah never became a province of thought in which they felt themselves strangers. In their interpretation of the Laws, of religious commandments, they did not represent them as allegories of more or less profound ideas but rather as the performance of a secret rite, or mystery, in the same sense in which the term was used by the ancients. As for Aggadah, the Cabbalists lived in a world historically continuous with it, and they were able to enhance it in a spirit of mysticism. Aggadaic productivity had been a constant element of Cabbalistic literature. *The Zohar* (The Book of Splendor) was the unique work of Moses De Leon in twelfth-century Spain.

After the Jewish community was expelled from Christian Spain in 1492, Safed, in Palestine, became the center of Jewish mysticism and a gathering place for poets, mystics, and philosophers. There the philosophy of Isaac Luria was formed. Lurian Cabbala had a pronounced influence upon Jewish life in Eastern Europe through Hassidism, which later evolved in the eighteenth century as a religious folk movement. The attitudes and outlooks of Hassidism remained active through modern times and permeated the childhood environment of many modern Hebrew poets.

Secular Hebrew poetry began to develop in the tenth century C.E. Adopting the conventions of Arabic literature, Hebrew poets approached the secular mode through its popular themes. However, the outstanding Hebrew poet-philosophers who lived in Moslem Spain from the tenth through twelfth centuries went beyond a merely conventional style; they not only were gifted in structuring language and developing ideas but also in evoking the imagery of human emotions and the tensions of human existence. Their wide scope and variety of forms influenced Hebrew poetry for four hundred years. While they sang of the beauty of nature, the nobility of love, friendship, and valor, their religious conscience could not abide a peaceful existence at a time when Europe was filled with Jewish persecution. A dominant theme in their poetry was a personal longing for Zion which often spoke with nationalistic intensity. The lyric, philosophic, and liturgical poetry of Solomon Ibn Gabirol and Yehuda

Halevi—indeed the entire body of poetry of this great Spanish period—was considered an important legacy for modern poets by both Bialik and Tchernichovsky.

After the Spanish center was destroyed, the restrictions placed upon Jewish communities in northern France and Germany almost muted their poetic voices for over two hundred years. It was within the atmosphere of the growing Italian Renaissance that Hebrew poetry shaped its humanistic voice. Although the Renaissance brought no release from the Ghetto for the Jews, persecutions were never severe in Italy, and general culture penetrated ghetto walls, allowing Jewish life to move closer to that of the general environment. The fortunate combinations of traditional Jewish scholarship and broad secular studies were again possible in Italy as they had been in Babylon and Moorish Spain. From the fifteenth century active groups of Hebrew writers and poets were discarding the Arabic modes and using Italian forms. It is necessary here to mention two important poets of the Italian period: Immanuel Haromi and Moses Hayyim Luzzato. Immanuel Haromi (of Rome), the thirteenth-century poet-physician, wrote secular, humanistic poetry. Still using Arabic forms, the *Mahberet*, or Notebook of Immanuel, was a collected work organized in the genre of the Arabic *maqua-ma*. In it the poetry demonstrated a variety of styles: lyric, epigram, sonnet, and poetic prose. Haromi's lyrics and love poetry were experimental, and he was the first Hebrew poet of his time to compose erotic verse. He also constructed the Hebrew sonnet in the Italian manner, with two quatrains and two tercets; among his work is an elegy mourning Dante's death. Saul Tchernichovsky, the poet-physician of the twentieth century—the first distinctly modern Hebrew poet—claimed Immanuel Haromi as his poet-ancestor.

It has been suggested that modern Hebrew poetry began in the eighteenth century with the diversified experimental poetry of Moses Hayyim Luzzato, who also lived in Italy. He had freed himself completely from Arabic meters, reshaped biblical lyric forms in his own style, and used Italian forms freely. Retaining aspects of medieval Hebrew rhyme, he created interesting new combinations. His lyrics were important in the Europeanization of Hebrew poetry, as was his translation of Don Luiz Vaz de Camões from the Portuguese. Actually Luzzato was a transitional figure in modern Hebrew poetry. A cabbalist and mystic pietist, he also wrote pastoral, allegorical dramas celebrating the sense of metaphysical wonder in his contemplation of the universe. It was his basically secular poetry, however, which was emulated by poets of the next hundred years. He also reawakened poetic interest in biblical poetry as he pointed the direction to a renascent humanism in Hebrew creativity.

Although Hebrew remained for the most part a literary language, we have evidence from the writings of these periods that Hebrew continued to be spoken sporadically in Palestine and in some countries of the Jewish dispersion. The degree of usage as a spoken language varied according to place and circumstance. In Europe—particularly in Italy, France, and Germany, where diverse languages divided national groups—Jews maintained Hebrew as a means of communication. They used Hebrew not only as a sacred language and as a literary instrument but also as the language of correspondence. That Hebrew was spoken in Jerusalem we know from the writings of Jewish and non-Jewish travelers. In Italy, Jewish intellectuals conversed in Hebrew. And in Holland, at the school where Spinoza was educated in Amsterdam, Hebrew was used as the language of instruction beyond the fifth grade. Through the seventeenth and eighteenth centuries Hebrew education was continued throughout the Jewish world.

By the middle of the eighteenth century, large centers of Jewish population were concentrated in Germany and Austria and in the countries of Eastern Europe. Still separated by social and economic restrictions from the general environment, Jews in the ghettos and in the "pales of settlement" found a glimmering of hope in the new spirit of science and in the libertarian impetus of various emerging nationalisms. In Germany the Jewish philosopher Moses Mendelssohn crystallized the ideology of a growing movement called the Haskalah or Enlightenment, which for the next one hundred and fifty years affected the westernization of the Jewish communities of Europe. In deference to the growing economic status of the Jewish communities, political reforms in Germany and Austria opened universities to Jews. These first scholars of the Haskalah relinquished not only archaic tradition but also their Jewish identity. They met every requirement including baptism to achieve entrée to what they considered to be the superior societies of Berlin and Vienna. This tendency explains the initial opposition of religious leaders to Haskalah.

The first attempts of the movement in Russia also followed the Austrian-German pattern. However, owing to the oppressive economic and social restrictions that shaped Jewish life in Eastern Europe until the twentieth century, the masses of Jews in Eastern Europe approached the modern world by a different path.

Elijah Gaon, the revered Rabbinic genius of the eighteenth-century Jewish city of Vilna in Lithuania, emerged as a strong champion of the blending of traditional learning with scientific study. It was he who insisted on a broader intellectual perspective for Jewish scholarship, as in earlier times. "Those who have no secular learning," he said, "do not even know Torah." He also insisted upon basing Jewish learning upon a rigorously critical study of texts, rather than upon traditional interpretations alone.

While this new attitude toward learning was filling an intellectual vacuum, the Hassidic movement developed to fill a growing spiritual void. The founder of Hassidism, Israel Baal Shem Tov (the Beloved Master of the Good Name), was concerned with human problems rather than with systems of learning. Accepting all the traditional obligations of the Jewish religion, he by-passed Rabbinic implications and interpreted Jewish reality in his own way. For an oppressed folk beset by poverty, he stressed humane instead of intellectual values. He denied the virtue of asceticism—physical and intellectual—and reiterated the sanctity of the human body and the natural desires. He united the ritual of melody and dance to the ritual of food and drink communally shared, and he reaffirmed not marriage alone but the sex act as a sacrament. For him the natural world was a miracle in process of continual creation. His concept of piety and community stressed reverence and enthusiasm for life, love for the Creator, for the creatures of the earth, and for the Jewish people. In the community of suffering, salvation was not possible; he proclaimed the community of joy.

Hassidism served to unify the fragmented lives of a crumbling people with a concept of wholeness. Keeping the Jews within the boundaries of religious tradition a hundred years longer, it possibly also kept them from physical dissolution. Classical Jewish mysticism had understood that men and the world had grown increasingly alienated from each other and from the source of life because of physical limitations and spiritual barriers. But Cabbala, like all secret philosophies, had been limited to a sensitive few. Hassidism as a folk movement applied the Lurian concept of *Tikkun* (mending) as a way of life based upon a more democratic principle of responsibility and hope. Hassidism's view brought Jews to a reconsideration of nature and natural existence, and reaffirmed the dignity of manual labor. It made the return to Zion—a millennial hope that had persisted in prophecy, liturgy, and messianic movements—a contingency for personal as well as communal redemption. One hundred years before the crystallization of this ideal into the secular concept of Zionism, three hundred followers of Israel Baal Shem Tov left Russia (in 1777) after the death of their master and teacher, to return to Palestine.

Classical Cabbala influenced the poetry of the Middle Ages,

of Spain, and of Safed, but it was Hassidism that influenced modern Hebrew poetry. The literature of Hassidism was relatively small and inaccessible, and it influenced poetry not through its themes but rather through its outlook. Poland, Galicia, southern Russia, Hungary, and Lithuania were the environments of Hassidism until after World War I. These, too, were the childhood environments from which came a great number of the first modern Hebrew poets. Most of them no longer accepted orthodox dogma or ritual, but they did remain within the social ethic of the Jewish faith. The ability of the modern Hebrew poets to visualize transcendent concepts in concrete images, to see positive creative forces immanent in nature, in man, and in society may be largely derived from the outlook of Hassidism. Song, Hassidism taught, is a ladder whereby man comes to a heightened consciousness. It has many rungs and must descend into dark depths before it can rise to luminous heights. It unites what is above with what is below and it evokes forms yet unseen. Great is the song composed of words and melodies, greater is the song in which melody suffices, but greatest is the song that needs neither words nor music.

From the early days of the Enlightenment a positive element in this ambivalent secular movement was the creation of an active secular literature. Hebrew writers concentrated on the translation of European poetry, particularly from the German into Hebrew, and they wrote quantities of original poetry. The style of this early Haskalah poetry related directly to the movement away from Talmudic language and Rabbinic style. Fabricated out of biblical phrases ingeniously linked, the new poetic style called *Melitzah* produced an artificial and ornamental genre. Long narratives, extended philosophic meditations, and exalted odes and elegies were characteristic of this poetry.

By 1850 protagonists of the later Haskalah movement were looking not so much for avenues of escape from tradition as for instruments for the reconstruction of Jewish values. In Odessa,

Petersburg, Vilna, and Warsaw, important literary circles were formed. At first, critical essay and satire dominated the belles-lettres of this period, but the short story and the novel began to develop as Hebrew genres. Under the influence of the developing prose techniques of the pioneer masters of the satiric prose story such as Mendele, and the craftsmanship of novelists, short-story writers, and essayists such as Peretz, Smolenskin, and Ahad Haam, the language of Hebrew poetry slowly became less stylized and stilted. Although it leaned to satire and polemic and still followed the earlier forms, the poetry of this later Haskalah period indicated the approaching change. Micah Joseph Lebenson wrote lyric poetry with a marked personal quality. Judah Leib Gordon was among the first to abandon the purely biblical language for a more natural synthesis. His poems were satirically realistic and portrayed the actualities of ghetto life. David Frishman's critical studies were the first Hebrew language introduction to the world of universal values, and his influence moved Hebrew literature away from a generalized view of the social environment to a concern for the inner lives of individuals. He wrote relatively few poems, but these combined lyric with legend and shaped the redemptive hope with charm and imagination.

By 1880, industrial changes had brought factories into the Jewish Pale in Russia and had developed a working class. Against a general background of widespread unrest throughout the Russian territories, the government-instigated pogroms in 1881–1882 spread massacre through Jewish Towns. Early hopes for liberalized laws came to nothing. On the contrary, greater economic restrictions spurred the socialist movement among the Jews. The developing Zionist movement sent the first *aliyah*, or wave of immigration, to Palestine, and more political upheavals in 1905 spurred a second wave of immigration. The years of World War I and the Bolshevik Revolution brought more terror to the Jewish communities of Russia, Poland, and Galicia.

Among the men who had gone to Palestine with the second aliyah in 1905 was Aron David Gordon. He was almost fifty when he joined Dagania, the first kibbutz or collective agricultural settlement, founded on the shores of the Sea of Galilee. The ideas of this group, who later became the backbone of social and political leadership in Palestine, were crystallized in the life and writings of A. D. Gordon. A secular Jew, Gordon believed that physical labor was a religious act and that work, as a redemptive process for the body and spirit of man, was holy. His writings developed this idea and influenced the generation that came in the 'twenties and the 'thirties. They believed, with him, that only those who loved a land enough to build it with their hands might call it the motherland. The young poets who came to Palestine after World War I, determined to be laborers, were all responding to Gordon's ideal. Later, when they turned to literary pursuits, their first experiences had shaped their poetry and filled it with Gordon's love for the land.

In the third wave of immigration after 1920, the Hebrew poets began to arrive singly in Palestine. Bialik and Tcherni-chovsky were already fifty years old. Cohen, Fichman, and Shimoni were in their middle forties, and they continued to work as editors, publishers, and poets. Karni and Hameiri were in their mid-thirties and became journalists for the new daily newspapers. Younger poets such as Greenberg, Shlonsky, and Lamdan had already been published in Hebrew journals in Europe, but they came to be workers rather than writers. S. Shalom and Amir Gilboa were not yet twenty when they arrived, and they did manual labor before they began to write their first poetry. Alterman was the first among the poets to complete his secondary education in Palestine.

For all of these poets Hebrew was the literary language of childhood. Whatever language they spoke at home, many of them began traditional Hebrew studies at the age of four and followed Talmudic disciplines until they were fifteen. Even those educated in modern schools were studying Hebrew at the age of eight. Nearly all of the Hebrew poets in the first part of the twentieth century were born in Eastern Europe. The secondary influences and social and literary ideologies that colored their writings were derived from their Slavic environment. Classic literatures as well as French, German, Italian, and English poetry reached them in their secular, secondary studies. A few began writing poetry in other languages, and for them Hebrew was the language of creative choice; for most, however, Hebrew was as natural as thought.

It is necessary to mention here the change that occurred in the Hebrew language during the first forty years of its modern existence. Hebrew was not firmly established as the unquestionable language of instruction in the schools of Palestine until 1918 when the Hebrew University in Jerusalem was founded. But as early as 1904, the Language Committee of the Teachers' Organization of Palestine was charged with the responsibility of fixing the pronounciation, the spelling, and the coining of new words.

The Ashkenazic pronounciation had been developed over the centuries by Jews living in Germanic and Slavic countries, and it had determined the mode of the early secular Hebrew poetry as well as that of the first modern Hebrew poetry. Sephardic pronounciation was still the common usage of Jews who had returned to Palestine from Middle Eastern, Oriental, and North African countries. The Language Committee of the Teachers' Organization designated the Sephardic pronounciation of Hebrew as the official one for the country, because it was thought to be closer to the phonics of the language spoken in pre-exilic Palestine. The Sephardic pronounciation differed from the Ashkenazic not only in the sound of certain vowels and consonants but also in stressing the last syllables of Hebrew words rather than the first. Differences such as these would affect cadence, stress, rhyme, and rhythm in a manner other than that which was common in

Hebrew prosody. Thus in this first period of development, the Ashkenazic ear was obliged to readjust itself to a variation of musical theme in modern Hebrew poetry. The flexible vitality of both language and poetry were reaffirmed by the grace of the readjustment. Today, early modern Hebrew poetry reads well, if not accurately, in the Sephardic accents; but when it is studied, it must be rhymed and scanned according to the rules of Ashkenazic prosody. In 1925 when Avraham Shlonsky and the modernists began their literary innovations, they had the new accents and rhythms of the spoken language to reinforce the difference of their new direction.

Since the days of the British Mandate in 1920 and the establishment of the State of Israel in 1948, Hebrew, Arabic, and English have been official languages of the country. English is a required language in the schools from the sixth grade on through the secondary schools. Arabic and French are introduced at the secondary level. Arabic expressions from daily life have entered into Hebrew colloquial speech, while English terminology is recognizable in legal and technical Hebrew vocabularies. English and American textbooks and literature are widely read both by students and by the general population. As inveterate movie fans, the Israeli are also exposed to the language of English and American films. French journals and newspapers are also extremely popular, as are French films. In spite of the official position of the English language, however, literary and artistic circles like to maintain educational ties with the traditions of continental Europe and think themselves closer to Paris than to London or New York. In the works of younger poets, however, one finds traces of the double influence of French and English poetry.

In Israel today, the Academy of Hebrew Language is the official legislator of the Hebrew tongue. Its appointed members are distinguished linguists, professors, prose writers, and poets who make the decisions to preserve the correctness of the language. To a large degree they influence not only the academic language but also newspapers and government-sponsored radio broadcasts. Another vital, unofficial legislator of the Hebrew language—common usage—is also very much at work on the Israeli scene. Common usage goes its own way, creating idioms and coining new words; thus it shapes literary styles. In the work of the young writers of both poetry and prose the standard and vernacular meet to create the living language.

Hayyim Nahman Bialik and Saul Tchernichovsky came from the Russian Ukraine and the Crimea respectively. Their first childhood years were spent in small Jewish villages in the environment of green woods and open fields. Out of their personal tensions, which grew out of the crisis in Jewish life, they created poetry that embodied the Jewish will to live. In this sense they may both be considered national poets. As they differed in character and experience, however, their outlook and their dictions differed as well. Future tensions inherent in modern Hebrew poetry, which went in search of native roots and also strove to reach the open air of universal context, were already evident in the varied idioms and poetic concepts of Bialik and Tchernichovsky.

Although he had been educated according to the conventions of Talmudic tradition, Bialik's personal interests and studies enabled him to draw on all the levels of Hebrew language and literature in order to construct and refine a flexible medium for contemporary use. He demonstrated how much Hebrew could express, and returned to Hebrew poetry the whole perspective of a long literary tradition. "The function of the poet," Bialik told Yakov Fichman, "is to revitalize dead words, to renew primary meanings that perish in men." He pointed out the differences between the language of prose and poetry in his critical essays. Beyond the denotative language of prose which rested upon parallel analogies in imagery and words, the language of poetry was connotative. It was weighted not only with implication but even mystery, pursuing the secret of organicism which as a unifying factor created a wholeness of the fragmentations of meaning. Bialik likened the prose writer to a man crossing a frozen river. He walked securely on the thick layers of ice. The poet, however, was in a much more dangerous position: he crossed the river when it was thawing and was obliged to make his way by leaping from one moving ice floe to another.

In his own poetry and prose Bialik enlarged and broke down conventional boundaries of language. In his poems he used the flexible prose rhythms of speech in lines that were still full of poetic connotation; and into his short stories and legends he wove connotative passages of poetic imagery and context.

Bialik's vision was that of the introspective eye which relates all external experience to the inner truth. As he believed self-knowledge lay within the inner consciousness of the poet, so he was convinced that Jewish awareness lay in folk sources, particularly in the Aggadah. After his father's death, Bialik was sent from home to be educated in the strict, pious environment of his paternal grandparents. His own orphanhood and exile symbolized for him the fate of the Jewish people and, in its broadest implications, the fate of modern man. He derived much of the symbolism of his poetic vision from his own blighted childhood.

Never did he forget or dim the sharp images of his early memories of people and of places. The first images he valued as primary intuitions; all else was recognition and reconstruction. He was a solitary poet contemplating not what had been lost, but what could not be fulfilled: the sense of love, the security of identity and belonging. Faithfulness to the Jewish people and compassion for all who suffer were the qualities with which he filled his void; but these were secondary to his sense of integrity which prevented him from rationalizing unpleasant truths. His empathy for the past and his compassion for the present did not blind him. He saw clearly the deterioration of Jewish life. Bialik recognized that tradition and learning had sustained the Jews just as his own identity had been preserved by memory and recall. Bialik pictured the devotion of the Talmud student in the house of study, but saw him as removed from life. He recreated the sanctity of the house of prayer, but showed the synagogue deserted. The world of nature drew him, and he went out to listen to the voice of field and forest only to discover that there, too, he was a stranger. Sensing that the Jew was cut off from the future in Europe, he wrote poems of prophetic invective against those who were deluded by false hope. Deriding passivity to suffering, he pointed to the complicity between the tortured and the torturer. Out of biblical imagery he dramatized the dead in the wilderness who threw off an age-old sleep to take a life of freedom by force.

Bialik spent half a lifetime gathering and reëditing the Aggadah, after which he began to gather and edit the poetry of the Spanish period. This work influenced all his own writings. While stressing the unified complex of Bialik's traditional Hebrew sources, it is necessary to acknowledge his debts, first of all to Mendele, the father of modern Hebrew prose, then to the influences of Belinsky, Tolstoi, and Pushkin. Concise or expansive, simple or profound, the organic unity in everything he wrote demonstrated a skill that related form to content. Lyric poetry, folk song, meditation, elegy, ode, dramatic narrative, allegory, legend, short story, and prose essay—he fashioned them all with lyric accents. In his clear imagery, his concern with precise language, his preference for inner rhythms rather than set metrics, and in his successful first efforts to merge and blend the reinforcing qualities of prose and poetic techniques, he was a modern poet.

By the time Bialik came to Israel in 1924, he was already a legendary figure. Becoming a dynamic influence upon the cultural life of Israel, he was invited to visit Europe and America as a spokesman for the people of Israel and the Hebrew language. In Tel Aviv, where his home was a meeting place for writers, a street was named for him; and the first large publishing house in Israel bears his name.

Tchernichovsky was a poet at home in the world. His childhood was serene in the Jewish village in Crimea where he first learned Hebrew from his father and later from tutors. He was given much freedom to wander, and the peasant children were his playmates. The only boy in the Russian village school that he attended, he delighted in his abundant vitality and found joy in life. Seeing nature with the eye of the physician as well as the poet, Tchernichovsky accepted change as a natural law, and for him the creative miracle was part of this law. A sensitive man, aware of pain, he had no patience with malignancy—either in history or in human nature; as a surgeon he respected the scalpel. He was unorthodox and yet maintained great pride in his Jewish origin. Later, when despair and mourning muted his poetic voice, he refused to accept the blood of martyrs. Instead he embraced those figures in Jewish history who had won freedom from tyranny. "For me poetry is always an act of love, an act of triumph," he wrote to Joseph Klausner, the first historian of modern Hebrew literature.

Tchernichovsky's early poems—songs of love, nature, and national hope—were fresh and concise, but they were strange to the readers of the new poetry. His language was sparsely Midrashic and drawn largely from the Bible, the Aggadah, and from the Hebrew poetry of Spain and Italy. He owed his debt to Immanuel of Rome and claimed him as his poet-ancestor. Tchernichovsky confirmed this influence by making light of tradition, tending toward eros, and being mildly blasphemous. His coined words pointed to some deficiencies of the Hebrew language; his broad outlook brought to Hebrew poetry the lyric and epic traditions of European literatures. Proficient in Latin, Greek, French, German, and English, as well as Russian, Tchernichovsky began early to translate epics from the English, Greek, Finnish, and Slavic literatures.

His first volume of poetry, published in 1899 shortly before he entered the university, did not bring him the immediate wide acclaim that Bialik had received for his first effort; but it brought him Bialik's friendship and Fichman's admiration, while Klausner became his champion. At Heidelberg he continued to write lyric poetry. Bialik faced squarely the contemporary situation of the Russian pogroms, whereas Tchernichovsky set his protest poetry in the environment of earlier historic times. He dramatically portrayed the massacre of the Jews in the German city of Mainz in the Middle Ages. At Heidelberg, influenced by Goethe's *Idyls*, Tchernichovsky began the composition of his Hebrew *Idyls*, which was to extend over a period of twenty years. Although he was called a pagan, Tchernichovsky portrayed Jewish folkways and religious festivals, including the rituals of birth and marriage as he remembered them from his childhood. He treated these themes in classic hexameters, which gave them an epic implication. Later he composed ballads and sonnets. His two sonnet cycles were the first in the Hebrew language.

After 1931, he lived permanently in Palestine and learned to love the austere landscapes of that country. There he also learned to mourn: "See oh earth, the best of our young men we have buried in you. . . !" Still, he saw the flowering wilderness as an omen of a better time and of a nobler generation of men, and he continued to write poetry until he died.

Bialik was a realist, Tchernichovsky a classicist, but both were ultimately romantics. Bialik gave expression to the circumstance and sorrow of the Jewish people, but his poetry expressed both personal and universal grief. Within the folk memory he had found again the sources of a more natural existence, and he called men to seek a more normal wholeness for their life. Tchernichovsky's worship of art and the ever-creative cosmic power of nature was only partially derived from Hellenism and the Italian Renaissance; it also stemmed from a purer mystic concept of spirit. His belief in the potential nobility of man and in a peaceful world of creative fulfillment was related to his faith in the continuity of his people. The humanization of mankind was for him, as it had been to the Hebrew prophets, not an abstract religious ideal but an active social principle.

Bialik and Tchernichovsky were separated in age by only two years, yet it became customary to call the poets who followed them the generation of Bialik. This new poetry, marked by its introspective quality, undoubtedly owed much to Bialik; however, the experimental spirit in the next twenty years revealed Tchernichovsky's influence upon Karni, Hameiri, Schneour, and others who preceded the modernists.

Yakov Fichman, Yakov Cohen, and David Shimoni wrote in an impressionistic vein. The influence of both the German romantics and the French and Russian symbolists touched their poetry. Cohen found equivalents in nature for his strong sense of paradox and expressed social dilemma through folklore. His world view was based on his own peculiar aesthetic. Fichman saw man as an active part of the cosmos but not at its center. He was concerned with "that which exists in the world and is not seen" and "with the inexpressible joy in the passing of all things." The acceptance of man's finite role in an infinite continuum formed the sense of tragic beauty and strength in Fichman's poetry. Shimoni, who began as an introspective individualist, later became known for his *Idyls*, which portrayed the acclimatization of the pioneer with the new land. These poets also served an important function as editors, critics, and translators. Fichman, especially, brought to Hebrew literature his fine understanding of contemporary European writing, and he later became one of the best interpreters of modern Hebrew letters.

Zalman Schneour was the powerful seminal writer of this group. A young rebel who fled the Hassidic environment of his childhood, he remained close in spirit to Tchernichovsky. Valuing the scope of Bialik's language as well, he worked to combine the essence of both poetic idioms. Schneour's originality brought to modern Hebrew poetry a new dimension of sensual vitality. His ability to evoke color, texture, and motion in poetry was sharpened by the imagistic and impressionistic influences of Russian and French poetry.

Schneour was an urban poet who saw the growing mechanical civilization as a degenerating influence upon man. In his prose stories and novels he portrayed for the first time the primitive character of the Jewish villagers; he especially loved to depict those whose lives were markedly *physical*—butchers, draymen, farmers.

In his poetry, however, Schneour built a mystique out of his sophisticated view of passion. Man was alive in the intensity of his physical, intellectual, and emotional being. In his recognition of himself as nature's creative equal lay his power. To the extent that man could return to nature to replenish his strength and creative imagination, he was awake; otherwise, he was less alive than a meadow or a tree.

Although he was an iconoclast, Schneour remained a deeply Jewish writer. He identified the hardening of life with idolatry, that Philistine denial of the worth of the spirit. He called upon his people to maintain their own values and to make them live again in history. His dynamic view of nature was shared and developed, in his own manner, by Shlonsky; his expressionist nationalism was given greater depth by Greenberg.

Poets of transition to Palestinian life were Rahel Bluwstein, Avigdor Hameiri, and Yehuda Karni. Rahel strove to achieve the "direct idiom cleansed of the literary." She accepted the tenets of the Acmeists, following Anna Achmatova of Russia and Francis Jammes of France. In 1909, at the age of nineteen, she abandoned academic studies in art and went to Palestine to work the land in the cooperative colony of Kinneret on Lake Galilee. Her earliest poetry reflected the experience of the pioneer woman upon the land: "Poetry that inscribes itself in memory to accompany us singing in daily life." When she was forced to leave this life and work by lingering tuberculosis, her poetry acquired a wistful, tragic perspective. Though limited in range, her songs are filled with the feeling for life and its potentialities.

Among the first Hebrew expressionists, Hameiri mirrored a generation of shock and change in the intensity of his poetry. He abandoned traditional idioms to compose daring metaphors, and he too worked for direct expression "to strip the veils from language."

Karni had the eye of the reporter, filling his poetry with the ordinary details of people and places. His concise poems written in vernacular speech picture the Israeli landscape and the psychological adjustment of growing new roots.

Uri Tzvi Greenberg is the foremost creator of expressionist poetry in Hebrew. A major poet and an outstanding craftsman of the Hebrew language, he combined traditional expression with new images, and the rare word with the most immediate picture of daily life. His poetry moves to extend the limitations besetting the renascent culture and to free it for its prophetic role. A heroic poet, he forged long lines in free verse, but also wrote in concise and concentrated forms. He speaks in an existentialist idiom, but it is that of a religious existentialist.

Until he was nineteen years old, Greenberg lived in the pious family environment of Hassidic rabbis. His service in the Austrian army during World War I precipitated an awareness of his own militant spirit. He wrote his first poetry in Yiddish and edited a journal of Yiddish expressionist poetry. Before coming to Palestine in 1924, he decided to write only in Hebrew and to join the extreme nationalist group within the Zionist movement. This group opposed the evolutionary socialism that is the major force in political Zionism. When he arrived in Palestine he joined the volunteer labor corps, and his experiences there are felt through his poetry.

Greenberg shaped his poetry out of the contemporary struggle, but he drew inspiration also from historic sources, particularly the struggle of the Zealots, the extremist party of the Second Jewish Commonwealth, who fought the Romans. Using all the levels of the past, he links time—past, present, and future—in an unbroken continuum. His poetry demands redemption, not as a fortuitous grace, but as the consequence of action.

Yitzhak Lamdan was an active editor as well as a poet. For eighteen years his journal *Gilyonot* made a place for unknown young writers and served as a platform for literary discussions. When he arrived in Israel in 1921, he did not intend to continue writing poetry. Seven years earlier, when the Jewish population was evicted from his village on the Ukrainian border, Lamdan, then fourteen, was separated from his parents. He wandered through the villages with his older brother and stopped at Jewish houses of study. Under the Kerenksy regime he volunteered for military service against the Germans. In October, 1920, his brother was killed in a pogrom. Lamdan made his way to Italy and from there to Palestine to work as an agricultural laborer.

His epic poem *Massadah* (see p. 130) became a psychological spur for a whole generation of Zionist youth. The poem was named after the mountain fortress in the southern wilderness where the last battle against the Romans was fought. As a contemporary symbol, it is Israel itself, the last station for the Jews. In the first parts of the poem the refugee on the wall retells his experiences and asks permission of the dead to continue the struggle for life. The poem continues as the night campfire reminds the men on guard of the flames into which their martyred fathers vanished, but this campfire poses another mystery which the sons rise to fathom in dance. The dance, the modern Hora, is a legacy from the Hassidim and earlier generations. It forms an unbroken circle and a joined line before the flame of life. The last parts of the poem deal with contemporary reality and end in a call for strength.

Shimon Halkin's poetry combines a lyric voice with a philosophic outlook. His themes are fragmentation, the search for wholeness, the problem of isolation and return, the landscape of reality, and the landscape of the heart. From the poetry of England and America he derives his moral search and many aesthetic forms. But his religiophilosophical view stems from the Hassidic group of HaBaD, which stressed the intellectual value inherent in the emotional experience.

Alienation from one's self and from others is a recurring theme in Halkin's poetry. In the poem "To Tarshish" there is a pointed statement: "I went far away from man, thus surely was I orphaned of God." Man's withdrawal, his inability to love, serves to paralyze his ability to believe. The poet escapes from the problematic landscape of his human existence to a green island of the aesthetic. But the guilt of separation from one's own world imposes an unbearable loneliness. As the poet magnifies his own thought and feeling, his loneliness reaches beyond himself to the pain and isolation of other men. The poem creates a unifying bond through meeting and recognition; thus ethic and aesthetic become one.

Not only as a poet, but also as a professor of Hebrew Literature in America and at the Hebrew University of Jerusalem, has Shimon Halkin influenced those young poets who have been his pupils as well as students of Hebrew literature. As a literary critic, he pointed away from a purely historical evaluation of Hebrew literature to an understanding of the social influences upon the development of attitude and style. It was Halkin who stressed the importance of explication of texts and of literate reading of the work itself as primary to any critical evaluation of the works of a poet.

The poetry of Yocheved Bat-Miriam reveals a highly personal symbolism relating objects to psychological states and images to inner feelings. The tension inherent in her poetry is developed through new image patterns which extend the dimension of Hebrew expression. Poetry is her response to her Hassidic home environment and to the Russian symbolist poetry which were fused in her own plastic grasp of the Hebrew language.

The poetry of Avraham Shlonsky had the impact of a delayed explosion upon the conventions of early modern Hebrew poetry. His poems were called strange and contrived even after he began to speak in more positive accents and portray more immediate and familiar scenes. To many, his mixed imagery and unorthodox metaphors were sources of consternation. But primarily his broken lines and loose stanzas, as well as highly vernacular cadences, freed Hebrew poetry from traditional metrics and made it open to the mode and tone of colloquial speech. Alterman and Goldberg, who were closely associated with him in the Yachdav group, continued this trend, which younger poets later assimilated as common practice.

The son of a Hassidic scholar active in the cultural groups of Odessa, Avraham Shlonsky emigrated to Palestine in 1924. His early poetry was influenced by Bloch and Mayakovsky. In long disjointed stanzas Shlonsky portrayed the gray futurist limbo of a meaningless existence. He pictured a diseased mankind searching for dubious cures at the old rivers of ancient civilizations. In his meeting with the land of Israel, however, Shlonsky found a new meaning beyond suffering and a new purpose beyond despair. The change was marked by the new tone that emerged in the midst of his futuristic writing. The sequence "Toil" and "Jezrael" came out of this first period. The other translations found here are from his middle and later work and they sustain this creative theme. Despite its secular view and new form, Shlonsky's poetry was not uprooted from the past. He transformed conventions, reinterpreted them to repattern traditional images into new metaphors with extended associations. He reintegrated old symbols, relating them to the new life and the building of the country.

Shlonsky's value as an innovator cannot be overestimated. Impatient with Fichman's concept of the evolutionary development of Hebrew style, Shlonsky joined with Eliezer Steinman to publish the literary weekly *Ketubim*, and the "new" writers centered themselves at first on this publication. After a while Shlonsky founded his own literary weekly *TURIM* and became the center of the publishing house of Yachdav, which encouraged the writers who were known by its name.

The poetry of S. Shalom combines personal intensity with social vision reminscent of Blake and a lyric mystique that recalls the world of Rilke. Shalom's "I" creates no differentiating mask for the ego, but merges the individual with the universal. His secular mysticism is humanistic, for it is the redeeming spark in man which the poet seeks and reveals—the creative spirit that prevails against terror and outlives despair.

Natan Alterman's serious poetry enchanted Israeli youth with its colorful fantasy, which was for them an intimate path to natural awareness. Influenced by French imagists and the troubadour poets, Alterman's early poetry ("Stars Outside") sang of an open world under the stars and the images of old forms in their moment of rebirth. The impact of Hitler on Europe gave his poetry a surreal quality — the poet's eye looked through a hole in a wall at his tortured beloved. In "Joy of the Poor" he used the rhythms of Yiddish folk songs and the imagery of East European life to evoke both compassion and a sense of finality. In "The Egyptian Plagues" he also used biblical themes for contemporary problems and biblical imagery to portray the alienation of the world from humane principles in man's lust for power.

In 1959 Alterman presented a new collection of poetry in the *Violent City*, which developed the theme of alienation and return in a new way. It portrayed haunted men fleeing the cities and harbors of Europe, their sea voyage becoming a journey back and forth into time and memory. But it was also a study of the imprisoning qualities of all cities, "where no living man sits under a green vine and no dead man lies under a stone. . .

whose commotion is mixed with daily silence." Alterman carried his refugees not to the cities of Israel but to its valleys and its newly built villages. He sought to recapture not only the spirit of the first pioneer days but to regain a longer perspective as a shield against the immediate, material stresses of contemporary life. He invoked Hebrew poets of the European past, the legend of the reviving magic of Hebrew words and letters. He stressed the family bond between the generations. He continued the development of imagery that seeks to unify distant worlds. In the last sequence of poems in the volume he shaped a contemporary legend: ten brothers, some living and some dead, meet at the crossroads in a valley inn; each brings his story and his song to be shared over a cup of wine. This is ritual storytelling, an invocation of memory to bind the shattered folk together in spirit as well as in body.

This ritual suggests a Hassidic parallel told by S. Agnon to Professor Gershon Scholem, who recorded it in his book *Major Trends in Jewish Mysticism:* When the Baal Shem Tov had a difficult task to perform he would go to a certain place in the woods, light a fire, and pray. When he had prayed, the task was accomplished. In another generation beset with the same task, the Rabbi remembered only the place and the prayer, but had forgotten how to light the fire. Even so, the task was accomplished. In the next generation both prayer and fire were forgotten, but the place was remembered, and then too the task was accomplished. At last there was only the memory of what had happened, but when the Rabbi sat down and *told the story*, the task was accomplished.

Although her earliest work reflects the Russian poetry of her childhood environment, Leah Goldberg's visual imagery and musical ear were formed by Verlaine and the French poets. Her style also mirrors her admiration for classical and contemporary Italian poetry. Fichman called her poetry "wisdom that sings." Despite its intellection, her poetry is the lyric of a woman's world, where the sense of beauty, love, and compassion prevail over loss and disappointment to find refuge in understanding. Her imagery is rooted in no tradition save art.

The writings of Avraham Shlonsky and Natan Alterman formed a bridge to the younger poets who first approached contemporary poetry largely in terms of these older poets. Although the younger poets' style and perspective differed from that of the poetry of the 'twenties and 'thirties, it is interesting to note the persistent influence of Greenberg, Shalom, Lamdan, and Halkin, as well as that of Shlonsky and Alterman. Some of these young poets were born in Israel; most of them came as children and were educated there. World War II and the War for Independence in 1948 precipitated their first creative years into an existence of violence and crisis. Their poetry stemmed from immediate confrontation with life, rather than from preconceived ideologies or theories of literature. They did not tend toward schools or factions. After the wars in which they fought, they completed their educations and most of them earned their livings as writers, teachers, editors, and translators. Some were members of kibbutzim. Thus, if these poets are not in the customary sense *engaged*, they are at least deeply *involved* in the society for which they speak.

In Amir Gilboa one is immediately aware of a wholly individual style. His poetry moves closer to life than to literature, and reveals the intellectual's will to comprehend, as well as to perceive, relationships. Growing out of consequence rather than circumstance, his poetry relates his perception to his inner truth, in imagery drawn from traditional as well as from contemporary sources.

David Rokeah chooses the images of Israeli landscape to express psychological states and to shape the emotional climate of his personal idiom. His is a self-contained poetry that draws neither upon the imagery of Hebraic tradition nor upon contemporary European forms. It maintains a lyric tone and an immediate awareness of nature. Rokeah's poetry has an objective character but, at the same time, a broad range of human values, and succeeds especially in communicating the direct impact of person and place.

Hayyim Guri has a deep sense of responsibility to his craft. He generates a sense of compassion which extends to all that his poetry touches. In the harshest circumstances and most cruel conditions, Guri's poetry evokes a concern for the humanity of the poet, the soldier, the victim, the enemy, and the man. His early war poetry was tragically alive with the perception of beauty in the face of death. Now his lyric skill extends toward the problematic in his unisolated world. Like Alterman, his literary ties were with French poetry. His musical ear and his adeptness with strict form demonstrate this influence. In his later work he has moved to the flat line and freer cadence of a contemporary idiom.

Yehuda Amihai's poetry is marked by the use of the prose line reinforced by poetic imagery. His short stories have grown out of this same technique. He is developing an original symbolism, merging the boundaries of poetry and prose. A blending of the vernacular and literary language is characteristic of his writing.

In the poetry of T. Carmi, early influences of the English language blend with his fine grasp of modern Hebrew. An emotional affinity to French poetry is often mirrored in his work. His clear imagery and musical ear blend with a sensitive but often cruel perception which he refines by intellectual control, probing his inner self and his personal relationships.

Young Israeli poetry is both sure and questioning. It continues to find inspiration in motifs of land and landscape, history, and tradition; but it differs from the earlier poetry in the close personal relationship of the poet to these motifs. Aware of the dynamics of native soil, majority culture, and the uses of the past, the young poets question the purpose of their particular destiny in the modern world. They are conscious of their identity, but they accept no absolute values from tradition for either the individual or the group. They continue to seek their own synthesis of physical and spiritual existence.

If young poets in Israel today look to the modern literatures of Europe and America, they imply no disregard of their own traditions. It is only that they have an intelligent dread of narrow provincialism. Mingling doubts and certainties, they pursue an introspective examination of aesthetic and social values derived from their Hebraic sources. Open to the world, they seek the living voice of their own art.

Note
An asterisk indicates that the reference is
discussed in the "Notes on the Poems" (pp. 347–356)

I

Bialik and Tchernichovsky

ביאליק וטשרניחובסקי

The Pool

I know a forest and in that forest

I know a hidden pool:

In the denseness of the wood, isolated from the world,

In the shades of a lofty oak, blessed by light and accustomed to storm,

Alone she dreams dreams of an inverted world

And spawns, secretly, her golden fish —

But no one knows what is in her heart.

In the morning

When the sun washes the locks of the forest's majesty

And pours a sea of radiance over his curls;

He, the mighty one, all of him an expanse of golden nets,

Stands willingly captive, like Samson in Delilah's hands,

With a faint smile and a lover's illumined face, aware of his strength.

In the golden mesh of himself, he accepts his bonds affectionately,

Lifts high his garlanded head beneath the powers of the sun,

As if to say: flood me, curl me, or bind me,

Do with me whatever your heart desires.

At this hour the pool, granted or not granted

A single golden ray from above —

Grows languid in the shade of her many-branched shield,

Quietly she nurses his roots and her waters grow tranquil;

As if rejoicing silent in her lot,

בָּאֵלֶּה מַעֲנוּ וְאֵין חֹפֶשׁ לָהֶם
בַּחֶדֶר וְלֹא מְקֹם הָאָדָם לְהָגֵד שְׁמֵךְ:
בּוֹנֵי־אֵל חֶרֶב חֶרֶב לֹא נִשְׁאֲרוּ
בְּכֹל שֵׁם יֵשׁ אֵת חֶדֶל —
מַעֲנוּ בַּמָּרוֹם ני׳ אֹ וְיֵשׁ אֶת לֹא־וְיֵשׁ
הָרֹק אֵת בַּר־מֶלֶךְ וְגֵל —
בָּאֵלֶּה לֹא: מֹאֹדֹת׳ הַאֲחָזֵת אֵל נֹאָל.
וְעָלִי אֵר לַחֶם תֵּלֶל וַוֹּו בְּכִלּוּ מֹעֶם׳
בְּלֹאֵי בַּר אֵר־בְּכֹל׳ אֲחֵר נֹאִלָּוֹ בְּוֵדְ׳
בַּאֵל מְאִידְ לֹא וְאֵל בֵּר נֶחָת בַּלֶּחֶם כַּלֶּ׳
אֲלֶינוּ׳ בְּמְדַמֵּל אֵל. לֵאֲלֶלְ׳ אֶלֶל תֵּלֶל׳
אֲלִישׁ׳ בְּאֵלֹל׳ בַּאֵֵנוּ וְלֵאֶל. אֶת חַל׳
אֵֹ מְאֵר־וְיֵל אֵר וּאֵוְאֶל מְאַגֵל:
בְּלֵלֶד בְּמֵעֶם בַּאֲלֵלוּ אֵלֵל בַּאֵל
בֵּחֵל׳

וְאֵל לֵאֵ בַּר־אֵלֵלֵל׳
וֵּלֵלוּ לֶל בֵּאֲר. אֵר־לֵל. אֶלֶל —
לֵאֵלוּ בָּאֵלֵ לֶל וֵאֵלֹ בַּלֶּ וֵלֵל
אֵר אֲר־אֵלֶל לֹא׳ בֵּלֶל אֵל לֵאַל בַּל׳
בֵּאֵֹ. מָלֶם׳ אֵלֵאֶ אֶל מַלֶּ׳
אֵל. לֵאֵ בֵּאֵל אֵלֵ אֵֵנוּ:
אֵל. לֵאֵ אֵל׳ בֵּאֵל

מַאֲנוּ

Privileged to be a mirror for the forest's mighty one.
And who knows, perhaps she dreams in secret
That not his image or his roots alone within her lie —
But that all of him grows within her.

On a moonlit night —
When a heavy mystery lies over the wood,
And hidden quiet light filters through its branches,
Stealing, passing over its trunks,
Embroidering there in silver and blue
Embroideries of its wonders —
Hushed is every thicket, hushed is every tree!
Each one darkens himself with his crown
And meditates there secretly the meditation of his heart.
The wood stands full of schemes, completely burdened with
Mystery, regal, glorious, singular, much honored and ancient
As if there, deep within the secret core of his might,
On a golden couch, hidden from living eyes, sleeps
In her very innocence, perfect majesty and eternal youth,
A princess from ancient times who was bewitched.
And the wood was charged to count her nostrils' breath
And guard in secret, watch the mystery of her virginity
Until the prince, her lover and redeemer, comes and sets her free —
At this hour the pond, granted or not granted

שֶׁזָּכִיתָ לִהְיוֹת רְאִי לַחֲסִין הַיַּעַר.
וּמִי יוֹדֵעַ, אוּלַי חוֹלְמָה הִיא בַּסֵּתֶר,
כִּי־לֹא רַק־צַלְמוֹ עִם יוֹנַקְתּוֹ בָּהּ –
אַךְ כֻּלּוֹ גָּדֵל הוּא בְּתוֹכָהּ.

וּבְלֵיל יָרֵחַ –
בִּרְבֹץ תַּעֲלוּמָה כְבֵדָה עַל הַחֹרֶשׁ,
וְאוֹר גָּנוּז חֲרִישִׁי זוֹלֵף בֵּין עֳפָאָיו
הִתְגַּנֵּב וַעֲבֹר עַל־גְּזָעָיו,
וְרוֹקֵם שָׁם בַּכֶּסֶף וּבַתְּכֵלֶת
אֶת־רִקְמוֹת פְּלָאָיו –
וְהַס כָּל־סְבָכְךָ, וְהַס כָּל־אִילָן!
כָּל־אֶחָד מַאֲפִיל עַל־עַצְמוֹ בְּצַמַּרְתּוֹ
וּמְהַרְהֵר לוֹ בִּצְנִעָה הִרְהוּר לִבּוֹ.
וְעוֹמֵד לוֹ הַחֹרֶשׁ רַב מְזִמָּה, כֻּלּוֹ טָעוּן
סוֹד מַלְכוּת נֶאְדָּר אֶחָד, גְּדָל־יְקָר וְקַדְמוֹן,
כְּאִלּוּ שָׁם לְפָנַי וְלִפְנִים, בְּחֶבְיוֹן עֻזּוֹ,
עַל־עֶרֶשׂ פָּז, מֵעֵין כָּל־חַי מְצֻנַּעַת, תִּישַׁן,
בְּעֶצֶם תֻּמָּהּ, כְּלִילַת הוֹד וַעֲלוּמֵי נֶצַח,
בַּת־מַלְכָּה מִנִּי־קֶדֶם שֶׁנִּתְכַּשְּׁפָה,
וְהוּא, הַחֹרֶשׁ, הָפְקַד לִמְנוֹת נִשְׁמוֹת אַפָּהּ
וּשְׁמוֹר מִשְׁמֶרֶת קֹדֶשׁ סוֹד בְּתוּלֶיהָ
עַד־יָבֹא בֶן־הַמֶּלֶךְ, דּוֹדָהּ גּוֹאֲלָהּ, וּגְאָלָהּ –
הַבְּרָכָה בְּשָׁעָה זוֹ, אִם־תִּזְכֶּה וְאִם לֹא־תִזְכֶּה

A liquid silver ray from on high —

Withdraws into the shadow of her many-branched shield,

Grows doubly silent,

As if the silence of the wood and the glory of its mystery

Were doubled there in the mirror of her slumbering waters.

Who knows, perhaps secretly she dreams

That the prince is roaming, wandering in vain,

Searching in primordial forests, in sandy wastes, and in the beds of seas

For the lost princess —

This hidden delight, this great radiance,

Is she not secreted here within her depths —

In the heart of the slumbering pond.

And on a day of storm

In the forest, overhead, already congregates a coven of clouds

And battle is in their hearts,

While still controlling, repressing their anger a moment,

With essential thunder their belly rages,

Cloud to cloud, like a herald of approaching evil

Sends flashes of lightning in haste:

"Prepare!"

And yet before the enemy is known,

Or from where the enemy will come —

The forest all in gloom stands prepared

For disaster in the world.

בְּקֶרֶן כֶּסֶף קְלוּשָׁה מִנֹּבַהּ –
תִּתְכַּנֵּס־לָהּ בְּצֵל מָגִנָּה רַב הַפֹּארוֹת,
וּמִשְׁנֶה דְמָמָה תִּדֹּם,
כְּאִלּוּ דְמִי הַחֹרֶשׁ וְהַדְרַת סוֹדוֹ
נִכְפְּלִים שָׁם בִּרְאִי מֵימֶיהָ הַנִּרְדָּמִים.
וּמִי יוֹדֵעַ, אוּלַי תְּחַלֵּם בַּמִּסְתָּרִים,
כִּי אַךְ לַשָּׁוְא יְשׁוֹטֵט, יֶתַע בֶּן־הַמֶּלֶךְ
וִיחַפֵּשׂ בְּיַעֲרוֹת עַד, בְּצִיּוֹת חוֹל וּבְקַרְקַע יַמִּים
אֶת־בַּת הַמַּלְכָּה הָאֹבֶדֶת –
וְחֶמְדָּה גְנוּזָה זוֹ בִּזְהָרָהּ הַגָּדוֹל
הֲלֹא הִיא כְמוּסָה פֹה עִמָּהּ בְּמַעֲמַקֶּיהָ –
בְּלֵב הַבְּרֵכָה הַנִּרְדָּמֶת.

וּבְיוֹם הַסְּעָרָה –
עַל־רֹאשׁ הַיַּעַר נִצְבְּרָה כְּבָר חֲשֶׁרַת עָבִים
וּקְרָב בִּלְבָבָם,
אַךְ עוֹד מִתְאַפְּקִים הֵם וְכוֹבְשִׁים זַעְמָם רֶגַע
וּבְסֵתֶר רַעַם תִּרְגַּז בִּטְנָם,
וְעָב אֶל־עָב, כִּמְבַשֵּׂר רָעָה קְרוֹבָה,
שׁוֹלֵחַ רִמְזֵי בְרָקִים בְּחִפָּזוֹן:
„הַכּוֹנָה!“
וּבְטֶרֶם נוֹדַע מִי הָאוֹיֵב
וְאֵי מִזֶּה הָאוֹיֵב יָבֹא –
הַיַּעַר כֻּלּוֹ קוֹדֵר עוֹמֵד מוּכָן
לְכָל־פֻּרְעָנוּת שֶׁבָּעוֹלָם.

Suddenly — Spark! Lightning! The forest pales,

The world glows,

Crash Crash! Thunder explodes, the forest quakes

And seethes!

Sixty myriad blasts of wind

Seeing and yet unseen,

With wild shrieks swarms over its mighty ones,

Grasps them suddenly by their crown

Jerks them violently, beating their heads —

Thunder upon thunder!

From the midst of the storm comes the roar of the forest multitude.

Wide tumult, fierce clamor

Like the noise of distant breakers heavy with water,

And all says uproar, uproar, uproar —

In this hour's commotion, the pond,

Surrounded by a wall of forest lords,

Still hides deep down in her depth the golden fish,

And like a panicked infant on a terrored night, hides,

Shuts tight his eyes under his mother's wings

And blinks his eyes at every flash of sparkling light —

So with contorted face, black waters glum,

She withdraws into the shade of her many-branched shield

All of her shuddering, shuddering...

And who knows,

וּפִתְאֹם – זִיק! בְּרַק־נוּר! הַיַּעַר חָוַר,
הָעוֹלָם הִבְהֵב,
הַךְ־הָךְ! הִתְפּוֹצֵץ רַעַם, זָע הַיַּעַר –
וַיִּרְתַּח!
וְשִׁשִּׁים רִבּוֹא פְּרִיצֵי רוּחוֹת
הַרֹאִים וְאֵינָם נִרְאִים,
בִּשְׁרִיקוֹת פְּרָאִים פָּשְׁטוּ עַל אַדִּירָיו
וַיֹּאחֲזוּם פִּתְאֹם בִּבְלֹרִיתָם,
וַיְטַלְטְלוּם טַלְטֵלָה, הֲלֹמוּ רֹאשָׁם –
וְרַעַם אַחֲרֵי רָעַם!
וּבָא מִתּוֹךְ הַסְּעָרָה קוֹל הֲמוֹן הַיַּעַר,
רָחָב הֲמוּלָה, כְּבֵד תְּשׁוּאוֹת,
כִּשְׁאוֹן מִשְׁבָּרִים רְחוֹקִים כִּבְדֵי מָיִם,

וְכֻלּוֹ אוֹמֵר רַעַשׁ, רַעַשׁ, רָעַשׁ...
בִּשְׁעַת מְהוּמָה זוֹ – הַבְּרֵכָה,
מֻקֶּפֶת חוֹמָה שֶׁל־אַבִּירֵי חֹרֶשׁ,
עוֹד תַּעֲמִיק לַסְתִּיר בִּמְצוּלָתָהּ דְּגֵי זָהָבָהּ,
וּכְתִינוֹק נִבְעָת נֶחְבָּא בְּלֵיל זְוָעָה
עֲצוּם עֵינַיִם תַּחַת כַּנְפֵי אִמּוֹ
וּלְכָל־בְּרַק נוּר מְנַצְנֵץ יָנִיד עַפְעָף –
כֵּן נַעֲוַת פָּנִים, שְׁחֹרַת מַיִם וּקְדֹרַנִּית,
תִּתְכַּנֵּס־לָהּ בְּצֵל מָגִנָּה רַב הַפֹּארוֹת –
וְכֻלָּהּ רַעַד, רָעַד...
וּמִי יוֹדֵעַ,

Does she tremble for the glory mantle of the forest's pride,

For the summits of his split crowns,

Or does she grieve for all the beauty of her hidden world,

Bright dreamed, clear imaged

That a sudden wind passed over and muddied,

Multitude of splendid visions, her heart's darlings,

Musings by day, musings by night

That a spiteful moment turned to wrath.

At dawn —

The forest is quiet yet, sullen and trembling still,

The last shadows contract into their hiding place;

Warm, milky mists, creepers of dust

Begin to offer incense to the wood, wander up,

Hang scrap by scrap upon its crowns.

Tongues of breezes, sweet and cool

Like tongues of a soft infant mouth upon its mother's cheek,

Already have set out in darkness to appease the forest

For the night's chill and wrath.

They search soft genial light in the leaves,

Sailing from branch to branch, from tree to tree

Licking the whitish milky mists,

Or falling into a nest, unwittingly ruffle

The feathers of a soft sleeping bird —

And there above the forest heights rest

הַחֲרָדָה הִיא לִגְאוֹן אַדֶּרֶת יַעַר
וּלְתוֹעֲפוֹת צַמְּרוֹתָיו הַמְבֻלָּקוֹת,
אוֹ צַר לָהּ עַל־יְפִי עוֹלָמָהּ הַצָּנוּעַ,
בְּהִיר הַחֲלוֹמוֹת, זַךְ הַמַּרְאוֹת,
אֲשֶׁר עָבְרוּ רוּחַ פִּתְאֹם וַיַּעְכְּרֵנוּ,
וַהֲמוֹן חֶזְיוֹנוֹת הוֹד, טְפוּחֵי לִבָּהּ,
הִרְהוּרֵי יוֹם וְהִרְהוּרֵי לַיְלָה,
בְּרֶגַע זַעַם אֶחָד שָׁם לְקֶצֶף.ה

בַּשַּׁחַר –
הַיַּעַר מַחֲרִישׁ עוֹד, עוֹד זוֹעֲפִים וַחֲרֵדִים
מִצְטַמְצְמִים אַחֲרוֹנֵי צְלָלָיו בַּמַּחֲבוֹאִים;
אַךְ אֲדֵי חָלָב חַמִּים, זוֹחֲלֵי עָפָר,
הֶחֵלּוּ כְבָר מְקַטְּרִים לוֹ, וְהִנָּם תּוֹעִים
וְנִתְלִים קְרָעִים קְרָעִים עַל־צַמְּרוֹתָיו.
וּלְשׁוֹנוֹת רוּחַ קְטַנּוֹת, מְתוּקוֹת, פּוֹשְׁרוֹת,
כִּלְשׁוֹן פִּי־תִינוֹק רַךְ עַל לְחָיֵי אִמּוֹ,
כְּבָר יָצְאוּ בָעֲלָטָה לְפַיֵּס אֶת־הַיַּעַר
מִצַּנַּת לַיְלָה וּמִזַּעְפּוֹ.
וּבוֹלְשׁוֹת הֵן רַכְרַכּוֹת, קַלּוֹת, נוֹחוֹת, בֵּין־הֶעָלִים
מְשׁוֹטְטוֹת מִסָּבָךְ לִסְבָךְ, מֵעֵץ לַחֲבֵרוֹ,
מְלַקְּקוֹת אֶת־חֲלֵב הָאֵדִים הַלְּבָנוֹנִים
אוֹ נוֹפְלוֹת אֶל פִּי קֵן וּמְזַעְזְעוֹת שָׁם שֶׁלֹּא מִדַּעַת
נוֹצָתוֹ שֶׁל אֶפְרוֹחַ רַךְ וְיָשֵׁן – –
וְשָׁם עַל־מְרוֹמֵי יַעַר עָמְדָה לָפוּשׁ

The celestial court — a cumulus of clouds.

They are the clouds of glory, of dawn,

Whose form is like a host of ancient lords, celestial elders,

Carrying hidden scrolls, regal wrath, within their hands

From one world to another.

Then stood the forest silent and quaked,

Choking down in awe with bated breath

Each blink, each light chirp of a wakening bird,

All says tremor, reverence, honor —

And at this hour the slumbering pond

Envelops herself, serene, warm, smooth

In a light white sheet, a pallid mist,

And naps the sleep of dawn —

And who knows if now she does not dream

That in vain the august of the sky, the princes of the heights,

Wander far to seek another world,

At the ends of the sea, in the edges of the upper heaven —

And this other world is so near, so near —

For is it not here below, here below

In the heart of the hidden pool.

And I in my youth, my days' delight,

When first rustled over me the wings of the Presence*

And my heart still knew how to long and yearn and wonder silently

Seeking a hiding place for its prayers,

פַּמַלְיָא שֶׁל־מַעֲלָה – שִׁפְעַת עָבִים,
הֲלֹא הֵם עַנְנֵי הַכָּבוֹד, עָבֵי שַׁחַר,
שֶׁדְּמוּת לָהֶם כַּעֲדַת אַלּוּפֵי קֶדֶם, זִקְנֵי עֶלְיוֹן,
הַנּוֹשְׂאִים מְגִלּוֹת סְתָרִים, זַעַם מֶלֶךְ, בְּיָדָם
מֵעוֹלָם אַחֵר לְעוֹלָם אַחֵר.
וְעָמַד אָז הַיַּעַר זָע וּמַחֲרִישׁ,
מְחֻנָּק בַּחֲרָדָה וּבִנְשִׁימָה כְבוּשָׁה
כָּל־נִיד, כָּל צִפְצוּף קַל שֶׁל־צִפּוֹר מִתְעוֹרֶרֶת,
וְכֻלּוֹ אוֹמֵר רֶתֶת וְיִרְאַת כָּבוֹד – – –
בְּשָׁעָה זוֹ הַבְּרֵכָה הַנִּרְדֶּמֶת
תִּתְעַטֵּף־לָהּ, שַׁאֲנַנָּה, חַמָּה, חֲלָקָה
בְּסָדִין קַל וְלָבָן – אֵד חַוְרָוָר,
וּתְנוּמַת שַׁחַר תָּנֹם –
וּמִי יוֹדֵעַ, אִם לֹא־תַחֲלֹם עַתָּה,
כִּי אַךְ לַשָּׁוְא נִכְבַּדֵּי שַׁחַק, נְשִׂיאֵי מָרוֹם,
יַרְחִיקוּ נְדוֹד לְבַקֵּשׁ עוֹלָם אַחֵר
בְּעֶבְרֵי יָם וּבְקַצְוֵי שְׁמֵי שָׁמָיִם –
וְעוֹלָם אַחֵר זֶה כֹּה־קָרוֹב הוּא, כֹּה־קָרוֹב –
הֲרֵי הוּא כָאן מִלְּמַטָּה, כָּאן מִלְּמַטָּה
בְּלֵב הַבְּרֵכָה הַמֻּצְנַעַת.

וַאֲנִי בִּימֵי נְעוּרַי, חֶמְדַּת יָמַי,
אַךְ־רִפְרְפָה עָלַי רִאשׁוֹנָה כְּנַף הַשְּׁכִינָה,
וּלְבָבִי יָדַע עוֹד עֲרוֹג וְכָלּוֹת וְתָמוֹהַּ דּוּמָם
וּלְבַקֵּשׁ מַחֲבֵא לִתְפִלָּתוֹ,

I used to journey at the heat of a summer's day
To the kingdom of magnificent tranquillity —
To the forest's dense thickets.
There between God's trees which had not heard the ax's echo,
On a path known only to the wolf and mighty hunter,
I used to wander whole hours by myself,
Uniting with my heart and with my God until I came,
Stepping over, passing between golden snares,
To the Holy of Holies in the forest — the pupil of its eye.

Within a hanging of leaves
There is a small green island carpeted with grass.
A solitary island, like a small world in itself,
A tranquil, holy sanctuary, hidden between the shade trees
(Forest ancients, broad foliaged, heavy crowned):
Its ceiling — a small blue dome
Suspended over and actually imposed upon the trees;
Its floor glass: a pool with clear water,
A silver mirror framed in moist grass;
Within it was another world, a second world,
And in the center of the dome as in the center of the pool,
Facing each other, two agate gems were fixed,
Agates large and shining —
Two Suns.

הָיִיתִי מַפְלִיג לִי כְּחֹם יוֹם קַיִץ
אֶל־מַמְלְכוּת הַשַּׁלְוָה הַגֶּאְדָּרָה –
לַעֲבִי הַיָּעַר.
וְשָׁם, בֵּין עֲצֵי־אֵל לֹא שָׁמְעוּ בַּת קוֹל קַרְדֹּם,
בִּשְׁבִיל יָדְעוּ רַק רַעַל הַזְּאֵב וְגִבּוֹר צָיִד,
הָיִיתִי תוֹעֶה לִי לְבַדִּי שָׁעוֹת שְׁלֵמוֹת,
מִתְיַחֵד עִם לְבָבִי וְאֱלֹהַי עַד־בֹּאִי,
פָּסוֹחַ וַעֲבוֹר בֵּין מוֹקְשֵׁי זָהָב,
אֶל־קֹדֶשׁ הַקֳּדָשִׁים שֶׁבַּיַּעַר – אֶל־בַּת עֵינוֹ:

מִבֵּית לַפָּרֹכֶת שֶׁל הֶעָלִים,
שָׁם יֵשׁ אִי קָטֹן יָרֹק, רָפוּד דֶּשֶׁא,
אִי בוֹדֵד לוֹ, כְּעֵין עוֹלָם קָטֹן בִּפְנֵי עַצְמוֹ,
דְּבִיר קֹדֶשׁ שַׁאֲנָן, מֻצְנָע בֵּין צֶאֱלִים
שֶׁל־זִקְנֵי יַעַר רַחֲבֵי נוֹף וּמְסֻרְבְּלֵי צָמֶר:
תִּקְרָתוֹ – כִּפַּת תְּכֵלֶת קְטַנָּה,
הַכְּפוּיָה וּמֻנַּחַת עַל הָעֵצִים מַמָּשׁ,
רִצְפָּתוֹ – זְכוּכִית: בְּרֵכַת מַיִם זַכִּים,
רְאִי כֶסֶף בְּתוֹךְ מִסְגֶּרֶת דֶּשֶׁא רָטֹב,
וּבוֹ עוֹד עוֹלָם קָטֹן, עוֹלָם שֵׁנִי,
וּבְאֶמְצַע כִּפָּה זוֹ וּבְאֶמְצַע אוֹתָהּ בְּרֵכָה,
זוֹ נֶגֶד זוֹ, שְׁתֵּי אַבְנֵי כַדְכֹּד קְבוּעוֹת,
כַּדְכֹּדִים גְּדוֹלִים וּמַבְהִיקִים –
שְׁנֵי שְׁמָשׁוֹת.

And as I sat there at the pond's shore, visioning
The riddle of the two worlds, twin worlds,
Not knowing which of them comes first,
Bending my head under the blessing of the ancients of the wood
Dripping shadow and light, resin and song —
I clearly felt a silent flowing
A kind of new and fresh abundance to my soul;
My heart, thirsting for the great, holy mystery,
Continued to fill with silent hope,
As if demanding more and more, and yearning for
Revelation of the near Presence or of Elijah,*
And as my ear still strains and hopes,
And in its sacred desires my heart trembles, pines, expires —
The voice of the Withdrawing God
Bursts suddenly out of the stillness,
"Where are you!?"
And all the pleasant places of the forest fill with amazement,
The tall firs, supple dwellers,
Look at me with great majesty, wondering silently
As if to say: "What is he doing among us?"

There exists a silent immanent language, a secret tongue,
It has no sound, syllable, only shades of hues:
Enchantments, splendid pictures, hosts of visions.
In this tongue God makes himself known to those his spirit chooses,

וּבְשִׁבְתִּי שָׁם עַל־שְׂפַת הַבְּרֵכָה, צוֹפֶה
בְּחִידַת שְׁנֵי עוֹלָמוֹת, עוֹלָם תְּאוֹמִים,
מִבְּלִי לָדַעַת מִי מִשְּׁנֵיהֶם קוֹדֵם,
וּמַטֶּה רֹאשִׁי תַּחַת בִּרְכַּת שָׁבֵי חֹרֶשׁ
מַרְעִיפֵי צֵל וָאוֹר וְשִׁיר וְשָׂרָף כְּאֶחָד –
הָיִיתִי מַרְגִּישׁ בַּעֲלִיל בִּנְבֹּעַ חֶרֶשׁ
כְּעֵין שֶׁפַע רַעֲנָן חָדָשׁ אֶל נִשְׁמָתִי,
וּלְבָבִי, צָמֵא תַעֲלוּמָה רַבָּה, קְדוֹשָׁה,
אָז הוֹלֵךְ וּמִתְמַלֵּא דְּמִי תוֹחֶלֶת,
כְּאִלּוּ הוּא תוֹבֵעַ עוֹד וָעוֹד, וּמְצַפֶּה
לְגִלּוּי שְׁכִינָה קְרוֹבָה אוֹ לְגִלּוּי אֵלִיָּהוּ.
וּבְעוֹד קַשּׁוּבָה אָזְנִי וּמְיַחֶלֶת,
וּבְמַאֲוַיֵּי קָדְשׁוֹ לִבִּי יָחִיל, יִכְלֶה, יִגְוַע –
וּבַת קוֹל אֵל מִסְתַּתֵּר
תִּתְפּוֹצֵץ פִּתְאֹם מִן הַדְּמָמָה:
"אַיֶּכָּה?!"
וּמָלְאוּ נְאוֹת הַיַּעַר תְּמִיהָה גְדוֹלָה,
וּבְרוֹשֵׁי אֵל, אֶזְרָחִים רַעֲנַנִּים,
יִסְתַּכְּלוּ בִי בִּגְדֻלּוֹת הוֹד, מִשְׁתָּאִים דּוּמָם,
כְּאוֹמְרִים: „מַה־לָּזֶה בֵּינֵינוּ?"

שְׂפַת אֵלִים חֲרִישִׁית יֵשׁ, לְשׁוֹן חֲשָׁאִים,
לֹא־קוֹל וְלֹא הֲבָרָה לָהּ אַךְ גַּוְנֵי גְוָנִים;
וּקְסָמִים לָהּ וּתְמוּנוֹת הוֹד וְצָבָא חֶזְיוֹנוֹת,
בִּלְשׁוֹן זוֹ יִתְוַדַּע אֵל לִבְחִירֵי רוּחוֹ,

In it the Royal Emissary of the world reflects upon his thoughts,

The Artist Creator embodies the thought of his heart

And in it finds the solution of the unexpressed dream.

It is the language of images revealed

In a strip of blue sky and in its expanse,

In the purity of small silver clouds and in their dark mass,

In the tremor of golden wheat, in the pride of mighty cedars,

In the rustle of a dove's pure wing

And in the eaglewing's sweep,

In the beauty of a man's body, in the aura of a glance,

In the sea's wrath, in the wave's caprice and play,

In the overflowing night, in the silence of falling stars,

In the roar of light, in the rumble of sea flaming

With sunrises and sunsets.

In this language, tongue of tongues, also the pool

Formed for me her eternal riddle.

Hidden there in the shade, bright, serene, silent,

She looks at everything and all is envisioned in her, and with all

     she changes.

It seemed to me she was the open pupil, the eye

Of the forest Royal Emissary, great in mysteries

And in patient, profound meditations.

וּבָהּ יְהַרְהֵר שַׂר הָעוֹלָם אֶת־הִרְהוּרָיו,
וְיוֹצֵר אָמָן יִגְלֹם בָּהּ הֲגִיג לְבָבוֹ
וּמָצָא פִתְרוֹן בָּהּ לַחֲלוֹם לֹא־הָגוּי;
הֲלֹא הִיא לְשׁוֹן הַמַּרְאוֹת, שֶׁמִּתְגַּלָּה
בְּפַס רְקִיעַ תְּכֵלֶת וּבְמֶרְחָבָיו,
בְּזֹךְ עֲבִיבֵי כֶסֶף וּבִשְׁחוֹר גָּלְמֵיהֶם,
בְּרֶטֶט קָמַת פָּז וּבְגַאֲוֹת אֶרֶז אַדִּיר,
בְּרִפְרוּף כְּנַף צְחוֹרָה שֶׁל הַיּוֹנָה
וּבִמְטוֹת כַּנְפֵי נָשֶׁר,
בִּיפִי גֵּו אִישׁ וּבְזֹהַר מַבַּט עָיִן,
בְּזַעַף יָם, בִּמְשׁוּבַת גַּלָּיו וּבִשְׂחוֹקָם,
בְּשִׁפְעַת לֵיל, בִּדְמִי כוֹכָבִים נוֹפְלִים
וּבְרַעַשׁ אוּרִים, נַהֲמַת יָם שַׁלְהָבוֹת
שֶׁל־זְרִיחוֹת שֶׁמֶשׁ וּשְׁקִיעוֹתָיו –
בִּלְשׁוֹן זוֹ, לְשׁוֹן הַלְּשׁוֹנוֹת, גַּם הַבְּרָכָה
לִי חָדָה אֶת־חִידָתָהּ הָעוֹלָמִית.
וַחֲבוּיָה שָׁם בַּצֵּל, בַּהִירָה, שְׁלֵוָה, מַחֲשָׁה,
בְּכֹל צוֹפִיָּה וְהַכֹּל צָפוּי בָּהּ, וְעִם־הַכֹּל מִשְׁתַּנָּה,
לִי נִדְמְתָה כְּאִלּוּ הִיא בַּת־עַיִן פְּקוּחָה
שֶׁל־שַׂר הַיַּעַר גְּדָל־הָרְזִים
וְאֶרֶךְ הַשַּׂרְעַפּוֹת.

At Day's End

Through clouds of fire and clouds of blood
The sun sinks down to the ocean's edge.

The rays of light through clouds appear,
A vast array of burnished spears.

It waters the plain with lucid gleam
And sets afire the thicket's green.

It pours a light on the head of the wood
And blazes a fire in the river's flood.

It covers the top of the hill with gold,
Sprinkles, sprays the grain with a glow.

The wing of the day it bends to kiss
And goes down alive into the abyss —

Then all existence comes to shade,
The night comes as the night strides.

A light wind comes, blows, flees,
It kissed me and told me mysteries.

בַּעֲרֹב הַיּוֹם

בֵּין עָבֵי אֵשׁ וְעָבֵי דָם
הַשֶּׁמֶשׁ רַד לִפְאַת הַיָּם,

וְקַרְנֵי אוֹר בְּעַד הָעָב,
כַּחֲנִיתוֹת מִמֹּרָטוֹת רָב.

וַיִּשַּׁק הַכִּכָּר נֹגַהּ זָךְ,
וַיִּצַּת־אֵשׁ בִּירַק הַסְּבָךְ.

עַל־רֹאשׁ הַחֹרֶשׁ יָצַק אוֹר,
וַיִּתֶּךְ־אֵשׁ בְּמֵי־הַיְאֹר.

וַיְצַף אֶת־רֹאשׁ הַגִּבְעָה פָז,
בְּקָמָה זָרַק זִיו וָיָז.

וַיֵּט, וַיִּשַּׁק כְּנַף הַיּוֹם,
וַיֵּרֶד חַי אֶל־פִּי הַתְּהוֹם – – –

אָז יָבֹא כָל־הַיְקוּם בַּצֵּל,
הַלַּיִל הֹלֵךְ – בָּא הַלֵּיל,

וְרוּחַ קַל בָּא, נָשַׁב, נָס,
וַיִּשַּׁק לִי וַיְגַל לִי רָז.

To me it whispered: innocence, faith —
Like rays of light at end of day.

The days of youth, good child,
Quickly fly like birds in flight.

Here everything turns to dirt and dross —
There is a good, a festive world for us.

A lighted corner, a blessed space,
Its spirit — freedom, its sun — grace.

A place for us there I explored
Rise, let's fly together, my son, soar:

This is not peace, fly, go —
But why, my heart, do you pain so?

Who cast the shadow in your room,
God's darkness, eternal gloom?

Why do you glower, turn to —
There is God's expanse — narrow for you.

Are you afraid to watch the night's
Darkness prevail against the light?

הוּא לָאַט עִמִּי: אָמֵן, תָּם –
כְּקֶרֶן אוֹר בַּעֲרֹב הַיּוֹם.

וִימֵי הַנַּעַר, יֶלֶד טוֹב,
יָעוּפוּ חִישׁ כִּמְעוּף הָעוֹף.

פֹּה נֶאֱלַח הַכֹּל, הַכֹּל סָג –
יֶשׁ־עוֹלָם טוֹב שֶׁכֻּלּוֹ חָג.

יֶשׁ־קֶרֶן בְּרוּכָה, פִּנַּת־אוֹר,
שֶׁשִּׁמְשָׁהּ – צְדָקָה, רוּחָהּ – דְּרוֹר;

שָׁם תַּרְתִּי מָקוֹם לְךָ וָלִי –
קוּם נָעוּף יַחְדָּו, גְּדָאֵה, בְּנִי!

לֹא זֶה הַמְּנוּחָה, עוּף מִפֹּה –
אַךְ לָמָּה, לִבִּי, תִּדְוֶה כֹּה?

מִי הֵטִיל בַּחֲדָרֶיךָ צֵל,
אֲפֵלַת עַד וְחֶשְׁכַת־אֵל?

מַדּוּעַ אַתָּה זָעֵף, סָר –
יֶשׁ מֶרְחַב יָהּ – וּלְךָ הוּא צָר.

הֲלִרְאוֹת יֵרַע לְךָ בַּגֶּבֶר
אֱשׁוּן הַחֹשֶׁךְ עַל־הָאוֹר?

What is the pain, what is the dream
As day expires, which slowly come

And draw the heart, the innocent,
Beyond the seas to the infinite?

And If the Angel Should Ask

— My son, where is your soul? —

"Soar through the world, seek it my angel:
There is in the world a peaceful village surrounded by forest wall
This village has a blue sky, a boundless sky
In the middle of the blue sky an only daughter:
A single cloud, white and small.
On a summer's noon a child played there alone,
A child left to himself, fragile, unique and dreaming —
I am that child, my angel.
Once the whole world swooned and was still,
The two eyes of the child were drawn skyward.
They saw the only one, the pure, the clear.
As he saw her his soul went out as a dove from the cote
Toward the cloud, the delight."

— And it melted? —

כִּי מָה הַכְּאֵב וּמָה הַחֲלוֹם,
הַבָּאִים אַט עִם־צֵאת הַיּוֹם,

וּמֹשְׁכִים אֶת־הַלֵּב הַתָּם
אֶל־קַצְוֵי עַד, אֶל־אַחֲרִית יָם?

וְאִם־יִשְׁאַל הַמַּלְאָךְ

בְּנִי, נִשְׁמָתְךָ אַיֶּה? –

„שׁוּט בָּעוֹלָם, בַּקְּשֶׁנָּה, מַלְאָכִי!
יֵשׁ בָּעוֹלָם כְּפַר שַׁאֲנָן, מֻקָּף חוֹמַת יְעָרִים,
וְלַכְּפָר רְקִיעַ תְּכֵלֶת, בְּלִי מְצָרִים רָקִיעַ,
וְלָרְקִיעַ הַתְּכֵלֶת בַּת־יְחִידָה בָּאֶמְצַע:
עָב יְחִידָה, לְבָנָה וּקְטַנָּה.
וּבְצָהֳרֵי יוֹם קַיִץ בָּדָד שִׂחֵק־שָׁם יֶלֶד,
יֶלֶד עָזוּב לְנַפְשׁוֹ, רַךְ וְיָחִיד וְחוֹלֵם –
וַאֲנִי הוּא הַיֶּלֶד, מַלְאָכִי.
פַּעַם אַחַת הִתְעַלֵּף כָּל־הָעוֹלָם וַיִּשְׁתֹּק,
וּשְׁתֵּי עֵינֵי הַיֶּלֶד הַשָּׁמַיְמָה נִמְשָׁכוּ,
וַיִּרְאֶנָּה, הַיְחִידָה, הַזַּכָּה, הַבְּרוּרָה,
וְנַפְשׁוֹ יָצְאָה בִרְאוֹתוֹ, כְּצֵאת יוֹנָה מִשּׁוֹבָכָהּ,
אֶל־הָעָב הַנֶּחְמָדָה".

– וַתִּמּוֹג? –

"There is also a sun in the world, my angel:

A merciful golden ray saved my soul,

And on radiant wings many days it sparkled

Like a white butterfly:

Once at morning it rode astride a golden beam,

Looking for a pearl of dew among the grasses,

And a pure, innocent tear trembled then upon my cheek,

The beam shivered and my soul swooned —

And sunk into the tear."

— And it dried up? —

"No, for it fell upon a page of sacred Gemara.*

My grandfather had a Gemara, rough scrolled pages, crumpled

And in its belly — two of my grandfather's white hairs,

Threads of blemished fringes* of his small prayer shawl*

And marks of many drops of tallow and wax.

In this Gemara, in the belly of dead letters

Alone my soul fluttered."

— And it choked? —

"No, it fluttered and sang, my angel!

Out of the dead letters welled forth songs of life.

In my grandfather's bookcase the eternal dead quaked.

„גַּם־שֶׁמֶשׁ יֵשׁ בָּעוֹלָם, מַלְאָכִי!
אֶת־נִשְׁמָתִי הַצִּילָה קֶרֶן פָּז רַחֲמָנִיָּה,
וְעַל־כַּנְפֵי הַזֹּהַר יָמִים רַבִּים פְּזָזָה
כְּצִפֹּרֶת לְבָנָה;
פַּעַם רָכְבָה בַּבֹּקֶר עַל־גַּב קֶרֶן הַזָּהָב,
הָלוֹךְ הָלְכָה לְבַקֵּשׁ פְּנִינַת טַל בֵּין הַדְּשָׁאִים,
וְדִמְעָה זַכָּה וְתַמָּה אָז עַל־לְחָיֵי רָעָדָה, –
וַתִּזְדַּעֲזַע הַקֶּרֶן וְנִשְׁמָתִי צָנְחָה –
וַתִּשְׁתַּקַּע בַּדִּמְעָה".

– וַתִּיבָשׁ? –

„לֹא, כִּי נָשְׁרָה עַל־דַּף גְּמָרָא קְדוֹשָׁה.
גְּמָרָא הָיְתָה לְזִקְנֵי שְׁעִירַת גְּוִילִים וּמְעוּכָה,
וּבְכִרְכָּסָהּ – שְׁתֵּי שְׂעָרוֹת שֶׁל־זְקָנוֹ הַלָּבָן,
חוּטֵי צִיצִיּוֹת פְּסוּלוֹת שֶׁל־טַלִּיתוֹ הַקְּטַנָּה
וְסִמָּנִים שֶׁל־הַרְבֵּה טִפּוֹת חֵלֶב וְשַׁעֲוָה,
וּבַגְּמָרָא הַזֹּאת, בִּמְעֵי אוֹתִיּוֹת מֵתוֹת
בָּדָד פִּרְפְּרָה נִשְׁמָתִי".

– וַתֶּחָנֵק? –

„לֹא, פִּרְפְּרָה וַתְּשׁוֹרֵר, מַלְאָכִי!
בְּאוֹתִיּוֹת הַמֵּתוֹת שִׁירֵי חַיִּים הֵקֵרוּ,
וּבַאֲרוֹן סִפְרֵי זְקֵנִי מֵתֵי עוֹלָם נִזְדַּעֲזָעוּ.

Different were these songs: about a small clear cloud,

A golden sunbeam, a shining tear,

About blemished fringes and drops of wax —

But one song it did not know — the song of youth and love.

And it yearned to escape, it moaned and found no solace,

It fainted away, and was squeezed almost to death.

Once I visited my tattered Gemara —

And suddenly from it flew my soul.

And still it flies and soars in the world,

Soars and wanders and finds no solace.

On the dark nights at the beginning of each month

When the world prays over the imperfect moon,

It clings with its wings to the gate of love

Clings, knocks, secretly weeping,

And prays for love."

I Have a Garden
(from the folk song)

I have a garden and I have a well,

Upon my well there hangs a pail:

Every Sabbath comes my dear,

Drinks from my pitcher, water clear.

שׁוֹנִים הָיוּ הַשִּׁירִים: עַל־עָב קְטַנָּה וּבְהִירָה,
עֲלֵי קֶרֶן הַזָּהָב וַעֲלֵי דִמְעָה מַזְהִירָה,
עֲלֵי צִיצִיּוֹת פְּסוּלוֹת וַעֲלֵי טִפּוֹת שֶׁל־שַׁעֲוָה –
אַךְ שִׁיר אֶחָד לֹא יָדְעָה – שִׁיר עֲלוּמִים וְאַהֲבָה.
וַתְּכַל לָצֵאת, וַתֶּהֱמֶה, וְלֹא־מָצְאָה תַנְחוּמִין,
וַתִּתְעַלֵּף עַד־כְּלוֹתָהּ, וַיְהִי צַר־לָהּ עַד־מָוֶת.
פַּעַם אַחַת פָּקַדְתִּי אֶת־גִּמְרָתִי הַבָּלָה –
וְהִנֵּה פָרְחָה מִתּוֹכָהּ נִשְׁמָתִי.

וַעֲדַיִן הִיא טָסָה וּמְשׁוֹטֶטֶת בָּעוֹלָם,
מְשׁוֹטֶטֶת וְתוֹעָה וְאֵינֶנָּה מוֹצֵאת תַּנְחוּמִין;
וּבַלֵּילוֹת הַצְּנוּעִים שֶׁבִּתְחִלַּת כָּל־חֹדֶשׁ,
בְּהִתְפַּלֵּל הָעוֹלָם עֲלֵי פְּגִימַת הַלְּבָנָה,
הִיא מִתְרַפְּקָה בִכְנָפָהּ עֲלֵי שַׁעַר הָאַהֲבָה
מִתְרַפֶּקֶת, דוֹפֶקֶת וּבוֹכִיָּה בַחֲשַׁאי,
וּמִתְפַּלְּלָה עַל־הָאַהֲבָה".

יֵשׁ לִי גָן

(מִשִּׁירֵי עַם)

יֵשׁ לִי גָן וּבְאֵר יֶשׁ־לִי,
וַעֲלֵי בְאֵרִי תָּלוּי דְּלִי;
מִדֵּי שַׁבָּת בָּא מַחֲמַדִּי,
מַיִם זַכִּים יֵשְׁתְּ מִכַּדִּי.

Hush — the whole world slumbers there! ,
Also the apple and the pear;
My mother sleeps, my father naps,
Only my heart and I awake.

And like my heart, awake, the pail
Is dripping gold into the well,
Drips gold and crystal from above:
There comes my love, there comes my love.

Hush — the garden foliage stirred —
My love comes; fluttered the birds?
My love, my love! — hurry my dear,
No one is in the yard but me.

Upon the trough sit slowly down,
Head on shoulder, hand in hand.
I'll spin you riddles: why does
The pitcher to the fountain rush?

And why is it, you tell me,
The pail weeps, weeps silently?
Drips and drip-drops without cease
From eve to eve.

כָּל־הָעוֹלָם יָשֵׁן – הָס!
נָם תַּפּוּחַ וַאֲגָס;
אִמִּי נָמָה, נִרְדָּם אָבִי,
עֵרִים רַק אֲנִי וּלְבָבִי.

וְהַדְּלִי כִּלְבָבִי עֵר,
נוֹטֵף פָּז אֶל־פִּי הַבְּאֵר,
נוֹטֵף פָּז וְנוֹטֵף בְּדֹלַח:
דּוֹדִי הוֹלֵךְ, דּוֹדִי הוֹלֵךְ.

הַס, בַּגָּן נִזְדַּעֲזַע נוֹף –
דּוֹדִי בָא אִם־פִּרְכֵּס עוֹף?
דּוֹדִי, דּוֹדִי! – חוּשׁ מַחֲמַדִּי,
אֵין בֶּחָצֵר אִישׁ מִלְּבַדִּי.

עַל־הַשֹּׁקֶת נֵשֵׁב אַט,
רֹאשׁ אֶל־כָּתֵף, יָד אֶל־יָד;
אָחוּד חִידוֹת לָךְ: מַדּוּעַ
רָץ הַכַּד אֶל־הַמַּבּוּעַ?

וּמַדּוּעַ, הַגֶּד־לִי,
יֵבְךְּ בִּדְמָמָה, יֵבְךְּ הַדְּלִי –
טִיף, טִיף, נִים – וְכֹה בְּלִי־הֶרֶף
מִן־הָעֶרֶב עַד הָעֶרֶב.

And where does anguish start
Like a worm into my heart? —
Has my mother really heard,
Your heart away from me has stirred?

Answered my love, to me he said:
My foes against me speak falsehood!
Silly, this time next year we
Shall walk to the bridal canopy!*

A summer day will glimmer then,
Pour gold on our heads again.
From the fences, blessed salute,
The hands of trees loaded with fruit.

Brother and friend, uncle and kin,
A great assembly, candles and men,
And every kind of instrument
Lead us with bride's maids and best man.

Here the bridal canopy shall
Stand between the garden and the well;
And to me the lovely gift:
A small-nailed finger you will lift.

וּמֵאַיִן בָּא הַכְּאֵב
כְּתוֹלַעַת אֶל־הַלֵּב? –
הוֹי, הַאֱמֶת שָׁמְעָה אִמִּי,
כִּי לְבָבְךָ סָר מֵעִמִּי?

עָנָה דוֹדִי וְאָמַר לִי:
שׂוֹנְאַי שֶׁקֶר עָנוּ בִי!
וּבְעוֹד שָׁנָה, כְּעֵת חַיָּה,
אֶל־הַחֻפָּה גֵלֵךְ, פְּתַיָּה!

יוֹם שֶׁל־קַיִץ יַבְהִיק אָז,
עַל רֹאשֵׁנוּ יִיצֹק פָּז,
וִיבָרְכוּנוּ מִן הַגְּדֵרוֹת
כַּפּוֹת עֵצִים טְעוּנֵי פֵרוֹת.

אָח וָרֵעַ, דוֹד וּשְׁאֵר,
קָהָל גָּדוֹל, אִישׁ וָנֵר,
וּכְלֵי־זֶמֶר כָּל־הַמִּינִים
יוֹלִיכוּנוּ עִם שׁוֹשְׁבִינִים.

וְהַחֻפָּה תַּעֲמֹד כָּאן:
בֵּין הַבְּאֵר וּבֵין הַגָּן;
אַתְּ תּוֹשִׁיטִי לִי שָׁם דֶּרֶן:
אֶצְבַּע קְטַנָּה עִם צִפֹּרֶן.

"Behold, thou art," to you I'll quote,

"Forever unto me betrothed" —

My enemies shall stand and see

And they shall burst with jealousy.

Prophet, Go, Flee!

(Amos VII:12)

"Go, Flee?" — A man like me does not flee!

Walk calmly, my cattle taught me,

My tongue did not learn to say "yes"

And my word shall fall like a heavy ax.

Not my fault — if my strength was spent in vain,

It is your sin and you carry the blame!

No anvil underneath it did my hammer find

Into the tree's rot my ax came.

No matter! I accept my fate:

My tools to my belt I tie,

Day laborer without my wage

I shall return calmly the same way.

וַאֲנִי לָךְ: „הֲרֵי אַתְּ
מְקֻדֶּשֶׁת לִי לָעַד" —
שׂוֹנְאַי יִהְיוּ שָׁם וְרָאוּ,
וּמְקַנְאַה יִתְפַּקָּעוּ.

„חוֹזֶה, לֵךְ בְּרַח"

(עמוס ז׳, יב)

„לֵךְ בְּרַח?" — לֹא־יִבְרַח אִישׁ כָּמוֹנִי!
הָלוֹךְ בַּלָּאט לִמְּדַנִי בְקָרִי,
גַּם דַּבֵּר כֵּן לֹא לָמְדָה לְשׁוֹנִי
וּכְקַרְדֹּם כָּבֵד יִפֹּל דְּבָרִי.

וְאִם־כֹּחִי תַם לָרִיק — לֹא־פִשְׁעִי,
חַטַּאתְכֶם הִיא וּשְׂאוּ הֶעָוֹן!
לֹא־מָצָא תַחְתָּיו סְדָן פַּטִּישִׁי,
קַרְדֻּמִּי בָא בְּעֵץ רִקָּבוֹן.

אֵין דָּבָר! אַשְׁלִים עִם־גּוֹרָלִי:
אֶת־כֵּלַי אֶקְשֹׁר לַחֲגוֹרָתִי,
וּשְׂכִיר הַיּוֹם בְּלִי שְׂכַר פָּעֳלִי
אָשׁוּבָה לִי בַּלָּאט כְּשֶׁבָּאתִי.

Back to my cote I return, to its vales

And with sycamores my covenant I make.

And you — you rot and decay

Tomorrow storm shall carry you away.

אֶל־נָוִי אָשׁוּב וְאֶל־עֲמָקָיו
וְאֶכְרֹת בְּרִית עִם שִׁקְמֵי יָעַר.
וְאַתֶּם – אַתֶּם מְסוֹס וְרָקָב
וּמָחָר יִשָּׂא כֻלְּכֶם סָעַר.

To the Sun

(from the sonnet sequence)

Our fathers who were in this place,
with their backs to the sanctuary, their faces to the East,
bowed eastward to the sun.
*(Succah 5:4)**

I

I have been to my God like the iris and the anemone*

   Which has nothing in its world save its pure sun,

   And a messenger taps it: "Rise, grow, small bud, open

Your song, festive song, amidst the prickly thorn!"

I sucked meadow-sap. Like wine overcame me

   This scent of fertile earth, its clod, clod fine.

   Had He no patriarch or priest in the city shrine

That He brought me here, his prophet proclaimed me?

More than resin on silver fir, shall I hold

Your good oil, on the head, shining gold,

   And all the scents of pear tree and field I guard

   More than dusts of Sheba's traders,* incense and nard?

Serenely I bow to you. In majesty I bow down

Like a gold-stalk of wheat heavy with grain.

לַשֶּׁמֶשׁ

(מִמַּחֲזוֹר הַסּוֹנֶטּוֹת)

אֲבוֹתֵינוּ שֶׁהָיוּ בַּמָּקוֹם הַזֶּה,
אֲחוֹרֵיהֶם אֶל הַהֵיכָל וּפְנֵיהֶם קֵדְמָה,
וּמִשְׁתַּחֲוִים קֵדְמָה לַשֶּׁמֶשׁ.
(סֻכָּה, פֶּ"ה, מִ"ד)

א

הָיִיתִי לֵאלֹהַי כְּיָקִינְטוֹן וְכַאֲדָנִי,
שֶׁאֵין בְּעוֹלָמוֹ לוֹ אַךְ שִׁמְשׁוֹ זֶה הַצַּח,
וּמַלְאָךְ דּוֹפֵק אוֹתוֹ: "קוּם גְּדַל, בֶּן־צִיץ, וּפְצַח
רִנָּתְךָ, רִנַּת־חַג, בְּחָרוּל הַנַּשְׁכָּנִי!".

וָאֵינַק רֹטֶב־נִיר. כַּיַּיִן עֲבָרַנִי
זֶה רֵיחַ אַדְמַת־בּוּל עַל רִגְבָּה, רֶגֶב רָךְ
הֲמִבְּלִי אֵין לוֹ אָב וְכֹהֵן בְּמִקְדָּשׁ־כְּרָךְ,
כִּי הֱבִיאַנִי לְכָאן וּלְנָבִיא לוֹ שָׂמָנִי?

הֲיֵקַל בְּעֵינֵי שְׂרָף עַל גַּבֵּי כֶּסֶף־בְּרוֹשׁ
מִשַּׁמְנֵךְ הַטּוֹב, הַמַּזְהִיב עַל הָרֹאשׁ,
וְרֵיחוֹת הָאַגָּס וְהַשָּׂדֶה שֶׁנָּטַרְתִּי

מֵאַבְקוֹת רוֹכְלֵי־שְׁבָא, מִנֵּרְדִּי וּמִקְטָרְתִּי?
וָאֵקַד לָךְ בַּלָּט. אֶשְׁתַּחֲוֶה בִּיקָר,
וּכְאַחַת שִׁבְּלֵי־פָז בַּקָּמָה כְּבַדַּת־בָּר.

XIII

Images of a faded world possessed me, I cannot flee!
 Images of this people, lovely grew all it touched,
 Beauty was its wisdom, and its wisdom was such
It spread beauty over the abyss and the sea.

Winds of the North sea charmed me through the trees
 Telling of the frost dressed in its design:
 Among sun-idols of On, as I sought him in the shrine,
I imagined this spark that resounds through me.

But it is an eastern spark I cherished from Canaan:
 Dan's idols demanded me, tamarisks striking awe.
I worshipped in Ur-Chaldees, Astarte's groves, sculptured stone.

Which road shall I pick, where is the path?
 Shall I choose Zeus or pour oil to Yah,
Or the image-kingdom's idol of the generation past?*

XIV

Or the image-kingdom's idol of the past generation
 Or a song, a dream of power, we shall ever form.
 Man's eye examined and discovered the secret of forms
In gold and in tin, fine atom combinations.

יג

אֱלִילֵי עוֹלָם גַּז תְּפָסוּנִי וְאֵין לִי מָנוֹס!
אֱלִילֵי גוֹי זֶה, יָיְף כָּל הַנּוֹגֵעַ בּוֹ,
גּוֹי הָיָה לְחָכְמָה לוֹ, וְחָכְמָתוֹ הָיְתָה גוֹי,
וַיִּז מִיָּפְיוֹ לוֹ עַל שְׁאוֹל וְעַל אוֹקְיָנוֹס.

קְסָמוּנִי רוּחוֹת צָפוֹן־הַיָּם מִבֵּין אִילָנוֹת,
מְסֻפָּרוֹת מִן הַכְּפוֹר הָעוֹטֶה תַשְׁבֵּץ שְׁבוֹ;
וּבֵין חַמָּנֵי־אוֹן, וּבְמִקְדָּשׁ תַּרְתִּי בוֹ,
דְּמִיתִי נִיצוֹץ זֶה, הָאוֹמֵר בִּי הַשָּׁנוֹת,

אַךְ זִיק מִמִּזְרָח הוּא, מִכְּנַעַן אֲנַצְּרֶנּוּ;
תְּבָעוּנִי פְּסִילֵי־דָן, אֲשָׁלִים מְלֵאִים חִיל,
אֲשֵׁרוֹת, גָּלְמֵי צוּר, בְּאוּר־כַּשְׂדִּים אֶעֶבְדֶנּוּ.

אֵי דֶרֶךְ אֶבְחַר בָּהּ וְאֵיפֹה הוּא הַשְּׁבִיל?
הַאֶמְשַׁח שַׁמְנִי לְיָהּ אוֹ זֵאוּס אֶבְחָרֶנּוּ,
אוֹ פֶסֶל אַחֲרוֹן־דּוֹר בְּמַמְלֶכֶת־הָאֱלִיל?

יד

אוֹ פֶסֶל אַחֲרוֹן־דּוֹר בְּמַמְלֶכֶת־הָאֱלִיל,
אוֹ שִׁיר חֲלוֹם־אֶיָּל נָקִימָה לְעוֹלָמִים.
וּבְחַנֶּה עֵין־אִישׁ וְגִלְּתָה סוֹד־הַגַּלְמִים
צֵרוּפֵי אָטוֹם דַּק בַּזָּהָב וּבַבְּדִיל.

From the inanimate he turned, stretched a line a path
    To the kingdom of trees and to plants without feeling,
    To spotted mushroom, and all are one chain of being:
Pond algae, the almond and the elephant calf.

Comprehended was the secret of heat, light, electricity,
The wonder of flowering barley seed, the magnet's mystery,
    The pulsing of live nerve, taut without relief,

And they were one, a secret, secret of secrets — life,
    Then was this poem sung to him: this is my Sun that warms me, ,
    I have been to my God like the iris and the anemone.

XV

I have been to my God like the iris and the anemone,
    Like a gold-stalk of wheat heavy with grain;
    He commanded mountain mists, prepared for me heat's rain,
Turquoise, purple, scarlet, light and shadow's symphony.

My wisdom was an era's anguish, each nation's song charmed me,
    Voice of spirit wrapped in light, in the strange dark a voice lost.
    As I stood among the living and those giving up the ghost;
Was I born too soon, or too late did God form me?

וּמִן הַדּוֹמֵם יֵט וּמָתַח קַו וּשְׁבִיל
לְמַמְלְכוֹת הָעֵץ וְהַצּוֹמְחִים הַנַּעֲלָמִים.
וְשַׁלְשֶׁלֶת אַחַת לוֹ: פִּטְרִיָּה שֶׁבַּכְּתָמִים,
יְרֹקֶת הָאֲגַם, הָאֱגוֹז וּשְׁגַר־הַפִּיל.

וְנִקְלַט סוֹד הַחֹם, הַחַשְׁמַל וְהָאוֹרָה,
מִסְתּוֹרֵי הַמַּגְנֵיט, רָז פְּרִיחַת עִנְבַת־שְׁעוֹרָה,
זַעֲזוּעֵי עֶצֶב עֵר, הַנִּמְתָּח וְאֵין לוֹ פְּנַי,

וְהָיָה לְאֶחָד סוֹד, סוֹד כָּל הַסּוֹדוֹת – חָי.
אָז יוּשַׁר לוֹ הַשִּׁיר: זֶה שִׁמְשִׁי חִמְּמָנִי,
הָיִיתִי לֵאלֹהַי כְּיַקִּינְטוֹן וְכָאֲדָנִי!

טו

הָיִיתִי לֵאלֹהַי כְּיַקִּינְטוֹן וְכָאֲדָנִי
וּכְאַחַת שִׁבֳּלֵי־פָז בַּקָּמָה כִּבְדַת־בָּר;
וַיְמַן לִי גִּשְׁמֵי־חֹם וַיְצַו עַרְפִּלֵּי־הָר,
סִמְפוֹנִיּוֹת אוֹר וָצֵל, וְכָחֹל, וְשָׂרֹק, וְשָׁנִי.

בִּינוֹתִי צַעַר־דּוֹר, שִׁיר גּוֹי וְגוֹי קְסָמָנִי,
קוֹל נֶפֶשׁ עוֹטָה אוֹר, קוֹל תּוֹעָה בְּמַחְשָׁךְ זָר,
בְּעָמְדִי בֵּין הַחַי וּבֵין הַגּוֹסֵס כְּבָר;
הַאִם קַדְמָתִי בָּא אוֹ אַחַר צוּר בְּרָאָנִי?

In my heart still lies dew that falls on fields of Edom,

On the Summit of Mount Hor, the eastern God's home,

   For my heart prays a song to the Sun and Orion.

When the bean sheathed, fruit ripened on the tree,

I cannot flee, by images of a faded world possessed —

   Or the image-kingdom's idol of the generation-past?

Levivot*
(an idyl)

I

Truly it was morning, and few to equal it,

And the first of the months of Spring, lovely over the steppes of Ukraine,

Steppes and plains sea-broad — and who was the first,

First of all, to see this fresh morning's delight,

Still washed in dew and the glow of the morning star

That day and hour? — The lark was first

And raised himself on his wings skyward and rained down his melodies.

Waking the swallow in the roof and the sparrows in the thicket's branches.

Second, the sun awoke from her sleep, her face blazing

With shame that she rose late, hurried to her work,

Paint-brushing the buds, putting blue to the young bird's wing,

Curling with sparks a low wave, gilding the scales of the sea,

עוֹד בִּלְבִּי לָן הַטַּל, הַיּוֹרֵד עַל שְׂדֵה־אֱדוֹם,
עַל פִּסְגַּת הַר־הָהָר, מְעוֹנָה אֱלֹהֵי קֶדֶם,
כִּי לִבִּי דוֹבֵב שִׁיר לַחַמָּה וְלַכְּסִיל.

מִשֶּׁיִּתְרַמֵּל פּוּל וְגָמַל פְּרִי־אִילָנוֹת
אֱלִילֵי עוֹלָם גַּז תְּפָסוּנִי וְאֵין לִי מָנוֹס —
אוֹ פֶסֶל אַחֲרוֹן דוֹר בְּמַמְלֶכֶת־הָאֱלִיל?

לְבִיבוֹת

(אִידִילְיָה)

1

אָכֵן בֹּקֶר, שֶׁאֵין דֻּגְמָתוֹ רַבִּים, אָז הָיָה
וְרִאשׁוֹן בְּחָדְשֵׁי הָאָבִיב, הַנָּאוֶה עַל שַׂדְמוֹת אוּקְרָיְנָה,
שַׂדְמוֹת וַעֲרָבוֹת נִרְחָבוֹת כַּיָּם! — וּמִי זֶה הָרִאשׁוֹן,
רִאשׁוֹן לַכֹּל, אֲשֶׁר רָאָה אֶת חֶמְדַּת הַבֹּקֶר הָרַעֲנָן,
עוֹדוֹ רוֹחֵץ בַּטַּל וְהֵילֵל בֶּן־שַׁחַר עוֹד מַבְהִיק,
בְּאוֹתוֹ הַיּוֹם וְהַשָּׁעָה? — עֶפְרוֹנִי — הוּא הָיָה הָרִאשׁוֹן
וְעָלָה עַל כְּנָפָיו אֶל עָל וְהִמְטִיר מִשָּׁם מַנְגִּינוֹתָיו,
מֵעִיר הַדְּרוֹרִים בַּגַּג, וְעַל פֹּארוֹת הַסְּבָךְ הָאַנְקוֹרִים. —
שְׁנִיָּה אָז תִּיקַץ מִשְּׁנָתָהּ הַחַמָּה וְלוֹהֲטִים פָּנֶיהָ:
בּוֹשָׁה כִּי אַחֲרָה קוּם, נֶחְפְּזָה הִיא אֶל עֲבוֹדָתָהּ
לְהַעֲבִיר מַכְחוֹל עַל צִיץ וְלָשִׂים בַּפּוּךְ כְּנַף צִפֹּרֶת,
לְסַלְסֵל בְּרִצֵּי גַל נִדָּח, קַשְׁקַשּׂוֹת הָאֲקוֹנוּס לִהֲפֹז,

Warming frog eggs in the reedy recesses of fens.

She sent a waking ray to the bees: "Wake up, sleepy," and urged

A tardy grain of wheat. — Third, awoke the old woman,

The Rabbi's widow, Gittel, and she opened her shining eyes.

Pure blue, clear, without even a rack of light cloud,

The sky stretched and wrapped in fresh grasses,

Just now opening their eyes, pasture and steppes sparkle;

And tranquillity dreams in everything, a desolate sanctuary's silence,

As if sky above and earth below were amazed

At the aura's sight and at their own beauty.

Gittel hurriedly arose from her warm bed

(She covered herself with a quilt, though the cool days were already gone),

She washed her hands in a two-handle copper basin —

This basin was very old, massy and solid,

Polished to glowing with crushed brick.

(It had been a gift from her aunt, may she rest in peace,

Given to her on her betrothal day as a remembrance,

A precious utensil — and it was only twice repewtered after.)

The lips of the old woman whispered, for she prayed

Quietly as she did every day and her eyes laughed and shone.

It seemed to her as if the universe greeted her now with a charming smile,

As if everything was glad, rejoicing at life's abundant beauty.

Before her prayer was done she sensed her spotted cat

Lying at her feet, wailing and licking her dress.

לְהָחֵם בֵּיצֵי הַצְּפַרְדְּעִים בְּסֵתֶר קָנֶה וּבִצָּה.
שָׁלְחָה קַו מֵקִיץ לַדְּבוֹרִים: "הָקִיצוּ, יְשֵׁנִים" וּמְזָרְזָה
בְּגַרְגֵּר שֶׁל דָּגָן שֶׁפָּגֵר. – וּשְׁלִישִׁית נֵעוֹרָה הַזְּקֵנָה
גִּיטְל, אַלְמְנַת הָרַב, וַתִּפְקַח עֵינֶיהָ הַמְּאִירוֹת.
צָחִים וּכְלִילֵי־הַתְּכֵלֶת, בְּאֵין זֵכֶר לְעָב קַל בַּמָּרוֹם,
הֶאֱהִילוּ שָׁמַיִם, וַעֲטוּפֵי עֲשָׁבִים רַעֲנַנִּים,
פָּקְחוּ זֶה עַתָּה עֵינֵיהֶם, הִבְרִיקוּ הַמִּגְרָשׁ וְהַשָּׂדֶמָה;
וְשַׁלְוָה חוֹלֶמֶת בַּכֹּל, דּוּמִיַּת בֵּית־מִקְדָּשׁ שֶׁשָּׁמֵם,
כְּאִלּוּ שָׁמַיִם בָּרוֹם וְהָאָרֶץ מִתַּחַת בְּתִמָּהוֹן
הֵכוּ לְמַרְאֵה הַזִּיו וּתְמֵהִים בְּעַצְמָם עַל יָפְיָם.

מְהֵרָה גִּיטְל וַתָּקָם מֵעַל מִטָּתָה הַחַמָּה
(הָיְתָה מִתְכַּסָּה בַּשְּׂמִיכָה וְאִם עָבְרוּ כְּבָר יְמֵי צִנָּה),
נָטְלָה יָדֶיהָ בְּסֵפֶל נְחֹשֶׁת בֶּן־יְדוֹתָיִם.
עַתִּיק הָיָה הַסֵּפֶל מְאֹד, כָּבֵד מִשְׁקָל וּמוּצָק,
מַבְרִיק וּמַזְהִיר, כְּבָא מִמֵּרוּק בִּלְבָנָה כְתוּתָה
(דּוֹרוֹן לָהּ הָיָה מֵאֵת דּוֹדָתָהּ, עָלֶיהָ הַשָּׁלוֹם,
וְנָתְנָה לָהּ אוֹתוֹ בְּיוֹם חַג כְּלוּלוֹתֶיהָ לְזִכָּרוֹן,
כְּלִי מְאֹד יָקָר – וּבְדִיל מֵאָז אַךְ פַּעֲמַיִם צִפּוּהוּ).
לָחַשׁ לְשִׂפְתֵי הַזְּקֵנָה, כִּי אֶת תְּפִלּוֹתֶיהָ הִתְפַּלְּלָה
חֶרֶשׁ וּכְדַרְכָּהּ יוֹם יוֹם, וְעֵינֶיהָ צוֹחֲקוֹת וּמְאִירוֹת;
נִדְמָה לָהּ, כְּאִלּוּ הַיְקוּם בְּצָחוֹק־חֵן יְקַדְּמֶנָה הַפַּעַם,
וְהַכֹּל שָׂמֵחַ וְשָׂשׂ עַל שִׁפְעַת־הַחַיִּים וְיָפְיָם.
וְטֶרֶם תְּפִלָּתָהּ תְּכַלֶּה כְּבָר הִרְגִּישׁ בָּהּ חֲתוּלָהּ הַבָּרֹד,
נָח לְרַגְלֶיהָ וּמְיַלֵּל בְּתַחֲנוּנִים וּמְלַקֵּק שִׂמְלָתָהּ;

He had grown thin and his hair was falling out
(it is the season of cats, their wailing is heard in the nights).
"Shame on you, old fool," the old woman fumed at him
And she filled a potsherd with milk and gave it to the spotted cat,
And the animal lapped hungrily, famished from its night wanderings.

Gittel watched the cat lapping the milk and felt
Suddenly in her soul hunger and in her nostrils
The smell of *levivot* filled with cheese
And washed in buttermilk — steam rising in the pot from the boiling water.
A smile was on the old woman's lips, she laughed at herself in her heart.
How comes this desire? — She turned her step to the cellar
Heavy with coolness, for there were the cheeses and pitchers of buttermilk.
She is deep in the cellar — suddenly the sound of the dog's barking
Rasps her ear, and the voice of someone talking:
"Be off, go, son of Satan." It is Domaha's voice as she comes,
But Sirka still kept barking, and Domaha lifted
Her cane, a staff of light almond wood, over the dog's back,
Her blow came hard at his thin knee.
He began to set up a wail from the shrewd pain and fled,
Tucking his sparse tail between his legs and hobbling on three.
It was just then Gittel came to greet this Gentile woman:
"Good morning to you, Gittele." "And a good omen for you; see,
Here is a full pot in my hands and so I meet you, Domaha."
"Peace to you, Gittel, my dove!" — and Domaha stands her cane

בְּשָׂרוֹ כָּחַשׁ מִשֶּׁמֶן וּשְׂעָרוֹ הוֹלֵךְ וְנוֹשֵׁר
(וְהַיָּמִים יְמֵי הַחֲתוּלִים וִילֵלָם נִשְׁמַע בַּלֵּילוֹת).
"אִי לְךָ, זָקֵן מִשְׁתַּטֶּה!" – תִּתְרַעֵם עָלָיו הַזִּקְנָה, –
וְחֶרֶשׁ שֶׁל דּוּד מִלְאָה חָלָב וַתִּתֵּן לַחֲתוּלָה הַבָּרֹד,
וְלָקְקָה הַחַיָּה בְּתֵאָבוֹן, כִּי רָעֲבָה מִלֵּיל נְדוּדֶיהָ.

רָאֲתָה גִיטְל חֲתוּלָה הַלּוֹקֵק הֶחָלָב וְהִרְגִּישָׁה
פִּתְאֹם בְּנַפְשָׁהּ גַּם הִיא תַּאֲוַת־הָאֹכֶל, וּבְאַפָּהּ
רֵיחַ שֶׁל לְבִיבוֹת מְמֻלָּאוֹת בִּגְבִינָה עֲשׂוּיָה
וְרוֹחֲצוֹת בְּזֻבְדָּה – וְהָאֵד עוֹלֶה בַּסִּיר מִן הָרוֹתְחִים.
בַּת־צְחוֹק עַל שִׂפְתֵי הַזִּקְנָה, כִּי צָחֲקָה בְלִבָּהּ עַל עַצְמָהּ:
אוֹתוֹ הַחֵשֶׁק מִנַּיִן? – וַתָּשֶׂם פְּעָמֶיהָ לַמַּרְתֵּף,
כְּבֵד הַצִּנָּה, כִּי שָׁם הַגְּבִינָה וְכַדֵּי הַזֻּבְדָּה.
הִיא עוֹד בַּמַּרְתֵּף הָעָמֹק – וּפִתְאֹם קוֹל נִבְחַת הַכֶּלֶב
צוֹרֵם הָאֹזֶן מְאֹד, וְעוֹד קוֹלוֹ שֶׁל אָדָם בְּדַבְּרוֹ:
"סוּר לְךָ, סוּר בְּכוֹר־שָׂטָן!" –וְהַקּוֹל קוֹל דּוֹמְחָה בְּבוֹאָהּ,
אֶפֶס לֹא עָמַד סִרְקָה מִנְּבֹחַ; אָז תָּרִים דּוֹמְחָה
מַקְלָהּ, גֶּזַע לוּז רַךְ, עַל גַּבּוֹ שֶׁל אוֹתוֹ הַכֶּלֶב,
וְהָיְתָה פְּגִיעָתָהּ מְאֹד רָעָה בְּאַרְכֻּבָּתוֹ הַצְּנוּמָה;
הִתְחִיל בּוֹכֶה מְאֹד מֵעָצְמַת מַכְאוֹבוֹ – וַיָּנֹס,
תָּחוּב זְנָבוֹ הַמְדֻלְדָּל בֵּין רַגְלָיו, וְהוּא מְדַדֶּה עַל שָׁלֹשׁ.
וְיָצְאָה כְרֶגַע גַּם גִּיטְל לְקַדֵּם פְּנֵי אוֹתָהּ הַ"גּוֹיָה".
– "צַפְרָא טָבָא לָךְ, גִּיטְלִי!" – "סִמָּן טוֹב לָךְ, רְאִי נָא:
הִנֵּה בְיָדִי כְּלִי מָלֵא וְכָכָה פְּגַשְׁתִּיךְ, דּוֹמְחָה!"
– "שָׁלוֹם לָךְ, גִּיטְלִי יוֹנָתִי!" – וַתַּעֲמֵד דּוֹמְחָה אֶת מַקְלָהּ

In the corner of the small room that was the kitchen —

"And how is your health?" "Your eyes see, Domaha.

By the Master of the World's grace, I slowly make my way;

And where do *your* legs carry you?" "I go to the church

And here too is milk in a pitcher and a loaf of bread, I bring them

To Father Vassily for the holiday." "Oh, Oh, Domaha, what holiday is this?"

"Just so, is today a small matter?

This is the Saint's day of Little Mikola. You forgot? Our people too,

Many of them, healthy ones, go out to the fields on holidays, like today.

Faith has disappeared in the people. Who comes to the monastery service?

Two old men, three old women, while they are still alive.

No strength is left to struggle with children of these brazen days.

These little ones — every puppy of them — if you tell them, go to pray,

Wag their tongues immediately: Be off! Why *today* of all days? —

The generation dwindles, and how sad are the walls of the monastery.

When I come into the court, who is there? A blind man, a lame man,
        another pauper.

The sad walls of the house and Father Vassily in the midst.

Sad, too, the voice of the bells, as if weeping for forsaken holiness.

But here also among your own there are heretics, renegades.

Every unclean thing, they eat — and pig! They smoke on the Sabbath!

I remember when I was a child: Sabbath and life died down,

Tranquillity, silence in the market place. I was almost terrified.

Now — it is a shame, isn't it? The Sabbath, and they trade and sell.

I am too ashamed, I, by my head, to come on Sabbath,

בְּפִנַּת הַחֶדֶר הַקָּט, שֶׁהָיָה גַּם חֶדֶר־לַבְשׁוּל, –
– "הֲיֵנוּ הַךְ. וּבְרִיאוּתֵךְ?" – "עֵינַיִךְ הָרוֹאוֹת, דּוֹמָחָה:
בְּחַסְדֵי רִבּוֹנוֹ־שֶׁל־עוֹלָם אַשְׁרֵךְ דַּרְכִּי לְאִטִּי.
לְאָן יִשָּׂאוּךְ רַגְלַיִךְ?" – "אֶל בֵּית־הַתְּפִלָּה אָנֹכִי,
וְהִנֵּה גַם חָלָב בַּכַּד וְכִכַּר־הַלֶּחֶם, הֵבֵאתִי
לְאַבָּא בַּסִּילִי בֶּחָג". – "הוֹי, הוֹי, דּוֹמָחָה, מַה חַג זֶה?"
"הֲיֵנוּ הַךְ, גִּיטְל, אָטוּ מִלְתָא זוּטְרְתָא הַיּוֹם?
הַיּוֹם "מִיקוֹלַה הַקָּטָן"! שָׁכַחַתְּ? וְאוּלָם גַּם מִשֶּׁלָּנוּ
רַבִּים וְכֵן שְׁלֵמִים כַּיּוֹם הַשָּׂדֶה הֵם יוֹצְאִים בַּחַגִּים.
אָפְסָה אֱמוּנָה מֵעָם. מִי בָא אֶל עֲבוֹדַת הַמִּנְזָר?
יְשִׁישִׁים שְׁנַיִם וְשָׁלֹשׁ זְקֵנוֹת, כָּל עוֹדָם בַּחַיִּים;
כֹּחַ כְּבָר אֵין לְהִתְגָּרוֹת בְּעוֹלֵי־הַיָּמִים הַחֲצוּפִים.
אֵלֶּה הַקְּטַנִּים – כָּל כִּלְבַּלֵּב, כִּי תֹאמְרוּ לוֹ:
– לֵךְ אֶל הַתְּפִלָּה –

חוֹרֵץ לְשׁוֹנוֹ מִיָּד: – סוּרִי! מַה יּוֹם מִיָּמִים?
הוֹלֵךְ וּפוֹחֵת הַדּוֹר, גַּם כָּתְלֵי הַמִּנְזָר מַה־נּוּגִים!
בְּבוֹאִי בֶּחָצֵר – מִי שָׁם? עִוֵּר, פִּסֵּחַ וְעוֹד דַּלְפּוֹן,
כָּתְלֵי־הַבַּיִת הַנּוּגִים וְאַבָּא בַּסִּילִי בְּתוֹכָם.
וְנוּגֶה גַם קוֹל הַפַּעֲמוֹנִים, כִּמְבַכִּים עֲזוּבַת־הַקֹּדֶשׁ.
וְהִנֵּה גַם מִשֶּׁלָּכֶם מִינִים הֵם וְאֶפִּיקוֹרְסִים,
אוֹכְלִים כָּל טְרֵפָה וַחֲזִיר וּמַעֲלִים עָשָׁן בְּשַׁבָּת.
יַלְדָּה הָיִיתִי, זְכוּרַתְנִי: שַׁבָּת – וּמֵתוּ הַחַיִּים,
שַׁלְוָה וָשֶׁקֶט בַּשּׁוּק, כִּמְעַט אֲחָזוּנִי חֲרָדוֹת.
עַתָּה – חֶרְפָּה הִיא, כְּלוּם לֹא? שַׁבָּת – וְסָחֹר וּמָכֹר.
בּוֹשָׁה אָנֹכִי – אֲנִי, חַי רֹאשִׁי, מִלָּבוֹא בַשַׁבָּת

To buy something in a Jewish shop. Isn't it so, Gittel?

Zalman the sheep merchant was at our place the day before yesterday,

Buying and selling on the holiday. — Zalman! — I said, Will you truly

Deceive your soul, will you live forever and never die?

And your God, what will he say? Aren't you afraid of his law?

It is Sabbath today! – And what did he reply? This Zalman turned to my son

And said to him: 'Gritza! Do you feel like giving us your mother,

She shall be our Rabbi?' — By my head, so he said, that brazen one.

And so it is, but how are you? What is your cheese for, and the buttermilk?"

Ashamed, Gittel answered: "I don't know myself. The smell

Of *levivot* came to my nostrils and I was unable to control myself.

There is a folk-saying: An old person is like a child.

A man lives long, but without his good sense he is brought

To the grave. . . ." Then the peal of bells sounded from the monastery.

Domaha grasped her cane, her pitcher, and her loaf of bread.

"Peace to you." "Go in peace" — and she hurried to leave the house.

The words of the Gentile woman are true, Gittel thought in her heart.

The generation dwindles. What are we? Moreover, what are our children?

Zalman the merchant... and my son? And my granddaughter, Razele,
    may she live.

Woe, Woe! Were we and our fathers so?

Gittel went and took a large pastry board down from the wall,

Tablets of sumach. It was made heavy and pink,

A dark reddish embroidery of veins spread over its surface.

She put the pastry board on the table and took up the sieve,

לִקְנוֹת דָּבָר בַּחֲנוּת־יְהוּדִית, הַיְנוּ הַךְּ, גִּיטְלִי.
וְזַלְמָן הַסּוֹחֵר בַּצֹּאן, אַךְ שִׁלְשׁם הָיָה אֶצְלֵנוּ,
קוֹנֶה וּמוֹכֵר בְּחָג. – זַלְמָן! – אָמַרְתִּי – הַאֻמְנָם
מַשְׁלֶה אֶת נַפְשְׁךָ אַתָּה, לְעוֹלָם תִּחְיֶה וְלֹא תָמוּת?
וֵאלֹהֵיכֶם מַה יֹּאמַר? הַאֵינְךָ יָרֵא אֶת דִּינוֹ? –
שַׁבָּת הַיּוֹם! – וּמַה שָּׂח? אֶל בְּנִי אֲזַי יִפְנֶה זֶה זַלְמָן
וְאוֹמֵר לוֹ: גְּרִיצָה! הֲיֵשׁ אֶת נַפְשְׁךָ לָתֵת אֶת אִמְּךָ,
וְהָיְתָה הִיא לָנוּ לְרַב? – חֵי רֹאשִׁי, כֹּה אָמַר הֶחָצוּף.
הַיְנוּ הַךְּ, וּמָה אַתְּ? וּמַה לָּךְ הַגְּבִינָה וְהַזֻּבְדָּה?״
בּוֹשָׁה גִּיטְל עָנָתָה: ״נַפְשִׁי בַּל אֵדַע... בָּא רֵיחַ
לִבִיבוֹת בְּאַפִּי, וְכָךְ לֹא יָכֹלְתִּי לִמְשׁוֹל בְּרוּחִי;
הַיְנוּ דְּאָמְרֵי אִינְשֵׁי: דּוֹמֶה זָקֵן לְיָלֶד.
רַבּוֹת יִחְיֶה הָאָדָם וְנִבְעָר־מִדַּעַת לַקֶּבֶר
יוּבָל...״ – וּבְאוֹתוֹ הָרֶגַע בָּא צִלְצוּל פַּעֲמוֹנֵי הַמִּנְזָר,
אָחֲזָה דּוֹמָחָה בַּמַּקֵּל, בַּכַּד וּבְכִכַּר־הַלֶּחֶם.
– ״שָׁלוֹם לָךְ!״ – ״לְשָׁלוֹם לְכִי!״ – וַתְּמַהֵר לַעֲזוֹב הַבַּיִת.
״צָדְקוּ דִבְרֵי הַ״גּוֹיָה״ – כֵּן גָּמְרָה בְלִבָּהּ הַזְּקֵנָה,
הוֹלֵךְ וּפוֹחֵת הַדּוֹר; מָה אָנוּ, וְכָל שֶׁכֵּן בָּנֵינוּ?
זַלְמָן הַסּוֹחֵר... וּבְנִי? וְנֶכְדָּתִי רִיזְלֶ׳ה תִּחְיֶה?
אוֹי וַאֲבוֹי! הֲכֵן הָיִינוּ אֲנַחְנוּ וַאֲבוֹתֵינוּ?״

בָּאָה וְנָטְלָה מֵעַל הַקִּיר הַמַּעֲרוֹךְ הַגָּדוֹל:
לוּחוֹת עֲצֵי־הָאֱגוֹ, אַדִּירִים וּוְרָדִים עָשׂוּהוּ,
וְרִקְמָה אֲמָצָה שֶׁל גִּידִים מְבַצְבֶּצֶת וְעוֹלָה עַל גַּבּוֹ.
שָׂמָה הַמַּעֲרוֹךְ עַל פְּנֵי הַשֻּׁלְחָן וַתִּקַּח הַנָּפָה,

She put very fine wheat flour into the sieve.

She sieved and scattered quickly and it danced in her nimble hands.

Like dust of clear snow into the holes of the sieve pushed

Grains of flour and so they rested on the whole board,

Grain after grain of dust. And the surface grew

Shining, glowing, and pure as the first snow that falls

And kisses the autumn earth: Bear greetings from the Prince of Winter!

Actually like grains of dust that fall, descend at their leisure,

Grain after grain, alone, caught and drifted the drama

Of Gittel's months. And everything that had happened to her was before her

Good and bad, years of work, moments of joy: —

She was a child ... a bride ... already a mother. Once alert, here

She is already old, a grandmother with a granddaughter, Razele, may she live.

Dust of pure snow pushed through the holes of the sieve,

Grain after grain, alone, they fall and descend at their leisure.

Then with her hands Gittel gathers the flour and makes of it

A circular mound and in the mound's center a hole.

Silently she gathers the flour, and her hands are light as she gathers,

And before her eyes her granddaughter smiles: Razele, may she live.

II

Clean, pure, and soft — the child will open its eyes:

Wrapped up in itself, the foreign element has not thrust into its soul.

Good and evil slumber and all its spirit's strength lies within.

נָתְנָה בַּנָּפָה הַהִיא קֶמַח־סֹלֶת מְאֹד דַּקָּה,
נִפְתָּה וְזָרְתָה מִיָּד וַתָּרֶקֵד בְּיָדֶיהָ הַמְּהִירוֹת.
כְּאַבְקוֹת הַשֶּׁלֶג הַצַּח נִתְחַבּוּ בְּנִקְבֵי הַנָּפָה
גַּרְגְּרֵי הַקֶּמַח וְכֹה נָחוּ עַל פְּנֵי כָל הַמַּעֲרוֹךְ,
גַּרְגֵּר שֶׁל אָבָק עַל גַּרְגֵּר. וְהָלַךְ הַמַּצָּע וְגָדֵל,
מַבְרִיק וּמַבְהִיק וְצַח, כַּשֶּׁלֶג הָרִאשׁוֹן, הַיּוֹרֵד
וְנוֹשֵׁק אֶת אַדְמַת הַסְּתָו: שְׂאִי שָׁלוֹם מֵאֵת שַׂר שֶׁל חֹרֶף!
מַמָּשׁ כְּגַרְגְּרֵי הָאָבָק, הַנּוֹפֵל, הַיּוֹרֵד לְאָטוֹ,
גַּרְגֵּר וְגַרְגֵּר לְבָד, נֶאֱחָזוּ, חָלְפוּ בַּמַּחֲזֶה
יַרְחֵי גִיטְל וְכֹל שֶׁעָבַר עָלֶיהָ – לְפָנֶיהָ,
טוֹבָה וְרָעָה, שָׁנִים שֶׁל עָמָל וְדַקּוֹת שֶׁל אֹשֶׁר: –
יַלְדָּה הִיא... כַּלָּה... כְּבָר אֵם... וּפַעַם נְעוֹרָה – וְהִנֵּה
זְקֵנָה כְּבָר, וְהִיא סַבְתָּא וְנֶכְדָּה לָהּ, רֵיזְ'לֶה תִּחְיֶה.

כְּאַבְקוֹת הַשֶּׁלֶג הַצַּח נִתְחַבּוּ בְּנִקְבֵי הַנָּפָה
גַּרְגֵּר וְגַרְגֵּר לְבָד, נוֹפְלִים וְיוֹרְדִים לְאָטָם;
בְּיָדָהּ אָז תֶּאֱסֹף גִּיטְל הַקֶּמַח, וְתַעַשׂ מִמֶּנּוּ
סוֹלְלָה הוֹלֶכֶת בְּעִגּוּל וְחוֹר בַּסּוֹלְלָה בַּתָּוֶךְ.
דּוּמָם אָסְפָה הַקֶּמַח, וְרַכּוֹת יָדֶיהָ בָּאָסְפָהּ,
וְנֶגֶד עֵינֶיהָ מְצַחֶקֶת נֶכְדָּתָהּ רֵיזְ'לֶה תִּחְיֶה.

II

נָקִי, וְטָהוֹר וָרַךְ – כֵּן יִפְקַח עֵינֵיהוּ הַיֶּלֶד.
כֻּלּוֹ כְּמַתְכֻּנְתּוֹ שֶׁלּוֹ, וְאֵין לְזָר חֵלֶק בְּנַפְשׁוֹ.
נָמִים הַטּוֹב וְהָרָע, כָּל כֹּחוֹת נַפְשׁוֹ בְּקִרְבּוֹ.

The child grows in the shadow of wings in the parents' hiding place,
Its soul like theirs, and it absorbs into itself their being.
Days pass and there comes a day (Gittel took six eggs,
She cracked them and put white and yolk into the wheat flour,
She kneaded the dough properly, kneading and kneading vigorously
And its appearance changed quickly, easily, and it was like clear amber)
When the child stands outside the nest of its parents who guard him,
And all who go back and forth before him lay upon him their hand
That injects him with filth, that scratches an abscess on his back —
It is done by main force daringly against the gentle parent hand.

Razele grew and was beautiful, the house was filled with gaiety.
In early morning, like the lark, she greeted the sun with song
And when the sun turned down to evening she closed her eyes, wearied
By her day's toil, chirping, skittering, singing
Dashing up the sand, teaching her dolls to pray
"I thank Thee." Then Gittel's son left the village,
And went away to live in the city. And after five long years
Gittel again saw her granddaughter who had left the nest.
She saw her but did not recognize her fledgling:
Then the child fell on the grandmother's bosom,
Her spirit subdued by the voice of the past yet living in her heart;
This moment gone, she opened lovely eyes
To pierce the old woman's heart with looks,
Canvassing and questioning: in spirit she was already a stranger to her.

הוֹלֵךְ וְגָדֵל הַיֶּלֶד בְּצֵל כַּנְפֵי הוֹרִים וּבְסִתְרָם,
נַפְשׁוֹ דּוֹמָה לְנַפְשָׁם וְהוּא סוֹפֵג אֶל תּוֹכוֹ יְשׁוּתָם.
וְיָמִים יַחֲלֹפוּ; וְיֵשׁ יוֹם (וְגִיטְל לָקְחָה שֵׁשׁ בֵּיצִים,
טָרְפָה וְשָׂמָה הַחֶלְבּוֹן וְהַחֶלְמוֹן בְּקֶמַח-הַסֹּלֶת,
לָשָׁה הַקֶּמַח כַּחֹק, לִישָׁה וְלִישָׁה חֲזָקָה,
וְהָפַךְ עֵינוֹ חִישׁ קַל וַיְהִי כְּעֵין הָעַנְבָּר הַשָּׁקוּף)
וְעָמַד הַיֶּלֶד מִחוּץ לְקַן אֲבוֹתָיו בָּם יֶחֱסֶה,
וְהָיְתָה בּוֹ יָדָם שֶׁל כָּל הָעוֹבְרִים וְהַשָּׁבִים עַל פָּנָיו,
וְנָתְנָה בּוֹ מִזֻּהֲמָתָהּ, וְשָׂרְטָה עַל גַּבּוֹ שָׂרָטֶת,
וְנִחֲתָה בְּכֹחַ וָעֹז, לְעֻמַּת יַד-אָבוֹת הָרַכָּה.

רֵיזְ׳לֶה גָּדְלָה וַתִּיף, וַתְּמַלֵּא הַבַּיִת עֲלִיצוּת.
הַשְׁכֵּם בַּבֹּקֶר בְּשִׁיר תְּקַדֵּם פְּנֵי שֶׁמֶשׁ כְּעֶפְרוֹנִי,
וְנָטְתָה הַשֶּׁמֶשׁ לַעֲרוֹב וְסָגְרָה עֵינֶיהָ, עֲיֵפָה
מֵעֲמָלָהּ בַּיּוֹם, מִצַּפְצֵף, מִכַּרְכֵּר, מְרַגֵּן
וּמֵהִתְפַּלֵּשׁ בַּחוֹל, מְלַמֵּד בְּבָתָּהּ הִתְפַּלֵּל
„מוֹדָה אֲנִי״. אַךְ אָז יַעֲזוֹב בְּנֵה הָעֲיָרָה –
יָצָא וַיִּגַּר בִּכְרַךְ. וּמִקֵּץ חָמֵשׁ שָׁנִים אֲרֻכּוֹת
רָאֲתָה שֵׁנִית אָז גִּיטְל נֶכְדָּתָהּ, שֶׁיָּצְאָה אֶת קַנָּהּ,
רָאֲתָה אוֹתָהּ, אַךְ לֹא הִכִּירָה נֶכְדָּתָהּ-אֶפְרוֹחָהּ;
רֶגַע עוֹד נָפְלָה אֶל חֵיק הָאֵם-הַזְּקֵנָה הַיַּלְדָּה:
נַפְשָׁהּ נִכְנְעָה לְקוֹל הֶעָבָר הַחַי עוֹד בְּלִבָּהּ;
וְאוּלָם הָרֶגַע כִּי חָלַף – פָּקְחָה עֵינֶיהָ הַיָּפוֹת,
שׁוֹאֲלוֹת וְחוֹדְרוֹת לְלֵב הַזְּקֵנָה, לָדַעַת מָה אַתְּ,
לָתוּר וְלִדְרֹשׁ הַכֹּל, כִּי זָרָה כְּבָר הָיְתָה לָהּ בְּרוּחָהּ.

Truly Gittel saw that changes had taken place;

And her son was different too, but she looked away,

Refusing to see it all, as if frightened at the sight.

The dough took on the redness of an Indian topaz,

And Gittel palmed the smoothness of the rolling pin.

Over the dough she passed it, over the four corners

She rolled and smoothed hard to make a single layer,

One thickness and one texture in all its parts;

She took the greatest care there were no gaps and breaks:

It turned out round and thin, as if fashioned with a saw and plane.

For a while it seemed as if the dough fought back,

Caught at the wood's smoothness, held on with great stubbornness,

Leaned on the surface of the rolling pin, clung with audacious strength,

But Gittel carefully overcame it with her quick movements.

Again, but after two years, she saw her.

Razele came from the Gymnasium, for she was a student,

Her thin body in the standard reddish uniform —

They are squeezing this little body with a mighty hand.

The same measure for everything, order and a book of rules.

Her hand gesticulated to her teacher's words, the voice of authority.

She bowed very properly, she spoke with judgment.

She brought with her a prize: *The Poems of Pushkin* in a binding

Of elegant purple cloth embossed with gold

("For good behavior and for devotion to studies").

אָמְנָם, רָאֲתָה גִיטְל, כִּי רַבּוֹת הַחֲדָשׁוֹת צָמְחוּ
וְאַחֵר הָיָה גַם בְּנָהּ, אֲבָל הֶעֱלִימָה עֵינֶיהָ,
מְמָאֲנָה לִרְאוֹת הַכֹּל, כִּירָאָה מִפְּנֵי הַמַּרְאֶה.
כְּפִטְדַּת־הֹדוּ אֲמָצָה כֵּן נַעֲשָׂה מַרְאֵה הַבָּצֵק.
לָקְחָה אָז גִּיטְל בְּכַף אֶת הַמַּעֲגִילָה הַחֲלָקָה,
אוֹתָהּ הֶעֱבִירָה עַל פְּנֵי הַבָּצֵק אֶל אַרְבַּע פְּנוֹתָיו,
הֶעֱבֵר וְהַחֲלֵק בְּעֹז לְהַיְשִׁירוֹ, לַעֲשׂוֹתוֹ לִשְׁכָבָה
אַחַת, וּמִדָּה וְקֶצֶב אֶחָד לְכָל הַחֲלָקִים;
וְשָׂמָה אֶת לִבָּהּ לְבַל יֵצְאוּ בּוֹ פְּרָצִים וְחַדּוּדִים.
עָגֹל הָיָה וָדַק, כְּעָשׂוּי בְּמַשּׂוֹר וּבְמַעֲצָד.
וְנִדְמֶה לָרְגָעִים כְּאִלּוּ עוֹמֵד עַל נַפְשׁוֹ הַבָּצֵק,
אוֹחֵז בְּחֶלְקַת הָעֵץ, וְנֶאֱחַז בְּרֹב קַשִׁיּוּת־עֹרֶף,
דָּבֵק בְּחָזְקָה וּבְעֹז, מִתְרַפֵּק עַל פְּנֵי הַמַּעֲגִילָה...
וְטִפְּלָה בּוֹ גִיטְל מְאֹד וּזְרִיזָה הָיְתָה בְמַעֲשֶׂיהָ.

...וְעוֹד הַפַּעַם אַךְ כַּעֲבֹר שְׁנָתַיִם, אוֹתָהּ רָאֲתָה:
רֵיזְ׳לֶה בָּאָה מִבֵּית־הַגִּמְנַסְיוֹן, כִּי הָיְתָה "תַּלְמִידָה";
בְּגָדִים אֲמָצִים כַּחֹק עַל פְּנֵי גִזְרָתָהּ הַדַּקָּה,
אוֹסְרִים וּמְכַוְּצִים בְּכַף אַדִּירִים הַגְּוִיָּה הַקְּטַנָּה.
מִדָּה וּמְשׁוּרָה לַכֹּל, וְסֵדֶר וּמִשְׁטָר קָבוּעַ.
יָדָהּ הִנִּיעָה כְּדַבֵּר מוֹרָתָהּ וּגְזֵרַת רָאשֵׁיהָ,
עוֹשָׂה הַקִּדָּה כַּדָּת, וּבְמִשְׁפָּט כִּלְכְּלָה דְבָרֶיהָ.
תְּשׁוּרָה הֵבִיאָה אָז אִתָּהּ: שִׁירֵי פּוּשְׁקִין בִּכְרִיכָה
יָפָה וְנֶהְדָּרָה מִבַּד אַרְגָּמָן, וְזָהָב צְפוּיֶהָ,
"עֵקֶב הַנְהָגָהּ כַּדָּת וְכַדִּין וְהַתְמָדָהּ בְּלִמּוּדִים".

All day the girl sat over the book and read

Poem after poem in a high-tuned voice like a melodious singer,

And her eyes were fire and her cheeks flame.

The book was precious in the eyes of the old woman and the girl:

Each day the granddaughter read it till she rested in the evening

And the old woman placed it in the bookcase among the other books,

"Tzena Urena"* and the beloved "Supplications of Sara Bat-Tuvim."*

When first she did so, her heart pounded

But she excused the unclean blemish,*

For it was not like the other books her granddaughter brought

To stack in the corner of the room... (and the old woman took a glass

Bottle, thin and round, and thrust it into the prepared dough,

She pressed the mouth of the bottle — circles formed.

The glass entered the dough and its opening cut like a knife.

All alike were the many circles she made;

They came out every one a twin, like objects poured in a factory).

The vise of discipline and law that presses on the student's soul

Will press, cut, form his being to the approved shape,

Straight and standard; one never thinks to alter it.

Rejected, stepped on, wounded, the soul of the little one contracts

Under the mighty force whose long pressure alienates it —

It dwindles like a candle struggling with a storm wind.

With almost no resources left, at the end of many days,

The child will leave the threshold of its school, its thoughts

כָּל הַיּוֹם אֶל הַסֵּפֶר יָשְׁבָה הַנַּעֲרָה וַתִּקְרָא
שִׁירָה וְשִׁירָה בְּקוֹל רָם וּבְנִגּוּן, כִּמְזַמֵּר בְּרִנָּנִים,
וְהָיוּ עֵינֶיהָ כָאֵשׁ וְעַל פְּנֵי לְחָיֶיהָ הַלָּהַב.
יָקָר הָיָה הַסֵּפֶר בְּעֵינֵי הַזְּקֵנָה וְהַנַּעֲרָה:
יוֹם־יוֹם בּוֹ קָרְאָה הַנֶּכְדָּה, וּבְנוּחָהּ בָּעֶרֶב הֶעֱמִידָה
אוֹתוֹ הַזְּקֵנָה בַּאֲרוֹן־הַסְּפָרִים בֵּין יֶתֶר סְפָרֶיהָ:
„צְאֶינָה וּרְאֶינָה” וְהַתְּחִנּוֹת הַחֲבִיבוֹת שֶׁל „שָׂרָה בַת־טוֹבִים”.
אָמְנָם, נוֹקְפָה מִתְּחִלָּה הָיָה לִבָּהּ בַּעֲשׂוֹתָהּ,
אוּלָם הִיא לִמְּדָה זְכוּת עַל אוֹתָהּ הַ„טְּרֵפָה־וְהַפְּסוּלָה”,
יַעַן לֹא הָיְתָה כִּשְׁאָר הַסְּפָרִים הֵבִיאָה נֶכְדָּתָהּ,
לְהַעֲמִיד בְּפִנַּת־הַחֶדֶר ... (וַתִּקַּח הַזְּקֵנָה צְנַצֶּנֶת־
זְכוּכִית דַּקָּה עֲגֻלָּה וַתִּתֵּן בַּבָּצֵק הַמּוּכָן,
נָטְלָה וְלָחֲצָה אֶת פִּי הַצְּלוֹחִית – וַיֵּצְאוּ עֲגוּלִים.
נִכְנְסָה הַזְּכוּכִית בַּבָּצֵק וּפִיהָ בָּא חוֹתֵךְ כַּשַּׁכִּין.
מִדָּה אַחַת לְכָל הָעֲגוּלִים הָרַבִּים עָשָׂתָה.
תּוֹאֲמִים יָצָאוּ, כְּכֵלִים בְּבָתֵּי־הַחֲרֹשֶׁת יוּצָקוּ).

צֶבַע הַמִּשְׁמַעַת וְהַחֹק, הַמְּעִיקָה עַל נֶפֶשׁ הַתַּלְמִיד,
תִּגְזֹר וְתִלְחַץ וְתָצוּר יֵשׁוּתוֹ בַּצּוּרָה, שֶׁמְּצָאָהּ
טוֹבָה וִישָׁרָה, שֶׁאֵין לְהַרְהֵר אַחֲרֶיהָ לְשַׁנּוֹתָהּ.
וְנֶפֶשׁ הַקָּטָן תִּתְכַּוֵּץ, וְהִיא נִדְחָהּ, נִרְמֶסֶת וּדְוֻיָה,
מִפְּנֵי הַנּוֹגֵשׂ הָעַז, הַשּׁוֹקֵד עָלֶיהָ לְהַחֲרִימָהּ:
הוֹלְכָה וּפוֹחֲתָה כַּנֵּר, הַנֶּאֱבָק עִם רוּחַ הַסָּעַר.
שָׂרִיד לָהּ אֵין כִּמְעַט, – וְהָיָה בְּאַחֲרִית הַיָּמִים,
וְעָזַב הַיֶּלֶד אֶת סַף בֵּית־סִפְרוֹ, וְהָיוּ מַחְשְׁבוֹתָיו

The thoughts of this one's book, its soul the creature of another book,

The sight of its eyes seen through the eyes of a dominating teacher,

Its voice the voice of this one or another,

It has gestures — peculiar gestures — and its soul is lost

To a cramping pressure...

                                    And the old woman took the cheese,

Crumbled it in a bowl and mixed it with eggs;

She took the cheese and poured it carefully

In the circles of prepared dough which she had cut with the glass bottle.

When she had poured the cheese, she pressed the dough with her hands,

Closed it over the cheese, and the two became one.

The spirit of the tender child had ceased to fight,

It absorbed whatever its tutors had to give.

It cherished up the stranger's teaching, emerging after many days,

To the joy of parents and teachers, at the gate — a learned calf.

But sometimes the child will free itself from the pressure of its bonds,

And its soul is filled with hidden hate, eternal grudge

Against its oppressors, who gave it things to sanctify

Against its will: having no weapon in its hands,

It will cleave to everything forbidden by its tormentors.

Years passed and Razele once more returned.

A young woman in her prime when she returned to the nest,

This time not at all gay as she used to be, her eyes

מַחְשְׁבוֹת סְפָרָיו שֶׁל זֶה, וְנַפְשׁוֹ – יְצִיר סֵפֶר שֵׁנִי,
וְעֵינָיו רוֹאוֹת מִבַּעַד לְעֵינָיו שֶׁל מוֹרוֹ הַתַּקִּיף,
וְהָיָה גַּם קוֹלוֹ כְּקוֹל מַדְרִיךְ זֶה אוֹ מִשְׁנֵהוּ,
תְּנוּעוֹת לוֹ – תְּנוּעוֹת הַלָּז, – וְנַפְשׁוֹ הוּא אָבְדָה בֵּינְתַיִם
בְּתוֹךְ הַלַּחַץ וְהַדֹּחַק...
וַתִּקַּח הַזְּקֵנָה הַגְּבִינָה,
מְעַכָּה אוֹתָהּ בַּסַּף וְעַל בֵּיצִים אוֹתָהּ עָשָׂתָה,
לָקְחָה הַגְּבִינָה הַזֹּאת וַתִּתֵּן אוֹתָהּ בִּזְהִירוּת,
בְּעִגּוּל הַבָּצֵק, הֵכִינָה בַּעֲשׂוֹתָהּ בְּצַלּוֹחִית הַזְּכוּכִית,
וְאַחֲרֵי תִתָּה הַגְּבִינָה, צָבְטָה הַבָּצֵק בְּיָדֶיהָ,
סָגְרָה עַל חֲתִיכוֹת הַגְּבִינָה – וַיִּהְיוּ שְׁנֵיהֶם לְאֶחָד.

...נֶפֶשׁ הַיֶּלֶד הָרַךְ כְּבָר פָּסְקָה מִלְּחוֹם עַל עַצְמָהּ,
וְסָפְגָה וְקִבְּלָה הַכֹּל מִיַּד מַדְרִיכֶיהָ. וַתִּטַּפַּח
בְּקִרְבָהּ תּוֹרַת הַזָּר, בִּרְבוֹת הַיָּמִים גַּם תֵּצֵא,
לְשִׂמְחַת הַהוֹרִים וּמוֹרִים, הַשַּׂעֲרָה – עֵגֶל מְלֻמָּד.
וְאוּלָם יֵשׁ שֶׁמִּלַּחַץ כְּבָלָיו יִשְׁתַּחְרֵר הַיֶּלֶד,
וְנַפְשׁוֹ שִׂנְאָה מְסֻתֶּרֶת, מַשְׁטֶמַת עוֹלָמִים נִמְלָאָה
לְכָל מַכְנִיעֶיהָ וְלַאֲשֶׁר אִנְּסוּהָ לְהַעֲרִיץ וּלְהַקְדִּישׁ
לַמְרוֹת רְצוֹנָהּ; וּבְאֵין מְחָאָה אַחֶרֶת בְּיָדֶיהָ,
תִּדְבַּק בְּכָל אֲשֶׁר אָסוּר מְעַנֶּיהָ חָל עָלָיו וַחֲרָמָיו.

...שָׁנִים עָבְרוּ, וַתָּשָׁב רֵיזֶל אֶל אִמָּהּ הַזְּקֵנָה.
עַלְמָה וּבְעֶצֶם נְעוּרֶיהָ שָׁבָה אֶל קִנָּהּ הַפַּעַם,
אֶפֶס עַלִּיזָה לֹא הָיְתָה כִּהְיוֹתָהּ מִקֶּדֶם, וְעֵינֶיהָ

Deep and full of melancholy. She was silent, reading

Day and night, as long as the kerosene lamp in her room stayed lit.

The old woman, thinking to give her some heart's-ease,

Took Pushkin out of the bookcase, where he was locked,

She gave it to Razele, and the young woman twisted her lips.

To see Pushkin insulted so made the old woman's soul grow sad;

She felt the insult, too, and it pained her heart.

With compassion she replaced this "unclean blemish" in the bookcase

Next to her supplications, her prayer book, and the "Tzena-Urena."

And even before the pancakes were prepared, in the depth of the stove
    water boiled,

Filling the pot and sending up vapor and bubbles.

The old woman took the *levivot* and put them into the boiling water

And the vapors covered them...

                         The sudden barking of Sirka

Came to Gittel's ears — the sound of words, abuse, a man's voice.

She went out and saw the postman of her village,

He brought her a letter. At once she recognized Razele's hand.

Heart pounding with joy, she tore off an edge of the envelope

And went close to the window pane to see the writing better.

At once a deathly pallor covered her lovely face;

Quickly she grasped the edge of the table, fearful of falling

To the ground. Her strength abandoned her then, but she recovered
    herself and sat on a chair.

The words of the letter were brief, ten lines, no more,

But how much the lines spoke to the old woman!

עָמְקוּ וְנִמְלְאוּ תוּגָה, וַתְּהִי מַחֲרִישָׁה וְקוֹרְאָה
יוֹמָם וָלֵיל, כָּל עוֹד הַנֵּפְטְ בַּמְּנוֹרָה בְּחַדְרָהּ.
חָפֵץ חָפְצָה הַזְּקֵנָה לַעֲשׂוֹת לָהּ נַחַת־רוּחַ –
לָקְחָה אֶת פּוֹשְׁקִין מִתּוֹךְ אֲרוֹן־הַסְּפָרִים, בּוֹ נִסְגָּר,
וְנָתְנָה לְרֵיזְ׳לֶה אוֹתוֹ – וַתִּעַקֵּם הָעַלְמָה שְׂפָתֶיהָ...
עָגְמָה נֶפֶשׁ הַזְּקֵנָה לִרְאוֹת אֶת פּוֹשְׁקִין בְּעֶלְבּוֹנוֹ,
חָשָׁה בְעֶלְבּוֹנוֹ גַּם הִיא, כְּאִלּוּ הִכְאִיבוּ אֶת לִבָּהּ,
שָׁמָה בְּרַחֲמִים רַבִּים הַ„טְּרֵפָה־וּפְסוּלָה" בָּאָרוֹן
יַחַד עִם כָּל תְּחִנּוֹתֶיהָ, הַ„סִּדּוּר" וְהַ„צֵּאֶנָה וּרְאֶינָה".

וְטֶרֶם נָכוֹנוּ הַלְּבִיבוֹת – וּבְיַרְכְּתֵי כִּירַיִם כְּבָר רָתְחוּ
מַיִם, שֶׁמִּלְּאוּ הַסִּיר וַיַּעֲלוּ אֵד וּבְעַבּוּעִים.
לָקְחָה הַזְּקֵנָה הַלְּבִיבוֹת וַתְּשִׂימֵן פַּעַם בְּרוֹתְחִים
וְאֵדֵי הַמַּיִם כְּבָר כִּסּוּן...
וְנִבְחַת סְרִיקָה הַפִּתְאוֹמִית
בָּאָה עַד אָזְנֵי גִיטְל – וְקוֹל דְּבָרִים, קוֹל גִּדּוּף, קוֹל גֶּבֶר.
יָצְאָה וְרָאֲתָה אֶת נוֹשֵׂא־הַמִּכְתָּבִים בִּכְפָרָהּ.
מִכְתָּב לָהּ הֵבִיא. מִיָּד הִכִּירָה כְּתַב־יָדָהּ שֶׁל רֵיזֶל.
בְּלֵבָב פּוֹעֵם מִגִּיל קָרְעָה אֶת קְצוֹת הַמַּעֲטָפָה,
קָרְבָה אֶל שִׁמְשׁוֹת הַחַלּוֹן לְהֵיטִיב לִרְאוֹת בַּכָּתוּב.
וְחִוְרַת־מָוֶת מִיָּד כִּסְּתָה פָּנֶיהָ הַיָּפִים.
מִהֲרָה לֶאֱחוֹז בִּקְצֵה הַשֻּׁלְחָן, כִּי יָרְאָה, פֶּן תִּפֹּל
אַרְצָה כִּי כֹחָהּ עֲזָבָהּ – וַתֶּחֱזַק וַתֵּשֶׁב עַל כִּסֵּא.
קָצְרוּ דִבְרֵי הַמִּכְתָּב, עֶשֶׂר שׁוּרוֹת, לֹא יוֹתֵר,
אֶפֶס הַשּׁוּרוֹת הָאֵל מָה רַבּוֹת הִגִּידוּ לְהַזְּקֵנָה!

"The fortress of Peter and Paul,* imprisoned, waiting for the trial . . ."

". . . A girl, a girl sitting in prison . . . Oh, Razele, Razele, my daughter!" . . .

The old woman felt some frightful thing, some overwhelming thing

Drawing near to step over her and to trample her,

And she had no energy or strength to save herself.

Her thoughts grew dim, faltered and expired,

Her eyes stared out and saw nothing . . .

The warm spring sun rose high and flooded with light

Field and forest and pasture; a ray stole in and caressed

The old woman's cheeks. She sits and hears

The boiling of the water in the pot: it steams, storms, rushes,

Raising up foam and mist, and the *levivot* are between the bubbles.

The Bells

(a ballad)

To the thunder of bells* a voice calls for blood!

Bom-Bom! Bom-Bom! Bom-Bom!

The town was stormed! Haidamaks*

Raped, slaughtered the folk! Everyone

Carried the booty in sacks.

„מְצוּדַת־פֶּטְרוּס־וּפַבְלוֹס אֲסוּרָה וּמְחַכָּה לַמִּשְׁפָּט"...
„נַעֲרָה יוֹשֶׁבֶת בַּתְּפִיסָה... הוֹי, רֵיזֶ'לֶה, רֵיזֶ'לֶה בִּתִּי!"...
חָשָׁה הַזְּקֵנָה, כִּי יֵשׁ נוֹרָא, וְאָם וּמַבְהִיל
הוֹלֵךְ וְקָרֵב, וּבָא וְחוֹנֶה עָלֶיהָ לְרָמְסָהּ,
וְכֹחַ לָהּ אָיִן, וְאֵין דֵּי אוֹן לְהִנָּצֵל מִמֶּנּוּ,
הוֹלְכוֹת מַחְשְׁבוֹתֶיהָ וְכָלוֹת, לְקוּיוֹת וְכֵהוֹת,
נִכְחָהּ הִבִּיטוּ עֵינֶיהָ – וּמְאוּמָה לֹא רָאֲתָה נֶגְדָּהּ...

וְשֶׁמֶשׁ הָאָבִיב הַחַם הִתְרוֹמֵם וַיָּצֶף בְּאוֹרוֹת
שָׂדֶה וְיַעַר וָכָר, וְקֶרֶן הִתְגַּנְּבָה – וּמְלַטְּפָה
לְחָיֵי הַזְּקֵנָה. וְהִיא יוֹשֶׁבֶת, מַבִּיטָה וְשׁוֹמַעַת
רְתִיחַת הַמַּיִם בַּסִּיר, שְׁקוֹדְחִים, וְרוֹעֲשִׁים וְסוֹעֲרִים,
מַעֲלִים קֶצֶף וָאֵד, וּלְבִיבוֹת בֵּין הַבַּעְבּוּעִים...

הַפַּעֲמוֹנִים

(בלדה)

אֶל רַעַם פַּעֲמוֹנִים – קוֹל קוֹרֵא לְדָם.
בָּם־בָּם! בָּם־בָּם! בָּם־בָּם!
הַבְקָעָה הָעִיר! הַיְּדַמְּקִים
הִכְרִיעוּ לַטֶּבַח הַקְּהִלָּה – הָעָם
נָשָׂא הַבִּזָּה בְּשַׂקִּים.

Two days corpses rolled in the town,
On the third, they threw them in a hole:
They fouled the synagogue (with feces of swine
They filthied each Torah scroll)*
Over it they built a steeple white and tall,
A choir of bells they hung there,
When the priest rose to prayer
They would answer him:
Bim-Bom! Bim-Bom!

One of the "Thirty-Six Just"* heard,
Alone on an autumn night he appeared:
He came, said the prayer for the dead.*
"Be magnified, be sanctified!"....
But finishing — there was no one,
Not a man, only the night asleep —
Groaned the big bell in the tall steeple
And the small bells answered then
"Amen!
Amen! Amen!"

The priest heard, he hurried there,
Crowd upon crowds came to the site,
The Metropolitan and Archimandrite
Sprinkled holy water, sang loud in the air

יוֹמַיִם הִתְגּוֹלְלוּ הַפְּגָרִים בָּעִיר,
בַּשְּׁלִישִׁי הִשְׁלִיכוּם הַבּוֹרָה;
וַיְחַלְּלוּ הַמִּקְדָּשׁ (בְּצוֹאַת־חֲזִיר
טִמְּאוּ כָל סִפְרֵי־הַתּוֹרָה),
וּמִגְדָּל לוֹ בָּנוּ לָבָן וָרָם,
וַיִּתְּנוּ בוֹ קְהַל־פַּעֲמוֹנִים.
וְהָיָה בְהִתְפַּלֵּל הַכֹּמֶר הַקָּם,
וְהָיוּ לוֹ עוֹנִים:
בִּים־בָּם! בִּים־בָּם!

וַיִּשְׁמַע הָאֶחָד מִלַּמֵּד־הַנָּא"ו,
וַיָּבוֹא יְחִידִי בַּלַּיְלָה וּסְתָו,
וַיָּבוֹא וַיֹּאמַר הַ„קַּדִּישׁ":
„יִתְגַּדַּל וְיִתְקַדֵּשׁ...".
וַיְהִי כְּכַלּוֹתוֹ – וְאִתּוֹ שָׁם אֵין
מֵאָדָם גַּם אִישׁ, אַךְ הַלַּיְלָה הַנָּם, –
וַיְנַהֵם הַפַּעֲמוֹן בְּמִגְדָּל הָרָם,
וַתַּעֲנֶינָה הַמְּצִלּוֹת גַּם הֵן:
„אָמֵן!
אָמֵן וְאָמֵן!

וַיִּשְׁמַע הַכֹּמֶר – הִזְדָּרֵז לְשָׁם,
הִתְקַבְּצוּ הֲמוֹנִים הֲמוֹנִים,
בָּא הֶגְמוֹן וְאַרְכִיהֶגְמוֹנִים.
וַיָּזוּ מֵי קֹדֶשׁ, שָׁרוּ בְּקוֹל רָם

To set the fault in the bells aright.

In the high steeple the bell responds

And the carillon,

In splendor and charm

Bim-Bom! Bim-Bom!

But during the watch of the midnight hour*

The sign is renewed:

Again groans the bell in the steeple

Sighs the carillon too

With a ringing of grace, with a ringing of pain,

"Amen!

Amen! Amen!"

They Say There Is a Country

They say there is a country

A land that flows with sunlight.

Where is that country?

Where is that sunlight?

They say there is a country

Where seven pillars* are.

There bloom on every hilltop

Seven wandering stars.*

לְתַקֵּן אֶת פְּגָם־הַפַּעֲמוֹנִים.
וַיֵּעָן הַפַּעֲמוֹן בַּמִּגְדָּל הָרָם,
וְהַמְצִלּוֹת גַּם הֵן
בְּהָדָר וָחֵן:
בִּים־בָּם! בִּים־בָּם!

וְאוּלָם בַּלַּיְלָה עִם תִּקּוּן חֲצוֹת
הִתְחַדֵּשׁ הָאוֹת:
שׁוּב נֶאֱנַח הַפַּעֲמוֹן בַּמִּגְדָּל הָרָם
הַמְצִלּוֹת נֶאֱנָחוֹת גַּם הֵן
בְּצִלְצוּל־יְגוֹנִים, בְּצִלְצוּל שֶׁל חֵן
„אָמֵן!
אָמֵן וְאָמֵן!"

אוֹמְרִים יֶשְׁנָהּ אֶרֶץ...

אוֹמְרִים: יֶשְׁנָהּ אֶרֶץ,
אֶרֶץ רְוַת שֶׁמֶשׁ...
אַיֵּה אוֹתָהּ אֶרֶץ?
אֵיפֹה אוֹתוֹ שֶׁמֶשׁ?

אוֹמְרִים: יֶשְׁנָהּ אֶרֶץ
עַמּוּדֶיהָ שִׁבְעָה,
שִׁבְעָה כּוֹכְבֵי־לֶכֶת
צָצִים עַל כָּל גִּבְעָה.

A land where is fulfilled
All a man can hope,
Everyone who enters —
Akiba* does approach.

"Shalom to you, Akiba,
Peace be with you, Rábbi.
Where are they, the Holy,
Where are the Maccábee?"*

Answers him Akiba,
Says to him the Rábbi:
"All Israel is holy,
You are the Maccábee!"

אֶרֶץ – בָּהּ יָקוּם
כָּל אֲשֶׁר אִישׁ קָנָה,
נִכְנַס כָּל הַנִּכְנָס –
פָּגַע בּוֹ עֲקִיבָא.

‎„שָׁלוֹם לְךָ, עֲקִיבָא!
שָׁלוֹם לְךָ, רַבִּי!
אֵיפֹה הֵם הַקְּדוֹשִׁים,
אֵיפֹה הַמַּכַּבִּי?”

עוֹנֶה לוֹ עֲקִיבָא,
אוֹמֵר לוֹ הָרַבִּי:
‎„כָּל יִשְׂרָאֵל קְדוֹשִׁים,
אַתָּה הַמַּכַּבִּי!”

II

The Generation of Bialik and Tchernichovsky

הדור של ביאליק וטשרניחובסקי

Tirzah

Day after day as the day sets,
    And the sun's heat is waning,
There walks Tirzah, lovely faun,
    Into the garden singing.

Day after day as day sets —
    To listen to her singing,
A cherub descends from the skies
    To the garden winging.

In mysterious quiet all is wrapped,
    The shadow spreading thickens —
And Tirzah singing, still sings on,
    And still the cherub listens.

Then as a sudden tremor moves
    Through leaves of tree about her,
Tirzah a slight moment shudders,
    Stares expectantly behind her.

But nothing whatever does she see,
    Completely unaware,
Confident she sings again
    For the cherub's listening ear.

תִּרְצָה

כָּל יוֹם וָיוֹם בִּפְנוֹת הַיּוֹם,
כִּי יֶרֶף לַהַט חֶרֶס,
לָהּ יוֹצֵאת תִּרְצָה, יַעֲלַת־תֹּם,
הַגַּנָּה וּמְשׁוֹרֶרֶת.

כָּל יוֹם וָיוֹם בִּפְנוֹת הַיּוֹם —
לִשְׁמוֹעַ אֶל הָרִנָּה,
אָז יֵרֵד כְּרוּב מִשְּׁמֵי־הָרוֹם
וּבָא אֱלֵי הַגַּנָּה.

הַכֹּל כְּבָר עוֹטֶה דְּמִי וָסוֹד,
וְעַב־צֵל מִשְׁתָּרֵעַ —
וְתִרְצָה שָׁרָה, שָׁרָה עוֹד,
וְעוֹד הַכְּרוּב שׁוֹמֵעַ.

וּבַחֲלוֹף פִּתְאֹם זִיז כִּמְעַט
בֵּין טַרְפֵּי־עֵץ סְבִיבֶיהָ —
וְחָרְדָה תִרְצָה רֶגַע קָט
וְצָפְתָה לַאֲחוֹרֶיהָ.

אַךְ הִיא לֹא תֵרֵא שָׁם עַד־מָה
וּמְאוּם אֵין הִיא יוֹדַעַת —
וְהָלְאָה בֶּטַח תָּשִׁיר לָהּ,
וְאֹזֶן כְּרוּב שׁוֹמָעַת.

Afternoon Light

Drink deep, my heart, of brightest noon,
But trust not its tranquillity!
Quietly, in the blue light, lurk
Mourning winds one cannot see.

Treacherous is the afternoon rest.
Do not trust it when it comes.
A bright canopy is woven slowly
By a hidden hand over horror's depths.

Dreams of purest white
Dig, for something, a grave:
You awake — their song stills:
Their gold tarnishes, their light pales.

Do not believe in the light of afternoon
Nor in its deceiving rest.
Sure is one hour, one hour alone,
Faithful in its distress.

This is the muted evening hour —
Lingering always in the day's edge.
It will not fail, believe in it.
Walk erect to meet it.

אוֹר צָהֳרָיִם

רְוֵה לְבָבִי, זִיו צָהֳרָיִם,
אַךְ אַל תַּאֲמֵן בְּמַרְגּוֹעָם!
חֶרֶשׁ אוֹרְבִים בְּאוֹר הַתְּכֵלֶת
רוּחוֹת אֵבֶל וְאֵין רוֹאָם.

בִּגְדָה מְנוּחַת צָהֳרָיִם.
אַל נָא תִבְטַח בָּהּ, אִם בָּאָה.
יָד נִסְתֶּרֶת אַט שׁוֹזֶרֶת
חֲפַת־אוֹר עַל תְּהוֹמוֹת־זְוָעָה.

וַחֲלוֹמוֹת־לִבְּךָ זַכִּים
כּוֹרִים קֶבֶר לְאֵיזֶה דָבָר;
וַהֲקִיצוֹתָ – נָדַם שִׁירָם;
זְהָבָם הוּעַם וְאוֹרָם חָוַר.

אַל תַּאֲמִינָה בְּאוֹר צָהֳרָיִם
וּמְנוּחָתָם הַכּוֹזֵבָה; –
שָׁעָה אַחַת, שְׁעַת בִּטָּחוֹן,
יֵשׁ נֶאֱמָנָה וַעֲצֵבָה.

שְׁעַת הָעֶרֶב הִיא הַדְּמוּמָה –
בְּשׁוּלֵי יוֹם הִיא תָּמִיד שׁוֹהָה.
הִיא לֹא תְכַזֵּב. בָּהּ רַק תַּאֲמִין.
וְשֶׁפִי תֵלֵךְ לִקְרַאת בָּאָה.

In the light of day, in the golden white
That it come, my heart, await!

Midnight

A tarrying moon still drips the redness of her blood
And the peaceful night grasses
Lean their little heads on each other
Dozing, hands under their cheeks,
In her tranquil light.
In the narrow lane a tired wayfarer kneels
And a horse in the meadow raises his head amazed.

Then someone stretches His hand over the world
And all motionless congeals beneath Him.
Like russet copper, light, mysteriously strange
Hangs over the earth grown dim.
From his chariot a star glides and in its lair
The sea lion mutely licks its paw.
No nurseling whimpers then, the cusp upon its branch
Holds its breath —
Only Chaos, a ravaging beast from its ambush,
Stretches out at the world's edge gaping his maw.
There is no rising and no setting at this hour.

בְּאוֹר הַיּוֹם וּבְלֶבֶן זָהָבוֹ
צִפָּה, לִבִּי, לָהּ כִּי תָבֹא!

חֲצוֹת

סַהַר מֵאַחַר רוֹעֵף עוֹד אֹדֶם דָּמוֹ
וְדִשְׁאֵי לֵיל שַׁאֲנַנִּים
זֶה עַל זֶה הִטּוּ רָאשֵׁיהֶם הַקְּטַנִּים
וּמְנַמְנְמִים, יְדֵיהֶם תַּחַת לְחָיָם,
בְּאוֹרוֹ הָרוֹגֵעַ.
בְּמֵצַר שָׂדֶה כָּרַע הֵלֶךְ עָיֵף
וְסוּס בָּאָחוּ יָרִים רֹאשׁ תָּמֵהַּ.

אָז אֶחָד יֵט יָדֵהוּ עַל הָעוֹלָם
וְהַכֹּל יִקְרַשׁ תַּחְתָּיו מִבְּלִי נוֹעַ.
אוֹר פֶּלְאִי זָר, כִּנְחֹשֶׁת אֲדַמְדַּמָּה,
יִתָּלֶה עַל הָאָרֶץ שֶׁהוּעַמָּה.
מֶרְכְּבוֹ יִצְנַח כּוֹכָב, וְעַל רִבְצוֹ
אֲרִי־הַיָּם כַּפּוֹתָיו יָלֹק אִלֵּם.
לֹא יִפְעֶה יוֹנֵק אָז, וְאָב עַל עַנְפוֹ
אֶת נְשִׁימָתוֹ יִכְלָא – –
רַק תֹּהוּ, כִּפְרִיץ־חַיּוֹת, מִמַּאֲרָבוֹ
יִתְמוֹדֵד בִּקְצֵה עוֹלָם, יִפְעַר לוֹעַ.
וְאֵין בְּשָׁעָה זוֹ לָקוּם וְאֵין לִשְׁקֹעַ.

There is one hour no man awaits:

The hour of final watch,

As the Nile hippopotamus, when darkness presses

And the universe is hidden from its lord,

Kneels down powerless upon the lair of night,

There is no watchful eye or witness for this hour and its anguish

As ailing yesterday is gathered to its forefathers.

Then fruit ripens on the tree, and like a scarlet forest

The vision of the world burgeons at its head.

יֵשׁ שָׁעָה אַחַת, אִישׁ לָהּ לֹא יְחַכֶּה,
הֲלֹא הִיא שְׁעַת אַשְׁמוֹרָה אַחֲרוֹנָה,
כַּבְּהֵמוֹת עַל יְאוֹר כִּי תִכְבַּד הָאֲפֵלָה,
וְתֵבֵל, נַעֲלָמָה מֵאֲדוֹנָהּ,
כּוֹרַעַת מִבְּלִי אוֹן עַל מַרְבֵּץ־לֵילָה.
אֵין עַיִן צוֹפָה וְעֵד לְשָׁעָה זֶה וִיגוֹנָהּ
בְּהֵאָסֵף תְּמוֹל נָגוֹעַ אֶל אֲבוֹתָיו.

אָז יִבְשַׁל פְּרִי עַל עֵץ, וּכְיַעַר אָדָם
חֲזוֹן הָעוֹלָם יָנוּב לְמֵרַאשׁוֹתָיו.

DAVID SHIMONI

The Flower Pot

There is an ancient forest, its giant trees
Support the skies;
And there is a clay pot; in it grows
A common flower.

On the window sill of a shabby hut
It quietly grows.
Each day to the flower pot an old woman comes,
She waters the bloom.

Her hand trembles, her back is bent with age,
Heavy the pitcher weighs:
Yet how she loves the plant, bends over it,
Washes its leaves.

Once I saw the old one
Watering her flower —
Suddenly as an eternal forest this lowly bud
Grew, spread.

Like the eternal forest, God's eye attends it
Day and night
Quenching its thirst from full deep and high domain
With streams, dew, rain.

עָצִיץ

יֵשׁ יַעַר עַד, עֵצָיו הָעֲנָקִים
תּוֹמְכִים שְׁחָקִים;
וְיֵשׁ עָצִיץ שֶׁל חֶרֶס, בּוֹ יִגְדַּל
רַק פֶּרַח דַּל.

עַל אֶדֶן שֶׁל אֶשְׁנָב, בְּאֹהֶל מָט
יִפְרַח בַּלָּאט;
יוֹם יוֹם זְקֵנָה תִגַּשׁ אֶל הָעָצִיץ,
תַּשְׁקֶה הַצִּיץ.

הַגַּב מִזֹּקֶן שַׁח, הַיָּד תִּרְעַד,
כָּבֵד הַכַּד;
אַךְ מַה תִּרְחַם הַשְּׁתִיל, תֵּכֶף עָלָיו,
תִּרְחַץ עָלָיו.

וְיֵשׁ שֶׁבְּרָאוֹתִי אֶת הַסָּבָה
פְּרֻחָה מַרְוָה —
פִּתְאֹם כְּיַעַר־עַד יִשְׂגֶּה, יִצְמַח
הַצִּיץ הַמָּךְ.

כְּיַעַר עַד, עָלָיו פְּקוּחָה עַיִן אֵל
יוֹמָם וָלֵיל
לִשְׁבֹּר צְמָאוֹ בְּשֶׁפַע תְּהוֹם וָעָל:
פְּלָגִים, גְּשָׁמִים וָטָל...

DAVID SHIMONI

Gleaning

Silence and aura. An ancient Yemenite woman gathers dry
                                   branches for a bonfire,
Her bent back between the green of grapevines darkens and
                                   gleams in harvest sheens.
Her dusky grandson with curly earlocks caught in mid-air in
                                   the branches of fig.
A slice of black bread between his teeth and his nimble fingers
                                   pick the last of the fruit.
A bird burst out of the fig thicket, chirped suddenly in
                                   the quiet world,
Dropped to warm earth and pecked the bread crumbs fallen below.
I too have joined the gleaners, silently as I lie on the
                                   vineyard hill:
I will furtively glean myself remnants of summer, sheens of
                                   harvest: delicate, serene ...

At Times Spirit Surges

At times spirit surges up from bodies' prison,
Flooding matter, overflowing their bounds.
Then comes the end of all flesh, only spirit pure and naked,
Only soul to soul utters word without sound.

לֶקֶט

דְּמָמָה וּנְהָרָה. תֵּימָנִית יְשִׁישָׁה מְקֹשֶׁשֶׁת
שׁוֹכוּת יְבֵשׁוֹת לִבְעֵרָה,
גַּבָּהּ הַכָּפוּף בֵּין יֶרֶק הַגְּפָנִים מַשְׁחִיר
וּמַבְהִיק בְּזָהֳרֵי־הַבָּצִיר.
נֶכְדָּהּ הַשְּׁחַרְחַר עִם פְּאוֹת־תַּלְתַּלִּים נֶאֱחָז
בָּאֲוִיר בִּסְבָכֵי הַתְּאֵנָה,
פְּרוּסַת פַּת־קֵיבָר בְּשִׁנָּיו, וְקוֹטְפוֹת יָדָיו
הַזְּרִיזוֹת אַחֲרוֹנֵי הַפֵּרוֹת.
צִפּוֹר הִתְפָּרְצָה מִמַּעֲבֵה הַתְּאֵנָה, צִפְצְפָה
פִּתְאֹם בְּשֶׁקֶט הָעוֹלָם,
יָרְדָה לָאָרֶץ הַחַמָּה וְנִקְּרָה פְּתוֹתֵי הַלֶּחֶם שֶׁנָּפְלוּ לְמָטָה.
אַף גַּם אָנֹכִי נִלְוֵיתִי לַמְלַקְּטִים, דּוּמָם
בְּשָׁכְבִי עַל גִּבְעַת הַכֶּרֶם:
שְׂרִידֵי הַקַּיִץ לִי אֶלְקְטָה חֶרֶשׁ, זָהֳרֵי
הַבָּצִיר הָרַכִּים, הַשְּׁלֵוִים...

וְיֵשׁ אֲשֶׁר הָרוּחַ

וְיֵשׁ אֲשֶׁר הָרוּחַ מִשְּׁבִי הַגּוּפִים יָרוֹם
וְעָבַר עַל גְּדוֹתֵיהֶם וְהֵצִיף אֶת הַחֹמֶר;
אָז יָבוֹא קֵץ כָּל בָּשָׂר, רַק רוּחַ זַךְ וְעֵירֹם,
רַק נֶפֶשׁ אֱלֵי נֶפֶשׁ בְּלִי קוֹל תַּבִּיעַ אֹמֶר.

And that stone in the field, muted and lowly,
No longer is field-stone — it is the spirit of acquiescence,
The creative understanding locked within its core
Gazes out from deep within to the edges of silence.

And this mule thigh bending low under burden
— How it glistens with sweat, how the thigh quivers —
Why, this is sadness, melancholy of duress
That creates and destroys, that binds and shatters.

Into space, the infant napping in his cradle
Stretches out the tiny tip of his foot in innocence —
Do you hear how round about angels lifted their voices
In sacred song of Creation, in pure melody's merriment?

And there a tree soars upward in a glow of sunset rays,
That into its verdant tangle drips the essence of their blood,
Lucent, tremulous hues gushing
Dusky green and rose, purple and gold —

And suddenly the tree fades.... Only anguished muteness blazes,
Only tender love whispers, only compassion's cry
Quivers there, against a flickering heaven yearning soars
To a beauty that has vanished, to a beauty not yet arrived.

וְאֶבֶן זוֹ בַּשָּׂדֶה הָאִלְמָה וְהַשְּׁחוֹחָה
שׁוּב אֵינָהּ אֶבֶן שָׂדֶה – הִיא רוּחַ הַהַשְׁלָמָה,
הַבִּינָה הָעִילָאִית הַסְּגוּרָה בְּתוֹךְ תּוֹכָהּ
וְצוֹפָה מִתּוֹךְ תּוֹכָהּ לְיַרְכְּתֵי הַדְּמָמָה.

וְיָרֵךְ זוֹ שֶׁל פֶּרֶד מִמַּשָּׂא מִשְׁתַּטֵּחַ
– מַה נּוֹצְצָה מִזֵּעָה, מָה רוֹטֶטָה הַיָּרֵךְ –
הֲלֹא זֶה הָעִצָּבוֹן, זוֹ תּוּגַת הַהֶכְרֵחַ
הַבּוֹרֵא וְהַמַּחְרִיב, הַמְחַבֵּשׁ וְהַמְפָרֵךְ.

וּקְצֵה כַּף רֶגֶל זְעִירָה לְתוֹךְ חֲלַל הָעוֹלָם
לְתֻמּוֹ הוֹשִׁיט תִּינוֹק מְנַמְנֵם בַּעֲרִיסָה –
הֲתַקְשִׁיב אֵיךְ מִסָּבִיב מַלְאָכִים נָתְנוּ קוֹלָם
בְּשִׁיר־בְּרֵאשִׁית קָדוֹשׁ, בִּנְגִינַת־תֹּם מַעֲלִיסָה?

וְעֵץ אֵל עַל עַל מִתַּמֵּר לְנֹגַהּ קַרְנֵי שְׁקִיעָה,
אֶל תּוֹךְ הַסְּבָךְ הָרַעֲנָן נוֹטֶפֶת תַּמְצִית דָּמָן,
וְכֻלּוֹ שָׁקוּף־רוֹטֵט בְּשִׁפְעַת גַּוְנֵי פְּלִיאָה
אֲפֵלוּלִי־יָרֹק־נָרֹד וְזָהָב וְאַרְגָּמָן –

וּפִתְאֹם גָּו הָאִילָן ... רַק יְלְהַט אֵלֶם־יָגוֹן,
רַק עֶדְנַת־אַהֲבָה תֶּהֱמֶה, בְּכִי־חֶמְלָה יִרְעַד רָעֹד,
וּמוּל רָקִיעַ דּוֹעֵךְ מִתַּמֵּר הָעֵרָגוֹן
אֶל יֹפִי שֶׁנִּסְתַּלֵּק, אֶל יֹפִי שֶׁלֹּא בָא עוֹד ...

The Middle Ages Draw Near!*

The Middle Ages draw near. Do you hear, sensitive man, do you feel
The whisper of crawling dust, the distant smell of sulphur?
That unseen pressure in the air, the heart and the land,
As during an eclipse; when houses silver and tremble,
And the blue sky turns lead, and cows low in panic,
And grasses and trees silver like greens sprouting in a cellar,
And the faces of men are frozen and strange like wax masks? —
From medieval oblivion returns the ancient mist,
As all streams return to the sea and the sun to the western clouds.
The ancient wheel revolves with the old rusty creaking.
The flow of blood budged it as a bursting flood surprises
The wheel of a desolate mill, haunt of ravens and demons,
But its axle is not wet enough, it creaks and curses dryly,
And the dust of its ancient victims billows from its cracked teeth.
The Gothic murk rises in flame and terrors on the horizon;
So has it always been. Thus fate returns to us
After every spring-like tiding seven storms and snows.
The conquering nations inherited the traits of their land and sun:
Day and darkness, summer and winter, returning, returning to the start.

Love, hatred, honesty, deceit.... And so it is forever;
Mighty is the approaching winter for summer tarried in the land —
The Middle Ages draw near!

יְמֵי־הַבֵּינַיִם מִתְקָרְבִים!...

יְמֵי־הַבֵּינַיִם מִתְקָרְבִים. הֲתַקְשִׁיב, הֲתָחוּשׁ, אִישׁ־נֶפֶשׁ,
אֶת רַחַשׁ הָאָבָק הַזּוֹחֵל, אֶת רֵיחַ־הַגָּפְרִית הָרָחוֹק? –
וְאוֹתָהּ מוּעָקָה נַעֲלָמָה בָּאֲוִיר, בַּלֵּב וּבָאָרֶץ,
כְּמוֹ בִשְׁעַת לִקּוּי־הַחַמָּה; עֵת בָּתִּים מַאֲפִירִים וְרוֹפְפִים,
וְעֵין שְׁמֵי־הַתְּכֵלֶת – עוֹפֶרֶת, וְגוֹעוֹת הַפָּרוֹת מִפַּחַד,
וּדְשָׁאִים וְעֵצִים מַכְסִיפִים כַּיֶּרֶק שֶׁעָלָה בַּמַּרְתֵּף,
וּקְפוּאִים פְּנֵי אָדָם וְזָרִים כְּמַסְווֹת הַדּוֹנַג? –
זֶה שָׁב הָעֲרָפֶל הַקַּדְמוֹן מִנְּשִׁיַּת יְמֵי הַבֵּינַיִם,
כְּשׁוּב כָּל הַנְּחָלִים לַיָּם וְהַשֶּׁמֶשׁ לְעַנְנֵי־מַעֲרָב.
חוֹזֵר הַגַּלְגַּל הָעַתִּיק בַּחֲרִיקַת חֻלְדָּה יְשָׁנָה,
שֶׁטֶף הַדָּם וְעָזְעָהוּ, כְּפֶרֶץ־יְאוֹר הַמַּפְתִּיעַ
אֶת גַּלְגַּל הַטַּחֲנָה שָׁמֵמָה – מִשְׁכָּן לְעוֹרְבִים וּלְשֵׁדִים;
אַךְ צִירוֹ לֹא רָטָב עוֹד דַּיּוֹ וְהוּא חוֹרֵק וּמְקַלֵּל מֵחָרָב
וַאֲבַק קַרְבְּנוֹתָיו הַקְּדוּמִים מִתַּמֵּר מִשִּׁנָּיו הַסְּדוּקוֹת.
עוֹלָה אֲפֵלַת־הַגּוֹתִים בְּאֵשׁ וּבְמוֹרָאוֹת בָּאֹפֶק;
כֹּה הָיָה מֵעוֹלָם, כֹּה חָזַר הַגּוֹרָל אֵלֵינוּ,
אַחֲרֵי כָל בְּשׂוֹרָה אֲבִיבִית שֶׁבַע סְעָרוֹת וָשֶׁלֶג.
יָרְשׁוּ הָעַמִּים הַמְנַצְּחִים אֶת סְגֻלּוֹת אַדְמָתָם לְשִׁמְשָׁם:
יוֹם וַחֲשֵׁכָה וְקַיִץ וָחֹרֶף וְחוֹזֵר וְחוֹזֵר חֲלִילָה;

אַהֲבָה, מַשְׂטֵמָה, תָּם־לֵב וְעַרְמוּמִית... וְכָכָה עַד עוֹלָם;
עַז הוּא הַחֹרֶף הַקָּרֵב, כִּי אָרַךְ הַקַּיִץ בָּאָרֶץ, –
יְמֵי־הַבֵּינַיִם מִתְקָרְבִים!

Like a cloud twisting in the distance. Open wide your eyes and ears,
     ancient people!
The wheel is... the turning wheel: and a wild wind before it
Skitters grotesque capers in the dust that crouches
On the paths of the old worlds....
Do not stand in its perverse way, do not run with it,
You be the axle and you also be the wheel! —
Your role has not been played yet, Eternal People, the play has
     not yet come to its end,

The heavy curtain is not lowered, myriad eyes are lifted yet
To you and the lofty drama, eyes of foe and lover alike.
If peoples whistle, envious, let your spirit not falter,
You must know — even their uncircumcised hearts still yearn in secret
For the end of the lofty drama prolonged before them thousands of years.
You must still go on. Go on. You will appear on the stage of the world
And your warm and mighty voice must split the whistling of the gentiles —
Until they grow mute, shaken and pale at the sight of surging courage,
Of your fiery spirit, as you conclude the play of world history:
Until they hide their confused faces in trembling hands,
Kneel, bellow in weeping, the weeping of generations confessing their sin...
Then you shall command the lowering of the curtain, to calm your
     stormy spirit
And to remain alone with your victory, before the world shall pass
Into the time of the great brotherhood and to the God the prophets
     did not imagine,

To the life the poets did not dream ... prepare for the mighty drama —
New days of transition draw near!

כְּעֵין עָנָן מִתְאַבֵּךְ בַּמֶּרְחָק, פְּקַח עַיִן וָאֹזֶן, עַם עַתִּיק!
הַגַּלְגַּל הוּא... גַּלְגַּל הַחוֹזֵר; וְרוּחַ פָּרוּעַ לְפָנָיו
מְכַרְכֵּר כְּרִכּוּרִים נִתְעָבִים בְּאָבָק הָרוֹבֵץ
בִּנְתִיבוֹת הָעוֹלָם הַיְשָׁנִים...
אַל־עֲמוֹד בְּדַרְכּוֹ הַגָּלוֹזָה וְאַל אִתּוֹ יַחַד תָּרוּצוּ,
הֱיוּ אַתֶּם הַצִּיר וְאַתֶּם הֱיוּ גַם הַגַּלְגַּל! – – –
עוֹד לֹא נִמְלָא תַפְקִידְךָ, עַם עוֹלָם, הַמַּחֲזֶה לֹא בָא עוֹד
אֶל קִצּוֹ,
הַמָּסָךְ הַכָּבֵד לֹא הוּרַד, עוֹד רִבְבוֹת עַיִן נְשׂוּאוֹת
אֵלֶיךָ וְאֶל גַּב־הַחִזָּיוֹן, עֵינֵי אוֹיְבִים וְאוֹהֲבִים יָחַד.
וְאִם יִשְׁרְקוּ עַמִּים וּמְקַנְּאִים אַל יִפֹּל רוּחֶךָ,
וְיָדַעְתָּ – לְבָבָם הֶעָרֵל אַף הוּא עוֹד יְצַפֶּה בַּסֵּתֶר
לְסוֹף הַחִזָּיוֹן הַנַּעֲלֶה, הַנִּמְשָׁךְ לִפְנֵיהֶם שְׁנוֹת אָלֶף.
עָלֶיךָ עוֹד לָצֵאת. עוֹד תֵּצֵא. עַל בָּמַת הָעוֹלָם תּוֹפִיעַ
וְקוֹלְךָ הַחַם וְהָאַדִּיר יְבַקַּע אֶת שְׁרִיקוֹת הַגּוֹיִים, –
עַד יֵאָלְמוּ נִדְהָמִים וְחִוְּרִים לְמַרְאֵה הָעֹז הַבּוֹקֵעַ
וְלַהַט־רוּחֶךָ, כַּהַתְמִךְ אֶת מַחֲזֶה תוֹלְדוֹת־הָעַמִּים;
עַד יַסְתִּירוּ אֶת פְּנֵיהֶם הַנְּבוֹכִים בְּיָדַיִם חֲרֵדוֹת,
וְכָרְעוּ וְנָעוּ בִּבְכִיָּה, בְּכִי דוֹרוֹת מִתְוַדִּים עַל חֶטְאָם...
אָז תְּצֻוֶּה לְהוֹרִיד הַמָּסָךְ, לְהַרְגִּיעַ רוּחֲךָ הַנִּסְעָר
וּלְהִשָּׁאֵר לְבַד עִם נִצְחוֹנְךָ, בְּטֶרֶם עֲבֹר כָּל הָעוֹלָם
לִתְקוּפַת הָאַחְוָה הַגְּדוֹלָה וְלֵאלֹהִים לֹא שְׁעָרוּם הַנְּבִיאִים

וְלַחַיִּים לֹא חָלְמוּם מְשׁוֹרְרִים... הַכּוֹנָה לַמַּחֲזֶה הָאַדִּיר, –
יְמֵי־מַעֲבָר חֲדָשִׁים מִתְקָרְבִים!

But should extinction be decreed upon all,

The light not shine after its setting, should the cruel wheel grasp you

To grind you in its teeth forever and grease its axle with your blood —

Should the nations make a murderous covenant to drag you into their
   savage way,

And not allow you to walk alone and complete your drama on this earth —

Then what is peace to you? Hasten the twilight of the world!

Grasp the turning wheel, cling to it tooth and nail,

As a leopard clings to the wild ox who would stab him with its horns.

And you shall be the terrible acid that destroys the solid iron,

And you shall take vengeance from the dark wheel for your shame and
   your father's shame.

Pierce it, devour it completely until its mighty links burst

And all the worn teeth fall with a cracking, angry shriek

And only its twisted axle remains revolving even after its destruction

Between mounds of ruins, idols, fences and shattered crowns.

And you shall dance around it in a circle the last cruel dance of freedom,

The last pure human beings around the deserted axle of abomination.

Enough, the martyr's death that leaves the earth to the unclean!

Die you shall, the death of all the creators that alter and perish on the earth

For the sake of the new, that rises pure with the mystery of Creation
   in its eyes.

Cease to be among the martyrs, learn to be heroes —

The Middle Ages draw near!

אַךְ אִם נִגְזְרָה כְּלָיָה עַל הַכֹּל,

וְלֹא יָאִיר הָאוֹר אַחֲרֵי שָׁקְעוֹ וּגְרַפְכֶם הַגַּלְגַּל הָאַכְזָר

לִטְחָנְכֶם בִּשְׁנָּיו לָנֶצַח וּלְהַשְׁמִין אֶת צִירוֹ מִדַּמְכֶם, –

וְכָרַתוּ בְרִית־רֶצַח הָעַמִּים לְסָחֲבְכֶם אֶל פִּרְאֵי דַרְכֵיהֶם,

לְלֹא תֵת לָכֶם לֶכֶת לְבַדְּכֶם וּלְכַלּוֹת חֶזְיוֹנְכֶם בָּאָרֶץ, –

אָז מַה־לָכֶם כֻּלְּכֶם וּלְשָׁלוֹם? הָחִישׁוּ אֶת שְׁקִיעַת הָעוֹלָם!

הֵאָחֵזוּ בַּגַּלְגַּל הַחוֹזֵר בְּשֵׁן וּבְצִפֹּרֶן בּוֹ דְבָקוּ,

כַּנָּמֵר הַדָּבֵק בָּרְאֵם הַמִּתְרוֹצֵץ לְדָקְרוֹ בְּקַרְנָיו;

וִהְיִיתֶם כַּחֹמֶץ הַנּוֹרָא הַמַּשְׁחִית כָּל בַּרְזֶל וּמוּצָק,

וּנְקַמְתֶּם מִגַּלְגַּל הָאֹפֶל חֶרְפַּתְכֶם וְחֶרְפַּת הָאָבוֹת.

חֲדַרוּהוּ, אִכְלוּהוּ עַד כָּלָה וְיִתְפּוֹצְצוּ אַדִּירֵי־חֶלְיוֹתָיו,

וְנָשְׁרוּ כָל שִׁנָּיו הַבָּלוֹת בַּחֲרִיקָה וּשְׁרִיקָה רוֹגֶזֶת,

עַד יִוָּתֵר רַק צִירוֹ הַמְעֻקָּל וְסוֹבֵב גַּם אַחֲרֵי חֻרְבָּנוּ,

בֵּין תִּלֵּי חֳרָבוֹת, אֱלִילִים וּגְדָרִים וּכְתָרִים נְפוּצִים.

וּרְקַדְתֶּם סְבִיבוֹ בַּמַּעְגָּל מְחוֹל־חֹפֶשׁ אַכְזָרִי וְאַחֲרוֹן,

בְּנֵי־אָדָם אַחֲרוֹנִים וּטְהוֹרִים סְבִיב צִיר־הַתּוֹעֵבָה

הַגַּלְמוּד ...

רַב לָכֶם לָמוּת מוֹת קְדוֹשִׁים וַעֲזֹב הָעוֹלָם לִטְמֵאִים!

וּמַתֶּם כְּמוֹת כָּל הַיּוֹצְרִים הַמְכַלִּים וְכָלִים בָּאָרֶץ

לְמַעַן הֶחָדָשׁ הָעוֹלֶה וְתֹם וְסוֹד־בְּרֵאשִׁית בְּעֵינָיו!

חִדְלוּ לָכֶם מִן הַקְּדוֹשִׁים, לִמְדוּ הֱיוֹת לְגִבּוֹרִים –

יְמֵי־הַבֵּינַיִם מִתְקָרְבִים!

ZALMAN SCHNEOUR

Song of the Snow

Oh, who crumbles up the heavens!
　　Here they fall in crumbs, in crumbs,
And the streets are merged — Be blessed
　　Who makes the changing seasons come!

There were fields — tell us where?
　　There were gardens — where are they?
Everything is white, white, white,
　　All colors hide themselves away.

Laughter, snow on every face.
　　Shadows — the sleighs go past;
In confusion of pure feathers
　　Melting are the steeple tops.

Snow is swirling — In his dance
　　Swept away is one black bird;
Kra-Kra-Kra... Oh raven, raven,
　　Everything is pure, is pure! . . .

שִׁירַת שֶׁלֶג

הוֹי, מִי פּוֹרֵר אֶת הַשַּׁחַק!
הִנֵּה יִפֹּל פְּתִים פְּתִים;
וּמִתְבּוֹלְלִים הָרְחוֹבוֹת –
בָּרוּךְ מַחֲלִיף אֶת הָעִתִּים!

שָׂדוֹת הָיוּ – אָמְרוּ אַיָּם?
גַּנִּים עָמְדוּ – אָנָה בָאוּ?
הַכֹּל לָבָן, לָבָן, לָבָן,
כָּל הַצְּבָעִים הִתְחַבָּאוּ.

צְחוֹק וְשֶׁלֶג עַל כָּל פָּנִים.
עוֹבְרוֹת עֶגְלוֹת-חֹרֶף – צְלָלִים;
וּבְעִרְבּוּבְיַת נוֹצוֹת צַחוֹת
נָמֹגִים רָאשֵׁי הַמִּגְדָּלִים.

סוֹבֵב שֶׁלֶג – וּבִמְחוֹלוֹ
נִסְחָף עוֹרֵב אֶחָד שָׁחוֹר;
קְרַע-קְרַע-קְרַע... הוֹי עוֹרֵב, עוֹרֵב,
הַכֹּל צָחוֹר, הַכֹּל צָחוֹר!...

The Fruited Month*

1

The green nut tree —

Many-stemmed tangled, tender-leaved and supple —

Has burgeoned nut twins.

To every leaf and twig these twins cling:

Together in pairs and triplets,

Look, their tanned backsides peep out in derision

From chartreuse trousers and checkered green.

So topaz yellows out of greening bronze.

Oh, who will believe she is a mother, this lovely nut tree —

And her children are so numerous!

Slender arms like a girl, thick locks like a bride.

Still she preens, longs for the wind's wooing.

The sculptures of her foliage are two hues of green;

Pale grainy green — the underleaf,

Deep darkening green — the overleaf.

When the field-wind blows he ruffles and fondles,

And she fevers, she lusts, this mother — the nut tree

Every branch winks, hints, each leaf cajoles —

Now all of her flickers, now again she fades. . . .

בְּיֶרַח - בּוּל

1

הָאֱגוֹזָה הַיְרָקָה –
רַבַּת-גֶּזַע וּפְרוּעָה, רַכַּת-עָלִים וּגְמִישָׁה, –
מְלֵאָה תְאֳמֵי-אֱגוֹזִים.
אֶל כָּל עָלֶה וְזַלְזַל דָּבְקוּ אֵלֶּה הַתְּאוֹמִים;
כְּפוּלֵי-כְפוּלִים בְּיַחַד וּמְשֻׁלָּשִׁים כִּסְגוֹלִים.
וַאֲחוֹרֵיהֶם הַשְּׁזוּפִים, שׁוּר, מְצִיצִים בְּלַעַג
מִתּוֹךְ מִכְנְסֵי-כַרְפַּס, מִתּוֹךְ מִשְׁבְּצוֹת-יֶרֶק.
כָּכָה תַצְהִיב הַפִּטְדָה מִתּוֹךְ בְּרוֹנְזָה נֶחְלָדָה.
הוֹי, מִי יַאֲמִין, כִּי אִם הִיא, זוֹ אֱגוֹזָה נֶחְמָדָה, –
וִילָדֶיהָ מָה רַבִּים!
דַּקַּת-זְרוֹעוֹת כִּילְדָּה, כִּבְדַּת-קְוֻצּוֹת כְּכַלָּה,
עוֹד תִּתְיַפֶּה אַף תַּעֲרֹג עַל חֲנֻפוֹת הָרוּחַ...
לַחֲטוּבֵי טְרָפֶיהָ שְׁנַיִם גְּוָנִים יְרֻקִּים:
יֶרֶק חִוֵּר מְחַסְפָּס פְּנֵי עָלֶיהָ מִלְּמַטָּה,
יֶרֶק עָמֹק וְקוֹדֵר – פְּנֵי הֶעָלִים מִלְמָעְלָה.
וּבְנֹשֵׁב רוּחַ-שָׂדוֹת – הוּא הַמְעַלְעֵל וּמְסַלְסֵל,
וְלַהֲטָה וְעָגְבָה זוֹ הָאֵם – הָאֱגוֹזָה:
שׁוֹקֵר, רוֹמֵז כָּל עָנָף, קְרִיאוֹת-חֵן לְכָל עָלֶה; –
הִנֵּה הִבְהֲבָה כֻלָּהּ, הִנֵּה שָׁבָה דָעֲכָה...

2

The melon's core fills with cold, sweet blood;
The heart fills with kernels — little black schemes.

He rounded his loins with plenty, bulged his belly with cunning,
Sunk his striped back into the gilded dust;
Lying supine, dozing in the sheen of the harvest sun —
Like an Arab, pampering himself on soft carpets,
Drawing, sucking juices from his green nargileh.*

Poppies

Once as it was morning and I was in the field,
The field was blazing with myriads of poppy bloom.
Like congealed cries of desire they burst from the earth,
Like lights of summer joys on stalks of festive green.

Fiery tongues in the green and the green is not consumed,*
And a morning wind blew rocking fiery tongues;
Poppy flames shimmered in clear crystal air
But sparks did not escape and no fine smoke.

Then I pushed through and stood fast in the flame meadow's navel,
Fire-tongues circled me and galloping waves of fire:
On my head burned the sun, at my feet flame-blossoms,
And, like gold white-heated, I was purified in the crucible.

2

דָּמִים קָרִים וּמְתוּקִים נִמְלָא תוֹךְ אֲבַטִּיחַ;
לִבּוֹ נִמְלָא גַרְעִינִים – מְזִמּוֹת קְטַנּוֹת, שְׁחַרְחָרוֹת.
עֲגֻל מָתְנָיו מְשֻׁבָּע, הִבְלִיט כְּרֵסוֹ בְּחָכְמָה,
שָׁקַע גַּבּוֹ הַמְנֻמָּר תּוֹךְ הֶעָפָר הַמְזֹהָב;
מֻטָּל פַּרְקְדָן, מִתְנַמְנֵם לְנֹגַהּ שֶׁמֶשׁ הַבָּצִיר –
כַּעֲרָבִי מִתְפַּנֵּק עַל טַפִּיטָיו הָרַכִּים,
מוֹשֵׁךְ, מוֹצֵץ עֲסִיסִים בַּנַּרְגִּילָה הַיְרַקָּה...

פְּרָגִים

וַיְהִי בִהְיוֹת הַבֹּקֶר וַאֲנִי בְתוֹךְ הַשָּׂדֶה,
וְהַשָּׂדֶה כֻּלּוֹ בּוֹעֵר בְּרִבְבוֹת פִּרְחֵי־פְרָג;
כְּצַעֲקוֹת־חֵשֶׁק קוֹפְאוֹת הִתְפָּרְצוּ מֵאֲדָמָה,
כְּאוּרֵי שָׂשׂוֹן הַקַּיִץ בְּגִבְעוֹלֵי יֶרֶק־חָג.

לְשׁוֹנוֹת־אֵשׁ בַּיֶּרֶק וְהַיֶּרֶק אֵינוֹ אֻכָּל,
וְרוּחַ בֹּקֶר נָשַׁב וַיְנַעֲנַע לְשׁוֹנוֹת אֵשׁ;
וְלַהֲבוֹת פְּרָגִים נָעוּ בָּאֲוִיר זַךְ כִּבְדֹלַח,
וּרְשָׁפִים לֹא מִתְמַלְּטִים וְעָשָׁן כָּל אֵין יֵשׁ.

אָז אֶחְתַּר וְאֶתְיַצֵּב בְּטַבּוּר שְׂדֵה־שַׁלְהָבֶת, –
וּלְשׁוֹנוֹת־אֵשׁ כִּתְּרוּנִי וְדַהֲרוֹת גַּלֵּי־נוּר;
עַל רָאשִׁי בּוֹעֵר שֶׁמֶשׁ וּלְרַגְלַי פִּרְחֵי־לַהַב,
וַאֲנִי כְזָהָב נִלְבַּן וְנִצְרַף תּוֹךְ הַכּוּר...

Passover in Jerusalem

Passionate angels serenaded today in Jerusalem —

Thousands of springs were concentrated in me today

And from its grave every dead skeleton breathes sun.

— Welcome fragrances, the crop-God's messengers,

I wait today, I wait this time

For the redeemer, the seducer — for whoever comes,

If only he comes:

Today is Passover and faith has no bounds.

Thousands of past kisses resound today in Jerusalem,

And the world begins to weep in God's choking provender

And from my ancestors' graves wells the song of blood.

— Jerusalem, Jerusalem, city of the arid and the prayer,

Today will you spread for me the warm nuptial couch,

For the kiss of the husband of your youth, bridegroom of blood,

Mourner of blood,

From under your heart, the King Messiah* to bear?

פֶּסַח בִּירוּשָׁלַיִם

מַלְאֲכֵי־עֲנָבִים זִמְּררוּ הַיּוֹם בִּירוּשָׁלַיִם –
אַלְפֵי אֲבִיבִים נֶדְחַסּוּ בִּי הַיּוֹם
וּמִקְּבָרוֹ יִנְשׁוֹם שֶׁמֶשׁ כָּל שֶׁלֶד מֵת.
– הֱיוּ בְרוּכִים לִי רֵיחוֹת, שְׁלִיחֵי אֵל־הַיְבוּל,
מְחַכֶּה אֲנִי הַיּוֹם, מְחַכֶּה אֲנִי כָּעֵת
לְמָשִׁיחַ, לְמַדִּיחַ – לְמִי שֶׁיָּבֹא
וּבִלְבַד שֶׁיָּבֹא:
חַג הַפֶּסַח הַיּוֹם וְלֶאֱמוּנָה אֵין חֵקֶר.

אַלְפֵי נְשִׁיקוֹת־עָבָר מְרִיעוֹת הַיּוֹם בִּירוּשָׁלַיִם,
הָעוֹלָם מִתְיַפֵּחַ בִּתְגוּבַת־אֵל נֶחֱנֶקֶת
וּמִקְּבָרוֹת אֲבוֹתַי בּוֹקֵעַ שִׁיר הַדָּם.
– יְרוּשָׁלַיִם, יְרוּשָׁלַיִם, עִיר הַתְּפִלָּה וְהַצִּחְיַח,
הֲתַצִּיעִי לִי הַיּוֹם מַצָּע־כְּלוּלוֹת חָם,
לִנְשִׁיקַת בַּעַל־נְעוּרָיִךְ, לַחֲתַן־הַדָּמִים,
לַאֲבֶל־הַדָּמִים.
לְהוֹלִיד מִתַּחַת לִבֵּךְ אֶת מֶלֶךְ הַמָּשִׁיחַ?

Purity

The door does not turn; in my window, no face:
No woman comes to visit my place.

The books dream in peace, no knowledge, no action:
In my heart is no doubt, no sin, and no passion.

My hand's-breadth days the clock does not measure.
Around me is silence, serene aura, pure glimmer.

All-wondrous shadow, past and future too.
And I am no infidel, no saint, no Jew.

Purity, song's echo; flower, joy's sheen,
Astound, shower, sport, gleam.

In my heart's abyss, small children play
And I am pure as a babe of one day.

טָהֳרָה

הַדֶּלֶת לֹא תָסֹב וְאֵין פָּנִים בְּחַלּוֹנִי;
וְאֵין נֶפֶשׁ אִשָּׁה מְבַקֶּרֶת אֶת מְלוֹנִי.

הַסְּפָרִים בַּחֲלוֹם־נָחַת, אֵין־דַּעַת, אֵין־מָעַשׂ;
וּבְלִבִּי אֵין סָפֵק, אֵין חֵטְא וְאֵין כָּעַס.

וּשְׁעוֹנִי לֹא יָמֹד אֶת יָמַי, יְמֵי־טְפָחוֹת,
וּסְבִיבִי: דוּמִיָּה, הוֹד שַׁאֲנָן, צַחְצָחוֹת.

וְהַכֹּל – צֵל־פֶּלֶא, צֵל עָבָר וְעָתִיד;
וְאָנֹכִי לֹא יְהוּדִי, לֹא כוֹפֵר, לֹא חָסִיד.

וּפִרְחֵי זִיו שָׂשׂוֹן וְטֹהַר הֵד שִׁירִים
מַפְלִיאִים, מַמְטִירִים, מִצְטַחֲקִים, מַזְהִירִים.

וִילָדִים מִשְׁתַּעַשְׁעִים בִּלְבָבִי, בִּתְהוֹמוֹ,
וְטָהוֹר אָנֹכִי כְּתִינוֹק בֶּן־יוֹמוֹ.

A Woman's Prayer

Guard me, oh God, from the cold winds that blow,
From the scorching wind's harm,
For the sake of the henhouse, the garden, and the cow
In the barn.

Because from an old father and mother,
Fragile from the womb, you have taken me
To bring forth bread from ascetic earth
And fruit from a fig tree.

And because in love and silence I accept
All good and evil due:
That the cow bellows, the grain is low,
And I am pregnant too.

תְּפִלַּת אִשָּׁה

שָׁמְרֵנִי, אֱלֹהִים, מֵרוּחַ קָרָה
וּמֵרוּחַ שׂוֹרֶפֶת
לְמַעַן שְׁלוֹם הַלּוּל וְהַגִּנָּה וְהַפָּרָה
שֶׁבָּרֶפֶת.

וְגַם בַּעֲבוּר שֶׁלְּקַחְתַּנִי, עֲנִיָּה מֵרֶחֶם,
מֵאָב זָקֵן וּמֵאֵם זְקֵנָה
לְהוֹצִיא מִקַּרְקַע סְגוּפָה לֶחֶם
וְגַם תְּאֵנָה.

וּבַעֲבוּר שֶׁקִּבַּלְתִּי עָלַי בְּאַהֲבָה וּבִדְמָמָה
כָּל הַטּוֹב וְהָרָע;
אֲשֶׁר גּוֹעָה הַבְּהֵמָה וּנְמוּכָה הַקָּמָה
וַאֲנִי גַם הָרָה.

Put Me into the Breach

Put me into the breach with every rolling stone,

With hammers fasten me in.

Perhaps I will placate my motherland and atone

The sin of the people who did not mend its ruins.

How good to know I am a stone like all the stones of Jerusalem:

With my bones bound up in the wall, happy am I.

Why should my body be less than my soul, in flood and flame

It accompanied this people in silence or keening cry?

Take me with the Jerusalem stone, place me in the walls,

Upon me daub cement,

And my pining bones will sing from the walls

Toward the Messiah's advent.*

שִׂימוּנִי בַּפִּרְצָה

עִם כָּל אֶבֶן מִתְגּוֹלֶלֶת שִׂימוּנִי בַּפִּרְצָה
וְחַזְּקוּנִי בַּמַּקָּבוֹת,
אוּלַי אֲכַפֵּר פְּנֵי מוֹלַדְתִּי, וְנִרְצָה
עֲוֹן הָעָם, אֲשֶׁר לֹא סָתַם הֶחֳרָבוֹת.

מַה טּוֹב וְיָדַעְתִּי, כִּי אֶבֶן אֲנִי כְּכָל אַבְנֵי יְרוּשָׁלַיִם,
וּמָה אֻשַּׁרְתִּי בְּהִתְקַשֵּׁר עַצְמוֹתַי עִם הַחוֹמָה,
לָמָּה יֵדַל גּוּפִי מִנַּפְשִׁי, אֲשֶׁר בָּאֵשׁ וּבְמַיִם
הָלְכָה עִם הָעָם בִּזְעָקָה אוֹ דְמוּמָה?

קָחוּנִי עִם הָאֶבֶן הַיְרוּשַׁלְמִית וְשִׂימוּנִי בַּכְּתָלִים
וְטוּחוּ עָלַי טִיחַ,
וּמֵחוֹמַת הַקִּיר יְרַנְּנוּ עַצְמוֹתַי הַכָּלִים
לִקְרַאת הַמָּשִׁיחַ.

Only of Myself I Knew How to Tell

Only of myself I knew how to tell,
My world like the ant's compressed.
Also my burdens I carried like her,
Too many, too heavy for my thin shoulder.

Also my path — like hers to the treetop —
Was a path of pain, a path of toil.
A giant hand, sure and malicious,
A teasing hand lay over all.

All my ways trembled and wept
At this giant hand, in constant fright.
Why did you call me, shores of wonder?
Why disappoint me, distant lights?

Here on Earth

Here on the earth — not in high clouds —
On this mother earth that is close:
To sorrow in her sadness, exult in her meager joy
That knows, so well, how to console.

רַק עַל עַצְמִי לְסַפֵּר יָדַעְתִּי

רַק עַל עַצְמִי לְסַפֵּר יָדַעְתִּי.
צַר עוֹלָמִי כְּעוֹלַם נְמָלָה,
גַּם מַשָּׂאִי עָמַסְתִּי כָּמוֹהָ
רַב וְכָבֵד מִכְּתֵפִי הַדַּלָּה.

גַּם אֶת דַּרְכִּי – כְּדַרְכָּהּ אֶל צַמֶּרֶת –
דֶּרֶךְ מַכְאוֹב וְדֶרֶךְ עָמָל,
יַד עֲנָקִים זֵידוֹנָה וּבוֹטַחַת,
יַד מִתְבַּדַּחַת שָׂמָה לְאַל.

כָּל אָרְחוֹתַי הִלִּיז וְהִדְמִיעַ
פַּחַד טָמִיר מִיַּד עֲנָקִים.
לָמָּה קְרָאתֶם לִי, חוֹפֵי הַפֶּלֶא?
לָמָּה כְּזַבְתֶּם, אוֹרוֹת רְחוֹקִים?

כָּאן עַל פְּנֵי אֲדָמָה

כָּאן עַל פְּנֵי אֲדָמָה – לֹא בֶּעָבִים, מֵעַל –
עַל פְּנֵי אֲדָמָה הַקְּרוֹבָה, הָאֵם;
לְהֵעָצֵב בְּעָצְבָּהּ וְלָגִיל בְּגִילָהּ הַדַּל
הַיּוֹדֵעַ כָּל כָּךְ לְנַחֵם.

Not nebulous tomorrow but today: solid, warm, mighty,
Today materialized in the hand:
Of this single, short day to drink deep
Here in our own land.

Before night falls — come, oh come all!
A unified stubborn effort, awake
With a thousand arms. Is it impossible to roll
The stone from the mouth of the well?

Aftergrowth*

Yes, I did not plow, I did not sow,
I did not pray for the rain.
Suddenly, see now, my fields have sprouted,
In place of thorn, sun-blessed grain.

Is it the aftergrowth, provender of the old,
Grains of delight harvested long ago?
They have remembered me in days of calamity,
Burst forth the secret way in me to grow.

Burgeon, flourish, plains of wonder,
Burgeon, flourish, ripen in haste!
I remember the words of comfort:
Aftergrowth and aftergrowth, you shall eat.

לֹא עַרְפִלֵּי מָחָר – הַיּוֹם הַמּוּמָשׁ בַּיָּד,
הַיּוֹם הַמּוּצָק, הֶחָם, הָאֵיתָן;
לִרְווֹת אֶת הַיּוֹם הַזֶּה, הַקָּצָר, הָאֶחָד,
עַל פְּנֵי אַדְמָתֵנוּ כָּאן.

בְּטֶרֶם אָתָא הַלֵּיל – בּוֹאוּ, בּוֹאוּ הַכֹּל!
מַאֲמָץ מְאֻחָד, עַקְשָׁנִי וָעֵר
שֶׁל אֶלֶף זְרוֹעוֹת. הַאֻמְנָם יְבָצֵר לָגֹל
אֶת הָאֶבֶן מִפִּי הַבְּאֵר?

סָפִיחַ

הֵן לֹא חָרַשְׁתִּי, גַּם לֹא זָרַעְתִּי,
לֹא הִתְפַּלַּלְתִּי עַל הַמָּטָר.
וּפֶתַע, רְאֵה נָא! שְׂדוֹתַי הִצְמִיחוּ
דָּגָן בְּרוּךְ שֶׁמֶשׁ בִּמְקוֹם דַּרְדָּר.

הַאִם הוּא סָפִיחַ תְּנוּבוֹת מִקֶּדֶם,
חִטֵּי חֶדְוָה הֵם, קְצוּרִים מֵאָז?
אֲשֶׁר פְּקָדוּנִי בִּימֵי הָעֹנִי,
בָּקְעוּ עָלוּ בִּי בְּאֹרַח רָז.

שִׁגָּשֵׂגְנָה, שִׂגֵּינָה, שַׂדְמוֹת הַפֶּלֶא,
שִׂגָּשֵׂגְנָה, שִׂגֵּינָה וּגְמֹלְנָה חִישׁ!
אֲנִי זוֹכֶרֶת דִּבְרֵי הַנֹּחַם:
תֹּאכְלוּ סָפִיחַ וְאַף סָחִישׁ.

III

The Modernists

המודרניזם העברי

By the Waters of the Sava*

Brother soldiers — With them in battle I reached the waters of the Sava.

They fell, feet up in the barbed wire,

Prolonged only the thin wail, their life's essence expiring,

Then they died, very dark.

I stood alone, like the last human being fighting in the world,

And I saw my growing brothers with their feet up,

Until they came to their death kicking at the sky:

I saw the moon, as if alive, scratching its silver face

On the blunted hobnailed soles of overturned soldiers.

This terrible radiance on the nails of the dead who kick the sky

Electrified my life with deadly shining terror.

The Divine in the mystery of fear* I visioned and man's downfall,
     with eyes of flesh.

As the last one who weeps, there I wept mightily.

In my life, I shall never weep again as I wept by the waters of Sava.

A Penny for You*

A penny for you, philosophers of eternity —

Of the spirit's life after death —

A penny for you, for the wrinkles on the forehead.

עַד מֵימֵי הַסַּוֶּה

– – אַחִים חַיָּלִים – אַתֶּם הִגַּעְתִּי בַּקְּרָב עַד מֵימֵי הַסַּוֶּה,
וְהֵם נָפְלוּ בְּרַגְלֵיהֶם־לְמַעְלָה אֶל סִבְכוֹת הַבַּרְזֶל,
וַיֶּאֱרַךְ רַק דַּק יְלֵל תַּמְצִית חַיֵּיהֶם הַגּוֹוֵעָה,
הֵם מֵתוּ אֲפֵלִים מְאֹד אָז.
אֶחָד עָמַדְתִּי, כְּאַחֲרוֹן לְגֶזַע הָאָדָם הַלּוֹחֵם בָּעוֹלָם,
וְרָאִיתִי אֶת אַחַי הַגְּדֵלִים בְּרַגְלַיִם לְמַעְלָה,
עַד אֲשֶׁר יַגִּיעוּ בְּמוֹתָם לִבְעוֹט בַּשָּׁמָיִם;
וְאֶת הַיָּרֵחַ רָאִיתִי מְחַכֵּךְ כַּחַי אֶת פָּנָיו הַכְּסוּפִים
בַּמַּסְמְרִים הַשְּׁחוּקִים עַל סֻלְיוֹת חַיָּלִים הֲפוּכִים.
וְהַזֹּהַר הַנּוֹרָא הַזֶּה עַל מַסְמְרִים הָאֵלֶּה בְּנַעֲלֵי מֵתִים הַבּוֹעֲטִים שְׁחָקִים,

חִשְׁמֵל אֶת חַיַּי בְּאֵימָה זוֹרַחַת עַד מָוֶת.
אֱלֹהוּת בְּסוֹד פַּחַד חָזִיתִי וּמַפַּל הָאָדָם, בְּעֵינֵי הַבָּשָׂר.
וְאָנֹכִי בָּכִיתִי אֲזַי שָׁם כְּאַחֲרוֹן הַבּוֹכִים
וְלֹא אֵבְךְ עוֹד בְּחַיַּי כַּבְּכִיָּה הַהִיא שֶׁבָּכִיתִי עַל מֵימֵי הַסַּוֶּה.

אֲסִימוֹן לָכֶם

אֲסִימוֹן לָכֶם, פִּלוֹסוֹפֵי הַנֶּצַח
לְחַיֵּי הָרוּחַ לְ א ַ ח ַ ר הַמָּוֶת...
אֲסִימוֹן לָכֶם בְּעַד קִמְטֵי הַמֵּצַח.

An aching body I choose to be
For the sake of the nail on my pink finger
That is dear to me.

A simple white pleasure I choose,
To put a white coat on my flesh —
That was dipped in water and came out so fresh —
Than to be a cosmic fragment in the dust.

A penny for you, for all your lovely words!

And the whole secret of sorrow, I comprehend,
And the perversity in all our life's events —
Is in death's end.

In the Covenant's Radiance

In the covenant's radiance that moment had come:
The emperor was pressed by the golden crown
That pressed like a crag:
And the emperor is a body: melancholy, fatigued.
Barefoot on the ground of the olive-press he stood
And the kingdom rolled off his heart like a stone —

וּבוֹחֵר אֲנִי הֱיוֹת גְּוִיָּה כָּאֶבֶת
לְשֵׁם הַצִּפֹּרֶן שֶׁל אֶצְבְּעֵי הֻרְדָּה
שֶׁהִיא לִי חֲמוּדָה.

וּבוֹחֵר אֲנִי עֹנֶג פָּשׁוּט וְלָבָן
בְּשִׂימַת כֻּתֹּנֶת לְבָנָה עַל בְּשָׂרִי,
שֶׁטֻּבַּל בַּמַּיִם וְיָצָא כֹּה טָרִי —
מֵאֲשֶׁר הֱיוֹת חֵלֶק קוֹסְמִי בֶּעָפָר...

אֲסִימוֹן לָכֶם בְּעַד כָּל אִמְרֵי שֶׁפֶר!

וְיוֹדֵעַ אֲנִי כִּי כָל סוֹד הָעַצֶּבֶת
וְהָעֶקֶשׁ הַזֶּה בְּכָל קוֹרוֹת חַיֵּינוּ —
בְּתַכְלִית הַמָּוֶת.

וּבְנֹגַהּ הַבְּרִית

וּבְנֹגַהּ הַבְּרִית בָּא הָרֶגַע הַלָּז:
וּמֵעִיק לַקֵּיסָר גַּם גֶּזֶר הַפָּז,
מֵעִיק כַּכֶּף.
וְהַקֵּיסָר הוּא גוּף: נוֹגַהּ דָּם וְעָיֵף.
וְעַל קַרְקַע הַקֶּטֶב הוּא נִצָּב יָחֵף.
וְהַמַּלְכוּת נָגְלָה כְּאֶבֶן מִלֵּב — —

The people would not know, nor his army.

His captains would not know in the fleet at sea

That the emperor stepped down,

That the emperor was gone —

He had conquered, who begged at the doors,

His head without crown,

That which the king in the world could not win,

That which no king in the world would win.

At Your Feet, Jerusalem

Kings cast wreaths at your feet and fall upon their faces

    And they are then wonderful servants to you and your God.

Rome too sends its marble, crystal and gold

    To build within you a summit sanctuary for fame and glory.

And we, we your barefoot sons and daughters

    Who come to you beggared from the ends of the world,

We are, as we here are, children

    Of Sovereignty: of the cactus growing by itself, of the waves of the cliffs.

We who leave Jewish community

    In the world, put our coat of many colors, like a lizard, into the bag.

Father scolded, mother wept, and the white bed was orphaned.

To you we have brought blood and fingers, love and muscles: unburdened

וְלֹא יָדַע צְבָאוֹ, לֹא יָדַע הָעָם,
לֹא יָדְעוּ קָבְרְנִיטָיו בַּצֵּי שְׁבַיִם:
כִּי הַקֵּיסָר יָרַד,
כִּי הַקֵּיסָר אָבַד – –

וְהַמְחַזֵּר עַל פְּתָחִים הוּא הַזֶּה שֶׁנִּצַּח
בְּלִי כֶתֶר עַל רֹאשׁ,
אֶת מַה שֶׁהַמֶּלֶךְ בַּיְקוּם לֹא כָבַשׁ
וּמַה שֶׁכָּל מֶלֶךְ בַּיְקוּם לֹא יִכְבּשׁ.

לְמַרְגְּלוֹתַיִךְ, יְרוּשָׁלַיִם

מְלָכִים מַטִּילִים עֲטָרוֹת לְמַרְגְּלוֹתַיִךְ וְנוֹפְלִים עַל
פְּנֵיהֶם וְהֵם אָז עֲבָדִים נִפְלָאִים לָךְ וְלֵאלֹהֵךְ.
גַּם רוֹמָא שׁוֹלַחַת אֶת שִׁישָׁהּ, בְּדָלְחָהּ וּזְהָבָהּ
לְהָקִים בָּךְ מִקְדָּשׁ עַל פִּסְגָּה לְשֵׁם וּלְתִפְאָרֶת.
וָאָנוּ, וְאָנוּ בָנַיִךְ וּבְנוֹתַיִךְ
הַיְחֵפִים, שֶׁבָּאוּ אֵלַיִךְ מִקַּצְוֵי הָעוֹלָם מְרוּדִים,
אֲנַחְנוּ כְּמוֹ שֶׁהִנְנוּ פֹּה בָנִים
לְמַלְכוּת: לַצָּבָר הַגָּדֵל מֵאֵלָיו וּלְגַלֵּי הַכֵּפִים.
אֲנַחְנוּ הַיּוֹצְאִים מִכְּנֶסֶת יִשְׂרָאֵל
בָּעוֹלָם, נָתְנוּ כְּתֹנֶת הַפַּסִּים כַּחוֹמֶט בַּיַּלְקוּט.
אָב זָעֵף, אִם בָּכְתָה וּמַטָּה לְבָנָה נְתָיַתְּמָה.
הֵבֵאנוּ לָךְ דָּם וְאֶצְבָּעוֹת, אַהֲבָה וּשְׁרִירִים; כְּתֵפַיִם מְפֻקָּרוֹת

Shoulders to carry the Hebrew globe with its open sores.

All our dreams and our ambitions we gave up

That we might be poor laborers in the wasteland.

Where in the world can you find its like? Ask, you who were burned by Titus!

Where do they love rusty sovereignty with eternal love?

Where is the wailing of jackals heard with great compassion?

Where do they fever in red song, where do they shrivel and grow silent,

And cool flaming foreheads and kiss the cliffs?

The heatwind here slowly burns away our dear youth

Whose dust is scattered daily over the crevices like gold

And we ask no compensation for our destruction.

And with our precious bodies we cover the swamps,

As our hands drive into them the eucalyptus trees.

We who provide a feast for the worms of Canaan,

We are prepared with faithful bodies, fevering

To be the warm bridge for the sovereignty that comes

Over the abyss of blood.

Should a sword be sharpened in Canaan against you —

We would make for you a witness-pile of bodies like an outer wall.

And someone who denies the glory in pain and in your disaster

Struggles from cliff to cliff here, cursing and reviling —

Yes, you will forgive him, and allow him to abuse:

To pass from cliff to cliff because his spleen has risen up.

It is impossible to snap the head off the body with one's hands

And throw it like a pot on one of the angry rocks.

לִנְשׂוֹא אֶת הַגְּלוֹבּוּס הָעִבְרִי בִּנְגָעָיו הַקָּשִׁים,
וְכָל הַחֲלוֹמוֹת וְכָל הַמַּאֲוַיִּים נָתְנוּ
בְּעַד הֱיוֹתֵנוּ פּוֹעֲלִים עֲנִיִּים בִּישִׁימוֹן.
אֵי מָשָׁל בָּעוֹלָם לָךְ? שַׁאֲלִי, שְׂרוּפָה מְטִיטוּס!
אֵי אוֹהֲבִים מַלְכוּת חֲלוּדָה בְּאַהֲבַת עוֹלָם?
אֵי שׁוֹמְעִים לְיִלַּלַת תַּנִּים בְּרַחֲמִים גְּדוֹלִים?
אֵי קוֹדְחִים בְּרִנָּה אֲדָמָה, אֵי צוֹמְקִים וְשׁוֹתְקִים
וּמְצַנְּנִים מְצָחִים לוֹהֲטִים – וְנוֹשְׁקִים – בַּכֶּפִים?
הַשָּׁרָב פֹּה שׂוֹרֵף לְאַט עֲלוּמֵינוּ
הַחֲמוּדִים וְאֶפְרָם יְפֻזַּר יוֹם יוֹם עַל נְקִיקִים כַּזָּהָב
וְאֵין אָנוּ דוֹרְשִׁים שְׁלוּמִים בְּעַד חָרְבָּנֵנוּ.
וְאָנוּ הַמְכֻסִּים הַבְּצָוֹת בְּגוּפִים
יְקָרִים, בִּתְקוֹעַ בָּהֶן הַיָּדַיִם עֲצֵי־אֶקְלִפְּטוּס,
אָנוּ הַנּוֹתְנִים אֲרִיסְטוֹן לְתוֹלָעֵי כְּנַעַן,
אָנוּ נְכוֹנִים בְּגוּפִים נֶאֱמָנִים
בְּקָדְחָם לִהְיוֹת הַגֶּשֶׁר הַחַם לְמַלְכוּתֵךְ הַבָּאָה
מֵעַל לִתְהוֹם דָּמִים.
לוּ חֶרֶב הוּחַדָּה בִּכְנַעַן וּבָאָה עָדַיִךְ –
וְעָשִׂינוּ לָךְ גַּלְעֵד מִגּוּפִים כְּחוֹמָה לַחוֹמָה!
וְאֶחָד הַכּוֹפֵר בַּהוֹד שֶׁבְּכְאֵב וַאֲסוֹנֵךְ,
מִתְלַבֵּט מִכַּף אֱלֵי כַף פֹּה וּמְחָרֵף – וּמְגַדֵּף –
הֵן תִּסְלְחִי, תִּסְלְחִי לוֹ וְתִתְּנִיהוּ לְחֶרֶף,
לָלֶכֶת מִכַּף אֱלֵי כַף פֹּה כִּי עָלְתָה מָרָתוֹ:
אִי־אֶפְשָׁר לְהַתִּיק הָרֹאשׁ מִן הַגּוּף בְּיָדַיִם
וּלְהַשְׁלִיכוֹ כִּקְדֵרָה אֶל אַחַד הַסְּלָעִים הַזּוֹעֲמִים.

But the hiss of this serpent is also the shadow of a melody!
And the soles of his feet danced a Hora* here,

Crying, "God will build the desolation,"* in the light of the stars.
And until he goes to Jaffa, to the office of the émigrés,

And puts his muddy coat, like a lizard, into the bag —
Yet many days

Will he stand and quarry your rocks — at your feet —
And he will eat his bread in a sweat — the shew bread —

Bitterly will he smoke a cigarette with his blood in his eyes.
Perhaps he will also dance another Hora

With his dragging feet — one last time —
And shout "God will build" in the light of the great stars!

We Were Not Likened to Dogs among the Gentiles

We were not likened to dogs among the Gentiles — They pity a dog,
Caress, even kiss him with the Gentile mouth. For like a puppy
Fondled at home, they pamper it, delight in it always:
And when this dog dies — how very much the Gentiles mourn him!

We were not led like sheep to the slaughter in the boxcars
For like leprous sheep they led us to extinction
Over all the beautiful landscapes of Europe...
The Gentiles did not handle their sheep as they handled our bodies:

וְלַחַשׁ הַנָּחָשׁ הַזֶּה הוּא גַם צֵל שֶׁל נְגִינָה!
וְכַפּוֹת רַגְלַיִם הַלָּלוּ הֵן רָקְדוּ פֹּה הוֹרָה
בִּזְעָקָה „אֵל יִבְנֶה הַשַּׁמָּה", לְאוֹר הַכּוֹכָבִים!
וְעַד אֲשֶׁר יֵלֵךְ לִיפוֹ אֶל לִשְׁכַּת הַיּוֹרְדִים
וְנָתַן כְּתָנְתּוֹ הַדְּלוּחָה, כַּחוֹמֶט בַּיַּלְקוּט –
עוֹד יָמִים עַל
יָמִים כֹּה יַעֲמוֹד וְיַחֲצוֹב בַּסְּלָעִים – לְמַרְגְּלוֹתָיִךְ.
וְיֹאכַל אֶת לַחְמוֹ בְּזֵעָה – אֶת לֶחֶם
הַפָּנִים; וִיעַשֵּׁן בִּמְרִירוּת סִיגָרָה וְדָמוֹ בְּעֵינָיו,
וְאוּלַי גַּם יִרְקוֹד עוֹד הוֹרָה
בְּרַגְלָיו הַכְּבֵדוֹת – רַק פַּעַם עוֹד אַחַד –
וְזָעַק „אֵל יִבְנֶה" לְאוֹר הַכּוֹכָבִים הַגְּדוֹלִים!

לֹא נִדְמֵינוּ לִכְלָבִים

לֹא נִדְמֵינוּ לִכְלָבִים בַּגּוֹיִים... כִּי הֵן כֶּלֶב אֶצְלָם יְרַחַם
יְלַטַּף וְיֵשׁ גַּם שֶׁיִּנָּשַׁק מִפִּי גּוֹי, כִּי כַוָּלָד
חָמוּד בְּבֵיתוֹ יְפַנְּקֵהוּ וְשָׂשׂ בּוֹ תָמִיד;
וּבְמוֹת כֶּלֶב זֶה, מַה מְּאֹד יֶאֱבַל עָלָיו גּוֹי!

לֹא הוּבַלְנוּ כַצֹּאן לְטִבְחָה בְּקְרוֹנוֹת רַכֶּבֶת
כִּי כַצֹּאן מִצְרַע הוֹבִילוּנוּ לְמוֹ כְלָיָה
דֶּרֶךְ כָּל הַנּוֹפִים הַיָּפִים בְּאֵירֹפָּה...
לֹא כִלְצֹאנָם עָשׂוּ הַגּוֹיִים בְּגוּפֵנוּ:

Before slaughter they did not pull out the teeth of their sheep:
They did not strip the wool from their bodies as they did to us:
They did not push the sheep into the fire to make ash of the living
And to scatter the ashes over streams and sewers.

Are there other analogies to this, our disaster that came to us at their hands?
There are no other analogies (all words are shades of shadow) —
Therein lies the horrifying phrase: No other analogies!
For every cruel torture that man may yet do to man in a Gentile country —
He who comes to compare will state: He was tortured like a Jew.
Every fright, every terror, every loneliness, every chagrin,
Every murmuring, weeping in the world
He who compares will say: This analogy is of the Jewish kind.

There is no recompense for our disaster, for its circumference is the world:
The whole culture of the Gentile Kingdoms to its peak — through our blood;
And all its conscience — through our weeping.

Lord! You Saved Me from Ur-Germany as I Fled

Lord! You saved me from Ur-Germany* as I fled
Mother's and father's threshold and I arrived whole
In body but with my soul torn, within it the lake-of-weeping...*
Now I live on my mourning. On me lies the agony of my word

בְּטֶרֶם שְׁחִיטָה לֹא עָקְרוּ אֶת שִׁנֵּי הַצֹּאן:
לֹא פָּשְׁטוּ מְגוּפָם אֶת צַמְרָם כַּאֲשֶׁר לָנוּ עָשׂוּ:
לֹא דָחֲפוּ אֶת הַצֹּאן אֶל הָאֵשׁ לַעֲשׂוֹת אֵפֶר מִן חַי
וְלִזְרוֹת אֶת הָאֵפֶר אֶל פְּנֵי נְחָלִים וּבִיבִים...

הֲיֵשׁ מְשָׁלִים עוֹד לְזֶה אֲסוֹנֵנוּ שֶׁבָּא לָן מִיָּדָם?
אֵין עוֹד מְשָׁלִים (כָּל הַמִּלִּים צַאֲלֵי צְלָלִים) –
וּבָזֶה הַבִּטּוּי הַמַּחְרִיד: אֵין עוֹד מְשָׁלִים!
כָּל עִנּוּי אַכְזָר שֶׁיַּעֲשֶׂה בֶן אָדָם בְּאֶרֶץ גּוֹיַת לְאָדָם,
יְדַמֵּהוּ הַבָּא־לְהַמְשִׁיל: הוּא עֻנָּה כִיהוּדִי
כָּל מָגוֹר כָּל זְוָעָה כָּל בְּדִידוּת כָּל עָגְמָה
כָּל בְּכִיָּה הוֹמִיָּה בָעוֹלָם
יֹאמַר הַמַּמְשִׁיל: זֶה מָשָׁל מִן הַמִּין הַיְּהוּדִי.

אֵין שְׁלֵם לַאֲסוֹנֵנוּ כִּי מִדַּת הֶקֵּפוֹ הוּא עוֹלָם:
כָּל תַּרְבּוּת מַלְכֻיּוֹת הַגּוֹיִים עַד שִׂיאָהּ – בְּדָמֵנוּ
וְכָל מַצְפּוּנָהּ – בִּבְכִיֵנוּ.

אֱלוֹהִים! הִצַּלְתַּנִי מֵאוֹר אַשְׁכְּנַז

אֱלֹהִים! הִצַּלְתַּנִי מֵאוֹר אַשְׁכְּנַז בְּבָרְחִי
מִסַּף בֵּית אָבִי וְאִמִּי וְהִגַּעְתִּי שָׁלֵם
בְּגוּפִי אַף עִם נֶפֶשׁ קְרוּעָה בּוֹ בִּכְנֶּרֶת־הַבְּכִי...
כָּעֵת חַי עַל אֶבְלִי, עֲלֵי עֲקַת דְּבָרַי הוּא

Knowing it is the order: To live: To carry that heritage
Dropped from my martyrs' shoulders and to deed the future
My beautiful-portion-in-the-heritage-of-Israel for generations,
Till it is brought to the mountain of yearning
And unloaded from my shoulders: like the fine marble blocks,
Like gold, silver and bronze bars, like precious stones:
For the building and the completion of the Sanctuary-of-Wondrous-Yearning
Where all yearning ceases to pain:
The heart delivers to the harp its beat and longing for the Omnipresent,
And the harp plays this heart —

Lord! I live, from your hand have I strength to live
On my mourning without its forcing me to perish...
On the dusts of my people this one time, I beg,
Endow me with the strength of speech,
With the secret strength of the Commandments at Sinai...
I will bring them to the ears of my multitude as I come to teach them:
Here you are the heirs, filling the place of martyrs,
Whose mouths are crushed in the dust of exile, in a sea of blood —
For their sake the miracle happened to you, the enemy did not pass through
        your land.
Each of their burdens slipping as they fell, their blood spilling,
Pray let us carry on our shoulders with love! With their world's song.

בִּידִיעָה כִּי הַצַו הוּא: לִחְיוֹת: כְּדֵי שֵׂאת בַּיְרֻשָׁה הַהִיא
שֶׁשָּׁמְטָה מִכִּתְפֵי קְדוֹשַׁי וּלְהוֹרִישׁ אֶל הַבָּא
אֶת חֶלְקִי־הַיָּפֶה־בִּיְרֻשַׁת־יִשְׂרָאֵל לְדוֹרוֹת,
עֲדֵי תוּבָא אֶל הָהָר הַנִּכְסָף
וּתְפֻרַק מִכִּתְפַיִם: כְּגוּשֵׁי הַשַּׁיִשׁ הַטוֹב,
כְּמִטִילֵי זָהָב כֶּסֶף וּנְחֹשֶׁת וְכַאֲבָנִים יְקָרוֹת:
בִּשְׁבִיל בִּנְיַן וְשִׁכְלוּל בֵּית־מִקְדָּשׁ־הַכִּסּוּף־הַנֶּאְדָּר
שֶׁבּוֹ כָל הַכֹּסֶף חָדֵל מִלְּכְאֹב:
הַלֵּב מוֹסֵר לָעֶגֶב אֶת דָּפְקוֹ וְחִשְׁקוֹ בַּמָּקוֹם
וְהָעֶגֶב מְנַגֵן לֵבָב זֶה – –

אֱלֹהִים! אֲנִי חַי, מִיָּדְךָ לִי הַכֹּחַ לִחְיוֹת
עַל אֶבְלִי, לְבַל זֶה יַכְרִיעֵנִי עַד כְּלוֹת...
עַל עַפְרוֹת עַמִּי הַפַּעַם אַחַת אֲבַקֵשׁ
הַעֲנִיקֵנִי מִכֹּחַ נִיבִים,
מִסוֹד כֹּחַ דִּבְּרוֹת מִסִּינַי,
אֲבִיאֵם בְּאָזְנֵי הַמּוֹנַי, בְּבוֹאִי לְלַמְּדָם:
הִנְּכֶם פֹּה יוֹרְשִׁים, מְמַלְאֵי מְקוֹמָם שֶׁל קְדוֹשִׁים,
שֶׁפִּיהֶם־הַמָּחוּץ בֶּעָפָר גְּלֻיוֹת וְיָם דָּם –
בַּעֲבוּרָם קַרְכֶם נֵס וְלֹא עָבַר הָאוֹיֵב אַרְצְכֶם.
כָּל מַשָּׂאָם שֶׁשָּׁמַט בְּנָפְלָם, בְּהַגֵּר שָׁם דָּמָם,
נָא נִשָּׂא עַל כְּתֵפַיִם בְּאַהֲבָה! בְּנִגּוּן עוֹלָמָם.

In the Khamsin
(excerpts from *Massadah*)

On roads beyond the camp the Khamsin* struck me.

From the flaming easterly wind to the shade of a bush I came,

But there was no shelter in the shade.

Without any hope I threw back a weary head

And I knew:

Here even shade melts in the Khamsin,

Here even God forgot to camp...

Orphaned of grace, like myself, over my head the bush bent

And I heard its plaint:

"How great is my insult, oh God, how great my pain

For shade you have given me

But in it, no shelter for the weary..."

*

The distant soughing of pine forests caresses my ear.

The basket of childhood* swam on Ikvah's* cold waters

In shady reeds —

Leave me visions of yesterday! Why have you beset me?

בַּחַמְסִין

(מתוך הפואימה „מסדה")

עַל דְּרָכִים אֲשֶׁר מְחוּץ לַמַּחֲנֶה הִכַּנִי הַשָּׁרָב,
מְלַהֵט רוּחַ הַקָּדִים בְּצֵל שִׂיחַ־דֶּרֶךְ בָּאתִי,
וְאֵין מַחֲסֶה בַּצֵּל.
הִפְשַׁלְתִּי רֹאשׁ עָיֵף בְּאֶפֶס תִּקְוָה
וָאֵדַע:
פֹּה גַם צֵל יָמֹג בַּשָּׁרָב,
פֹּה חֲנוֹת שָׁכַח גַּם אֵל...
יְתוֹם־חֶסֶד כָּמוֹנִי עַל רֹאשִׁי שָׂח הַשִּׂיחַ
וָאֶשְׁמַע תְּלוּנָתוֹ:
„מָה רַב עֶלְבּוֹנִי, אֱלֹהִים, וּמַה גָּדוֹל הַכְּאֵב
כִּי צֵל נָתַתָּ לִי
וְאֵין מַחֲסֶה בּוֹ לֶעָיֵף..."

★

...רַעַשׁ יַעֲרוֹת־אָרָנִים רָחוֹק יְלַטֵּף אָזְנִי.
...תֵּבַת־יַלְדוּת שָׁטָה עַל מֵי „אִיקָבָה"* קְרִירִים
בֵּין סוּף מֵצֵל – – –
עִזְבוּנִי, מַרְאוֹת־תְּמוֹל! מַה שַּׁתֶּם עָלָי?

From your rich earth I have plucked up all my roots,
And if Khamsin wither them here —
Let them wither!
To you when I anguish, I will not call again,
I will not plant them in your earth again.
Upon my back your sun was like a yellow badge* of shame.
Here have I come to shoulder burden of another sun,
And if it has become for me a curse —
Carry it, carry it too, my aching back!
I am a Jew still too proud
To go on begging
For another shelter and deliverance.

*

How little of God's grace caresses you, Massadah,
You lonely rejected one between wilderness and sea,
What will you do, poor mother, for your thirsty defenders,
As they nestle their heads into your lap
And it is their last refuge? —
In thirsty muteness I hang upon your throat
And I will not press you for I know your grief...
I know all — and why do you still offer me your breast...
When it is parched?

מֵאַדְמַתְכֶם דְּשֵׁנָה כָּל שָׁרָשַׁי עָקַרְתִּי,
וְאִם שָׁרָב פֹּה יְיַבְּשֵׁם –
יִיבָשׁוּ!
אֲלֵיכֶם, בַּצַּר לִי, שׁוּב לֹא אֶקְרָא,
בְּאַדְמַתְכֶם שֵׁנִית לֹא אֶטָּעֵם!
כִּטְלַאי־קָלוֹן צָהֹב הָיְתָה לִי שִׁמְשְׁכֶם עַל גַּבִּי
וְאָבֹא הֲלֹם לְכַתֵּף מַשָּׂא הַשֶּׁמֶשׁ הָאַחֶרֶת,
וְאִם הָיְתָה לִי לִקְלָלָה –
שָׂא גַם אוֹתָהּ, שָׂאֶהָ, גַּבִּי כּוֹאֵב!
אָדָם־מִיִּשְׂרָאֵל גֵּא מִדַּי אֲנִי,
כִּי אֵלֵךְ עוֹד לְבַקֵּשׁ
מִקְלָט אַחֵר לִי וְהַצָּלָה!

★

מַה מְּעַט חֶסֶד־אֵל יְלַטְּפֵךְ, מַסָּדָה,
אַתְּ הַנִּדָּחָה בֵּין יָם וִישִׁימוֹן,
וּמַה לְּלוֹחֲמַיִךְ הַצְּמֵאִים, אִם דַּלָּה, תַּעֲשִׂי,
בְּכָבְשָׁם רֹאשׁ בְּחֵיקֵךְ
וְהוּא לָהֶם אַחֲרוֹן?..
אֲנִי בְּאֵלֶם־צָמָא נִתְלֵיתִי עַל צַוָּארֵךְ
וְלֹא אָצִיקָה לָךְ, כִּי אֵדַע עָנְיֵךְ...
יָדַעְתִּי כֹּל... וּמָה עוֹד תַּחַלְצִי לִי שַׁד –
וְהוּא צָחִיחַ?..

*

Why did Hagar weep over Ishmael* when he thirsted
And the water in the skin dwindled?
She had no need to weep —
Ishmael grew up and he became savage desert-taught,
Great distances his bow now threatens.
Heavy with schemes, on the humps of his camel he sways and sings —
Where is Sarah here to weep over her son Isaac?
Whose every hope has been cast here
To the terror of the wasteland?
Reveal yourself, oh reveal yourself, Angel of God.
Show the well, reveal the shade
To those fleeing from stepmothers' wrath
Whom in their shelter
Heat welcomed
Thirst smote.
Reveal yourself! There is no mother left to raise her voice and weep
And call to you!
Beneath the orphaned bush in desert refuge
Not the son of the Egyptian woman has been thrown away —
Here in thirst is Isaac swooning,
Abraham and Sarah's seed.

★

וְלָמָּה בָכְתָה הָגָר עַל יִשְׁמָעֵאל כִּי צָמֵא
וַיִּכְלוּ מֵחֵמֶת מַיִם?
לֹא לָהּ הָיָה לִבְכּוֹת –
גָּדַל יִשְׁמָעֵאל וְהוּא פֶּרֶא לִמּוּד־מִדְבָּר,
עַל מֶרְחַקִּים רַבִּים עַתָּה קַשְׁתּוֹ תְּאַיֵּם
וּכְבַד־מְזִמּוֹת עַל דַּבְּשׁוֹת גְּמַלָּיו יִתְנוֹעֵעַ וְיָרֹן –
אֵי שָׂרָה כִּי תֵּבְךְּ לִבְנָהּ יִצְחָק
אֲשֶׁר כָּל יְהָבוֹ הָשְׁלַךְ פֹּה
עַל מוֹרָאוֹ שֶׁל הַיְשִׁימוֹן?
הִגָּלֵה, הָהּ, הִגָּלֵה, מַלְאַךְ אֱלֹהִים,
הַרְאֵה הַבְּאֵר, גַּלֵּה הַצֵּל
לִפְלִיטֵי זַעַם־חוֹרְגוֹת
אֲשֶׁר בְּמִקְלָטָם
קִדְּמָם שָׁרָב
וְצָמָא הֵכַם!
הִגָּלֵה! אֵין אִם עוֹד אֲשֶׁר תִּשָּׂא קוֹלָהּ וְתֵבְךְּ
וּלְךָ תִּקְרָא!
וְתַחַת שִׂיחַ־יָתוֹם בְּמִדְבַּר־מִקְלָט
לֹא בֶן־הַמִּצְרִית הָשְׁלַךְ –
פֹּה בַּצָּמָא יִתְעַלֵּף יִצְחָק,
זֶרַע אַבְרָהָם וְשָׂרָה !

Israel

> And he said: No longer Jacob shall your name be called
> but Israel for you have contended with Gods
> and men and you have prevailed.
> *(Genesis 32:28–29)*

And so night after night, God, you come to me,

Not to favor me do you come, but my strength to try,

And as I prevail against you until morning — again I am alone,

A poor strange wayfarer, limping upon my thigh.*

"You have contended with Gods and with men and you have prevailed" —

Is this all the blessing you apportioned me, mysterious one?

Woe is me, I know, against all of you I have prevailed, over everything,

But over one I could not, over myself alone —

Your blessings weigh heavily upon me, I cannot carry them,

Limping and alone over all the highways I go,

Vanquish me once, oh You, and let me rest at morn

The rest that all the vanquished know!

Again it is night. I am alone. Again God descends.

"Israel!" — Here I am, God, here I am!

Oh, why do you come down each night to wrestle with me,

And as dawn rises you forsake me limping again? —

יִשְׂ רָ אֵ ל

וַיֹּאמֶר: לֹא יַעֲקֹב יֵאָמֵר עוֹד שִׁמְךָ
כִּי אִם יִשְׂרָאֵל כִּי שָׂרִיתָ עִם אֱלֹהִים
וְעִם אֲנָשִׁים וַתּוּכָל – –
(בראשית לב, כח–כט)

וְכָכָה לַיְלָה לַיְלָה, אֱלֹהִים, אֵלַי תָּבוֹא,
לֹא לְחוֹנֵן תָּבֹאָה כִּי אִם נַסּוֹת כֹּחִי,
וּבְיָכְלִי לְךָ עַד בֹּקֶר – שׁוּב אֲנִי לְבַד,
הֵלֶךְ דַּל וָגֵר, צוֹלֵעַ עַל יְרֵכִי.

„שָׂרִיתָ עִם אֱלֹהִים וְעִם אֲנָשִׁים וַתּוּכָל" –
וְזֹאת כָּל הַבְּרָכָה אֲצַלְתָּ לִי, פִּלְאִי?
אֲלָלַי, יָדַעְתִּי, לְכֻלְּכֶם, לַכֹּל יָכֹלְתִּי,
וְלָאֶחָד לֹא אוּכָלָה, לֹא אוּכַל רַק לִי – –

כָּבְדָה בִרְכָתְךָ עָלַי, לֹא אוּכַל שְׂאֵתָהּ,
צוֹלֵעַ וּבוֹדֵד עַל פְּנֵי כָל הַדְּרָכִים,
נַצְּחֵנִי פַּעַם אַ תָּ ה וּתְגַנֵּי שְׁקֹט עִם בֹּקֶר
כַּאֲשֶׁר יִשְׁקְטוּ כָּל הַמְנֻצָּחִים!

שׁוּב לַיְלָה. אֲנִי לְבַד. וְשׁוּב אֱלֹהִים יוֹרֵד.
„יִשְׂרָאֵל"! – הַגֵּנִי, אֱלֹהִים, הַגֵּנִי!
הָהּ, לָמָּה לַיְלָה–לַיְלָה לְהֵאָבֵק עִמִּי תָבוֹא
וְעִם עֲלוֹת הַשַּׁחַר צוֹלֵעַ תַּעַזְבֵנִי? – – –

Before Your Wonders I Stand, My World

Before your wonders I stand, my world,
And know not yet to whom my blood sings:
Each day miracle blooms, sunrose anew,
Evening glides soft and deepens evening blue.

Before your wonders I stand, my world.
Who are you? My blood convulses as I envision you.
Somnambulist night is my life; alone, tremulous I wander.
Still earth starts my sap and sky grows fair.

Before your wonders I stand, my world.
Pray — reveal yourself, oh you, to whom my blood cries out!
Like a star from the mountain, deliverance looks to me:
Pray — reveal yourself, my bereaved soul is weary.

Reward

I know the reward of the secret tear as it humbly falls,
    Sensing refuge in the trembling eyelid even from merciful gaze:
    Night dew's blessing on the cold silent grass stalk's head,
    That the frost of the stalk, nestling in night's lap, moistens
        with its goodness —
    The tear's blessing to the soul that trembles lonely in the cold

לִפְנֵי פְלָאַיִךְ אֶעֱמוֹד, עוֹלָמִי...

לִפְנֵי פְלָאַיִךְ אֶעֱמֹד, עוֹלָמִי,
וְלֹא אֵדַע, מִי הוּא זֶה אֲשֶׁר לוֹ יָרָן דָּמִי:
יוֹם־יוֹם נֵס חָדָשׁ יִפְרַח שׁוֹשַׁן־שֶׁמֶשׁ
וְעֶרֶב יִגְלֹשׁ שֶׁקֶט וְעָמְקָה תְכֵלֶת־אֶמֶשׁ.

לִפְנֵי פְלָאַיִךְ אֶעֱמֹד, עוֹלָמִי:
מִי אַתָּה הוּא, אֲדַמְּךָ וְהִתְפַּלֵּץ דָּמִי?
לֵיל־סַחַרוּרִי חַיַּי: רוֹוֶה אֶתַּע לְבַדִּי
וְיָרֵף רָקִיעַ עוֹד וְאֶרֶץ תַּשְׁקְ לְשַׁדִּי.

לִפְנֵי פְלָאַיִךְ אֶעֱמֹד, עוֹלָמִי.
הִגָּלֵה־נָא, אֲשֶׁר לְךָ יְשַׁוַּע דָּמִי!
כַּכּוֹכָב מִן הָהָר צוֹפִיָּה לִי גְאָלָה;
הִגָּלֵה־נָא, כִּי עֲיֵפָה נַפְשִׁי הַשְּׁכוּלָה.

שָׂכָר

יָדַעְתִּי שְׂכָרָהּ שֶׁל דִּמְעָה חֲרִישִׁית, כִּי תַצְנִיעַ לָרֶדֶת,
חֲשָׁה לָהּ מִפְלָט בָּעַפְעַף הַמְרַתֵּת מִמַּבָּט גַּם חַנּוּן:
בְּרָכָה שֶׁבָּטַל־לַיְלָה לְרֹאשׁ הַגִּבְעוֹל הַצּוֹנֵן, הַחֲשַׁאי,
שֶׁקְפְאוֹן הַגִּבְעוֹל, הַנִּלְפָּת בְּחֵיק לַיְלָה, מַטְפִּיחַ טוּבוֹ —
בִּרְכַּת הַדִּמְעָה לַנְּשָׁמָה, הָרוֹעֶדֶת בָּדָד בַּקָּרָה

Returning to take shelter in her hiding place, that pure sanctuary,
    Where God's modest candle burns, illumines it and does not extinguish.
I know there is reward for whispers of each heart longing in darkness,
    For the tremor of each soul that pines away in unheard prayer.
    Silent the subdued prayer pours and grows pregnant, embroiders for itself
    Tapestries of mercy angels, on its ladder they climb heavenward
    And fly with Throne of Glory* filling their hands with white flame.
    On prayer's ladder* they return their modest mother to the soul
    Strewing in it sparks of holy flame, making luminous incurable orphancy.
Mute is man in his own orphancy, lonely he remains in his orphancy.
    The eye's gaze never tells its depth, nor sound suggests its weight.
    Fortunate is he who knows, envisions this truth from the prison of
        his aching flesh,
    Neither tries to flee his prisoned muteness, nor pines when he fails.
    And if he guesses who his torment is, only kisses the torment and forgets it
    As the light young snow kisses the bird's back and melts,
    So, mute necessity, as before, the secret, humble tear alone saves.
You too make peace, my being, with necessity make peace.
    Alone among lonely brothers I too shall mark my orphan path,
    And pity them, all the mute, although my pity they do not know.
    They will not know that, like them, I am mercy burdened too, also I.
    Alone, never proud, I heed the murmur of their silence — my own.
    The secret tear, both mine and theirs, the modest prayer I gulp,
    And pain and muteness in me shall sprout purity, this is the lot of man.

וְשָׁבָה לִמְצוֹא חָסוּת־מָה בְּחֶבְיוֹנָהּ, בַּמִּקְדָּשׁ הַטָּהוֹר,
שֶׁנֵּר אֵל צָנוּעַ יִדְלַק בָּהּ גַּלְמוּד, יָאִירָהּ וְלֹא יִכְבֶּה.
יָדַעְתִּי: שָׂכָר יֵשׁ לְלַחַשׁ כָּל לֵב מִתְגַּעְגֵּעַ בָּאֹפֶל
וּלְרֶטֶט כָּל נֶפֶשׁ יוֹצֵאת וְכָלָה בִּתְפִלָּה לֹא־נִשְׁמָעַת.
דּוּמָם תִּגָּרֵר הַתְּפִלָּה הַכְּבוּשָׁה וְהָרָתָה וְרִקְמָה לָהּ
רִקְמַת מַלְאֲכֵי־רַחֲמִים, הָעוֹלִים בְּסֻלָּמָהּ הַשָּׁמַיְמָה
וְטָסִים עִם כִּסֵּא־הַכָּבוֹד וּמְמַלְּאִים חָפְנֵיהֶם לִבְנַת אֵשׁ.
בְּסֻלָּם הַתְּפִלָּה, הוֹרָתָם הַבּוּשָׁה, אֶל הַנֶּפֶשׁ יָשׁוּבוּ
וְרִשְׁפֵּי אֵשׁ־הַקֹּדֶשׁ, יִזְרוּ בָהּ, יַגִּיהוּ יִתוֹם אֵין מַרְפֵּא־לוֹ.
אִלֵּם הָאָדָם בִּיתוֹמוֹ וּבוֹדֵד יִשָּׁאֵר בִּיתוֹמוֹ:
לֹא יַגִּיד מַבַּט־עַיִן עָמְקוֹ וְהֶגֶה כְבֵדוֹ לֹא יִרְמֹז.
וְאַשְׁרֵי אִישׁ יוֹדֵעַ, חוֹזֶה זֹאת מִכְּלֵא בְּשָׂרוֹ הַנִּכְאָב
וְגִיחַ מִכְּלֵא אִלְמוֹ לֹא יָנַס, וְלֹא יִדְוֶה כִּי נִכְשָׁל.
לוּא יֵשׁ וְנֵחָשׁ מִי מַדְוֵהוּ – וְנָשַׁק לַמַּדְוֶה וּשְׁכֵחוֹ,
כַּשֶּׁלֶג הַקַּל, הַצָּעִיר, הַגּוֹשֵׁק גֵּו־צִפּוֹר וְנָמָס,
וְכֹרַח הָאִלֵּם כְּקֶדֶם דִּמְעָה מַצְנִיעָה אַף תִּדְלֵהוּ.
הַשְּׁלִימִי גַם אַתְּ, הֱוָיְתִי, עִם הַכֹּרַח הַשְּׁלִימִי:
בּוֹדֵד בֵּין אַחִים בּוֹדְדִים שְׁבִיל שְׁתוּקִי אַתְוֶה גַם אָנֹכִי.
רַחֵם אֲרַחֵם אֶת כֻּלָּם, הָאִלְּמִים, וְלֹא יֵדְעוּ רַחֲמַי
וְלֹא יֵדְעוּ כִּי טָעוּן רַחֲמִים גַּם אֲנִי כְּמוֹהֶם, גַּם אָנֹכִי.
בָּדָד וְלֹא־גֵאֶה אַאֲזִין לְהֶמְיַת דִּמְמָתָם־דִּמְמָתִי;
דִּמְעַת־סֵתֶר, שֶׁלִּי כְּשֶׁלָּהֶם, וּתְפִלָּה מִבְיְשָׁה אֲעַלַּע
וְצַעַר וָאֵלֶם יָנִיבוּ בִּי טֹהַר, זֶה חֵלֶק אָדָם.

Here Is Much Burning Anger

Here is much burning anger, mighty hate,
  The prickly thorns spread like cactuses!
God, my God! Where is a man of vision, of indignation great,
  In whom, though one alone, wrath converges,

Bursts forth like fire, in an expanse of prairie,
  That hands have set against
Flashing conflagration, till it holds no strength or terror,
  And quench the rebel treason and intrigue with flame?

Where is the man of vision? Camel-like with covered eyes
  Men circle as if grinding bread:
Yet no kernel crumb between the millstones lies.
  With strong shoulder bent, circling in place, men tread.

This lying pride, this toiling without wheat;
  No man says to his friend: Be strong, Peace!
Though the heat of one day strikes their wounded feet
  And one frost, on a night without dream.

Only his bloody wound he shows repeatedly,
  My blood is redder, you who pass, look here!
And round about the people in a panic flee
  Too terrified to ask: Where is my people's comforter?

פֹּה רַב חֲרִי־הָאַף...

פֹּה רַב חֲרִי־הָאַף, רַבָּה הַמַּשְׁטֵמָה,
פָּשׂוּ הָעֲקָצִים כְּבִמְשׁוּכַת־צַבָּר.
אֵלִי, אֵלִי! אִי אִישׁ־חָזוֹן גְּדָל־הַחֵמָה,
בּוֹ, בְּאֶחָד רַק הוּא, הַזַּעַם יִצְטַבָּר,

וְיִתְפָּרֵץ כָּאֵשׁ בְּמֶרְחֲבֵי־שְׁדֵמָה,
יָדַיִם עֲרוּכוֹת לְמַעַן בּוֹא מִנֶּגֶד
לְתַבְעֵרָה מַבְלַחַת, אֵין־עֹז־וְאֵימָה,
וּלְכַבּוֹתָהּ בָּאֵשׁ כִּמְרֵי מְזִמָּה וָבֶגֶד?

אִי אִישׁ־חָזוֹן? הֵן כַּגָּמָל לוּט־הָעֵינַיִם
יָסֹבּוּ בְנֵי־אָדָם כְּטוֹחֲנִים לַלֶּחֶם:
וּשְׂרִיד זֵרְעוֹן לֹא יִמָּצֵא בֵּין הָרֵחַיִם, –
סוֹבֵב תַּחְתָּיו אָדָם וּבְאָן נָטוּי הַשֶּׁכֶם!

גְּאוֹן־הַשָּׁוְא הַזֶּה, יָגִיעַ אֵין־תְּבוּאוֹת;
אִישׁ לְרֵעֵהוּ לֹא יֹאמַר: חֲזַק, שָׁלוֹם!
לוּ חֶרֶב־יוֹם אֶחָד רַגְלַיִם יַךְ פְּצוּעוֹת
וְקָרַח גַּם אֶחָד בְּלַיְלָה אֵין־חֲלוֹם.

וְאִישׁ רַק דַּם־פְּצָעָיו יַצִּיג לִרְאֻאֶה:
הַבִּיטוּ, הָעוֹבְרִים – אָדָם יוֹתֵר דָּמִי!
וּמִסָּבִיב הָעָם אֲחוּז־הַזְּוָעָה
נָס, גַּם חָדֵל מִשְּׁאֹל: מִי יְנַחֵם עַמִּי?

Too late the comforter arrived, too late redemption's day.

    All the seers are busy sowing among thorns.

Weary Messiah trudges on the bogged roadway —

    Those who await him, wound his limbs with stones.

To Tarshish*

I

An elegy does not raise its wistful tone in downpour of southern shine,

Even wrapped in porous cloud, sheer as ashes vitreous.

Why then have you stirred in me, my heart, as my day declines,

Insisting on young, plaintive song, wailing like a flute breaking forth.

In the distances at the end of the earth the pines sough.

In the distances at the end of the earth the years are done.

Why then have you wakened, heart of my heart, and never hush?

Sivan's* heat wave set shrinking backward the sick sea.

And the green mold lay bare on a jagged-toothed cliff.

In such enchanted dusklight Jonah once rushed falteringly

To the boat, away from a God arousing, yet not quenching, thirst.

He too yearned for the sea, a fish hauled up by the hook,

Yet, never did he shatter his weary head against the rock:

To Tarshish, gullible heart, still hoping on the brink of the abyss!

אַחַר בּוֹא הַמְנַחֵם, אַחַר יוֹם הַגְּאֻלָּה:
טְרוּדִים חוֹזִים כֻּלָּם, זוֹרְעִים אֶל הַקּוֹצִים.
יִגַּע הַמָּשִׁיחַ בִּמְסִלָּה כְבוּלָה —
וּמִיַּחֲלָיו בָּאֲבָנִים כָּל אֲבָרָיו פּוֹצְעִים.

תַּרְשִׁישָׁה

א

אֱלֶגְיָה לֹא תַעֲגֵם קוֹלָהּ בְּשֶׁפֶךְ אוֹר דְּרוֹמִי,
לוּ גַם לוּט עָב תָּחוּחַ, דַּק כְּאֵפֶר הַדָּלִיל.
מַה־כֵּן אֵפֹא נִרְעַשְׁתָּ בִּי, לִבִּי, בִּנְטוֹת יוֹמִי
וְשֶׁוַע שִׁיר תִּדְרוֹשׁ צָעִיר, יִבְקַע, יֵבְךְ כֶּחָלִיל?
בַּמֶּרְחַקִּים, בִּקְצֵה הָאָרֶץ, יָשְׁקוּ אֲרָנִים,
בַּמֶּרְחַקִּים, בִּקְצֵה הָאָרֶץ, תַּמּוּ הַשָּׁנִים.
מָה הֱקִיצֹתָ, לֵב־לִבִּי, עַד לֹא תִדְמֶה כָּלִיל?

שְׁרַב־סִינָן הִרְתִּיעַ יָם חוֹלֶה אֲחוֹרַנִּית
וְנֶחְשְׁפָה הַיְרוֹקָה עַל שֵׁן־צוּק נַעֲוֶה.
בְּאוֹר־עַרְבַּיִם מְכֻשָּׁף כֹּה אַץ מְעַדֶּנֶת
יוֹנָה אֶל הַסְּפִינָה מֵאֵל מַצְמִיא וְלֹא יָרֶוֶה.
גַּם הוּא לַיָּם עָרַג, דָּג הֶעֱלָתוּ הַחַכָּה,
וְאֶת רֹאשׁוֹ יִגַּע אֶל הַסֶּלַע לֹא בָקַע:
תַּרְשִׁישָׁה, לֵב פּוֹתֶה, עַל פִּי הַתְּהוֹם עוֹד יְקַוֶּה!

Oh, Tarshish mine, you are there this moment, now
Your pine forests this moment expect me still.
In black-winged winter, in thicknesses of snow
The lean wolf, too desperate to howl, wanders the slopes of your hills.
But when the ever wistful, strange summer burgeons in you again,
I return to the coolness of your lap with the returning flock of cranes
Who from afar your murmuring lake reeds smell.

II

Your summer is ever Indian summer. Forever unscarred
Is your crystalline horizon, smoky sheerness that dying crystallized
In withheld wonder. A melancholy fruitfulness showered
From the coolness of your azure sheen at noon, a moist tremor waves
In it, as if the night had been washed in unheard rain.
You are a translucent depth and like seaweed your birch leaves wane
Within the mournful light that kisses them unstirred.

Oh that I might dip alive again, within your mournful light.
And yet, bereft of understanding press like drunken mole
My face within your tangled grass that wormwood blights
My senses till they swoon! Within you goes astray even the cautious soul:
But my faltering step will recognize again its print
Blood-spattered in your soil. Like a hungry rabbit may I sniff
Again the path of my destruction giddied by my blinded sight.

תַּרְשִׁישׁ שֶׁלִּי, הֲלֹא יֶשְׁךָ עַתָּה, בְּרֶגַע זֶה,
וְיַעַר־אֳרָנֶיךָ בְּרֶגַע זֶה לִי יְפַלֵּל.
בְּחֹרֶף שָׁחוֹר־כְּנָפַיִם, בְּעַב־הַשֶּׁלֶג, זְאֵב רָזֶה
בְּמִדְרוֹנֵי הָרֶיךָ נָע, נוֹאָשׁ גַּם מְיַלֵּל.
וְקַיִץ כִּי יָנוּב בָּךְ, עַגְמוּמִי תָּמִיד וָזָר,
אָשׁוּב אֶל קֹר חֵיקֵךְ עִם עֵדֶר עֲגוּרִים, חָזַר
בַּהֲרִיחוֹ רָחוֹק סוֹף־אֲגַמֶּיךָ הַמְמַלֵּל.

ב

קַיִצֵךְ קֵץ הַהֵדִים. עַד הָעוֹלָם לֹא יִפָּגֵם
אֲפִקֵךְ גֶּבֶשׁ, דֹּק הֶעָשָׁן גָּוַע וַיִּתְבַּדְּלַח
מֵעֹצֶר פֶּלֶא. עַד עוֹלָם יִרְעַף פִּרְיוֹן עָגֵם
מִצֶּנֶן זִיו תְּכֵלְתֵּךְ בַּצָּהֳרַיִם וְרַעַד לַח
בָּהּ יִתְנַחֵשׁ, כְּאִלּוּ גַם הַלַּיְלָה רְחָצָה
בְּגֶשֶׁם לֹא נִשְׁמָע. צוּלָה שְׁקוּפָה אַתְּ וְכָאַצָּה
עֲלֵי־לִבְנֵיךְ מַקְלִישִׁים בִּיגוֹן אוֹר יִשְׁקֶם.

הוֹ, מִי יִתְּנֵנִי שׁוּב טוֹבֵל עֶרֶן וּנְטוּל־בִּינָה
בִּיגוֹן־אוֹרֵךְ וְאֶכְבְּשָׁה פָּנַי כַּחֲפַרְפֶּרֶת
שְׁכוֹרָה בְּצַמֶּת עִשְׂבָּתֵךְ, הַמַּלְעִינָה
חוּשַׁי עַד הִתְעַלֵּף! תּוֹעָה בָּךְ נֶפֶשׁ גַּם נִזְהֶרֶת
וְכַף־רַגְלִי כּוֹשְׁלָה תָּשׁוּב תַּכִּיר אֶת עֲקֵבָהּ
עָקֹב מִדָּם בְּאַדְמָתֵךְ. כְּאַרְנֶבֶת רְעֵבָה
אָרַח שְׁבִיל־אָבְדָנִי וּתְסַחְרְרֵנִי הָעֶוֶרֶת.

Hunger for life stores within you each moment's essence,
As if in you the God himself crumbled to atoms
And moment after moment gulps the wine-lettings of his body.
Your summer is short; your spotted flies have grown so wise
Coupling in the hair of my arm in a seizure of intoxication. ‫ה‬;
Frog folk heat their virility all day;
And slowly returned atoms of the God become unities.*

But I who stalk about in a labyrinth of devious folly known
To the deniers of earth, and all my days regarded my soul
As the eye of a willfully barren God, was sucked down
Into the whirlpool of lusts storming your coolness,
A cheat caught in his deception. The erotic grasshopper leapt
About as if he had vanquished me, the whippoorwill's plaint
For its mate in the gloom bewails only the fate of my blood.

Oh fate of bloods yearning in the snort of an animal slaughtered,
When my own day was so ripe, how did your crying ensnare me?
I decreed annihilation upon my soul, buried it embalmed,
And here a bony arm of ancestors unknown reached for the pestle
To crush me, even myself, in the mortar of survival.
Oh ancestor of holy ancestors, be cursed for the revival
In me of your capricious will to be, night after night you lurk for me.

רְעַב־חַיִּים גּוֹנֵז קִרְבְּךָ כָּל רֶגַע מֶרְכָּז,
כְּאִלּוּ הִתְפּוֹרֵר הָאֱלֹהִים בָּךְ לִפְרָדִים
וְרֶגַע רֶגַע יְעַלַּע אֶת יֵין גּוּפוֹ מְקֻז.
קָצַר קִיצֵךְ וּמְאֹד חָכְמוּ זְבוּבֶיךָ מְנֻקָּדִים,
הַמִּזְדַּוְּגִים בִּשְׁעַר־יָדִי בְּחֶתֶף שִׁכְרוֹנָם.
עִם הַצָּפְרַדְּעַ יוֹם תָּמִים יֵחַמּוּ אוֹנָם
וְשָׁבוּ אַט פְּרָדֵי־הָאֵל לִהְיוֹת לַאֲחָדִים.

וְאָנֹכִי, הַמִּתְשׁוֹטֵט בְּמָבוֹךְ סִכְלוּת פְּתַלְתֹּלֶת
לִנְזִירֵי אֶרֶץ וְאֶת נַפְשִׁי דִּמִּיתִי כָל יָמַי
עֵין אֵל, עָקָר לָדַעַת, נְצוֹדוֹתִי בְּמַעַרְבֹּלֶת
הַחֲשָׁקִים הַמַּסְעִירִים אֶת צִנָּתֶךָ, רַמַּאי
נִתְפַּשׂ בְּרִמְיָתוֹ. נִתַּר חַרְגֹּל תַּאֲוָתֵנִי
כְּאִלּוּ הוּא נִצְּחַנִי וַאֲנִי יַת הַקּוֹלָנִי
אֶל בַּת־זוּגוֹ בָּאֹפֶל תְּתַנֶּה גּוֹרַל־דָּמָי.

גּוֹרַל דָּמִים עוֹרְגִים בְּנַחֲרַת בְּהֵמָה שְׁחוּטָה,
אֵיךְ לְכַדְתַּנִי שַׁוְעָתֶךָ בִּנְכוֹן יוֹמִי שֶׁלִּי?
כָּרַת גְּזֵרָתִי עַל נַפְשִׁי, קִבְרָתֶיהָ חֲנוּטָה,
וְיַד אָב מֵאָבוֹת שְׁלָחָהּ גְּרוּמָה אֶל הָעֵלִי
לִכְתֹּשׁ אוֹתִי גַם אֲנִי בְּמַכְתֵּשׁ הַהַשְׁאָרָה.
אָב מֵאָבוֹת קְדוֹשִׁים! אָרוּר אַתָּה, כִּי נִגְעֲרָה
בִּי אַוָּתְךָ לִהְיוֹת וְלַיְלָה לַיְלָה תּוֹחֵל־לִי.

Who am I to curse and who am I to bless?

The river of my blood is but a vat surging with ancient wines.

Whose mouth of all my ancestors, in my thirst, now sucks your flesh

Sweet to giddiness, oh woman, with a youthful surge not mine.

Not mine? Whose burning head cooled invisible on your breast which trembled

Small like a banished bird and weeping sang in dread

Of mercies from my hand groping toward your rounded thigh?

And grandmother shrouded in white, so like a bride,

Wrapped in her veil, upon my threshold silent lay

Within the pallor of my night and heard the howl

Rolling in my throat. One moment more,

The bereaved moon will take its sheen from your blue lips,

Your little body will crawl back into the darkness of its heaven —

But grandfather into the mortar yet will cast my panicked soul.

III

If only I could return again, at my day's end to seek

At evening, my Tarshish, the shadows of your trees

Like fingers caressing your darkening peaks —

I should not return God's chosen one who learned to see,

With acceptance in his heart, compulsive existence's abyss.

Ashamed to call the mosquito, brother, like a man passing through,

A man whose shadow will not recognize him, I would yet be drawn to you.

מִי אָנֹכִי כִּי אֲקַלֵּל וּמִי כִּי אֲבָרֵךְ?
נְהַר־דָּמַי רַק יֶקֶב הַמַּשִּׁיק יֵינוֹת־קְדוּמִים.
פִּי מִי מֵאֲבוֹתַי בִּצְמָאוֹנִי יָנַק בְּשָׁרֶךְ,
אִשָּׁה, מָתוֹק עַד מֹסֶךְ עֲוָעִים, בְּסַעַר־עֲלוּמִים
לֹא לִי, לֹא לִי? רֹאשׁ מִי יוֹקֵד שָׁדֵךְ סָמוּי צֹנֵן,
מַרְתִּית קָטָן כְּעוֹף נִדָּח, וּבְכִי מִי זֶה רַנֵּן
בְּפַחַד רַחֲמֵי־יָדַי לְקִרְאַת חַמּוּק יָרֵךְ?

וְסָבָתִי, צְחוֹרָה בְּתַכְרִיכֶיהָ כְּכַלָּה
עוֹטֶפֶת הַיָּנוּמָה, דּוּמָם גּוֹהֶרֶת עַל הַסַּף
בְּחַוְרוּרִית לֵילִי, מַאֲזִינָה לַיְלָלָה
הַמִּצְטַנֶּפֶת בִּגְרוֹנִי. עוֹד רֶגַע וְאָסַף
יָרֵחַ שְׂכוֹל נָגְהוֹ, סָבָה, מֵעַל שְׂפָתֵךְ כְּחֻלָּה,
גְּוִיָּתֵךְ קְטַנָּה תִּזְחַל אֶל מַאֲפֵל וְזִבּוּלָה —
וְסָב אֶל הַמַּכְתֵּשׁ יָטִיל נַפְשִׁי הַנִּבְהָלָה.

ג

לוּ שַׁבְתִּי עוֹד הַפַּעַם, בַּעֲרוֹב יוֹמִי, לִרְאוֹת
אֶת צִלְלֵי עֵצַיִךְ, הָהּ, תַּרְשִׁישׁ שֶׁלִּי, עִם עֶרֶב
לוֹטְפִים כְּאֶצְבָּעוֹת צַלְעֵי־הָרַיִךְ מַשְׁחִירוֹת —
לֹא בְחִיר הָאֱלֹהִים אָשׁוּב אֲשֶׁר לָמַד, בְּלִי סֶרֶב
בִּלְבָבוֹ, הַבֵּט תְּהוֹם קִיּוּמוֹ הַהֶכְרָחִי.
כְּאִישׁ חֲלֵכָה, לַיְתוּשׁ יְבוּשׁ מִקְּרוֹא: אָחִי,
אֵלַיִךְ אֶנָּהֶה, כְּאִישׁ צִלּוֹ לֹא יַכִּירוֹ.

And he recalls and does not recall his past's glory.

The roar of his life — he scents northern rain.

(Motherland, do not condemn me! How much I probe my heart,

I scatter its outcry to cloud form, vain enchantment,

Does it foretell on the pale horizon summer's rain?

Your transparent light — do not condemn me — starts like a barrier

Between me and, in its dearness, your heart's pain.)

My heart, also paining, does not yearn for tranquillity,

Tribute its meager remnant to the distance it will bear away.

I withdrew far from man, therefore I was orphaned of God,

And my soul does not know to what or to whom its tax to pay.

I have only a daughter. When frightened at night she wakes,

Leaping to my flesh from the murky deeps,

Woe, the death of my calamity, remains forever incomplete.

In her imagined safety in me my daughter will forget her fright

And my sin shall never die, that I bore her.

Tomorrow on the shore, her blind heart will be refreshed by a shell,

Petrified sea blossom, whose veins her tiny hand will lift

Drunk with love, to her mouth.

Far, far is the night. Father alone, O lovely daughter of my plight,

Will gather its black echoes in day's sly roar.

וְהוּא זוֹכֵר וְלֹא זוֹכֵר תִּפְאֶרֶת עֲבָרוֹ
וְנֶחְמַת־חַיָּיו – הָרֵיחַ גֶּשֶׁם בַּצָּפוֹן.
(אַל תַּרְשִׁיעֵינִי, הַמּוֹלֶדֶת! לִבִּי מָה אֲחַקְּרוֹ
וּכְשָׁוְא מִקְסָם אֶזְרֶה אֶת שַׁוְעָתוֹ אֶל עָב אָפֵן,
הַמִּתְנַבֵּא בְּאֹפֶק חָוַרְיָן לְגֶשֶׁם קָיִץ?
אַל תַּרְשִׁיעֵינִי, כִּי אוֹרֶךְ זְגִיג רוֹטֵט כַּחֲיִץ
בֵּינִי וּבֵין לִבֵּךְ דְּוַי בְּעֶצֶם יְקָרוֹ).

לִבִּי, דְּוַי גַּם הוּא, לֹא כַהוֹמֶה אֶל הַמַּרְגּוֹעַ
אֶת פְּלֵטָתוֹ דַלָּה לַמֶּרְחַקִּים תְּרוּמָה יִשָּׂא.
רָחַקְתִּי מֵאָדָם, עַל כֵּן יָתַמְתִּי מֵאֵלֹהַּ,
וְלֹא תֵדַע נַפְשִׁי לְמִי וּלְמָה תְשַׁלֵּם מִסָּה.
רַק בַּת יֵשׁ לִי. וְעֵת תָּקִיץ מִפַּחַד בַּלֵּילוֹת,
חוֹרֶגֶת אֶל בְּשָׂרִי מִן הַמְּצוּלוֹת הָאֲפֵלוֹת,
אֵילִילָה: עֲנוּתִי עַד נֶצַח לֹא תִתַּם לִגְוֹעַ.

פַּחְדָּה תִּשְׁכַּח בִּתִּי בְּחָסוּתָהּ בִּי הַמְדֻמָּה
וְלֹא יָמוּת חֶטְאִי לָנֶצַח, כִּי יְלִדְתִּיהָ.
צֶדֶף עַל הַחוֹף מָחָר יַרְנִין לִבָּהּ סוּמָא,
פֶּרַח־יָם אֶבֶן אֲשֶׁר תַּגִּישׁ עוֹרְקָיו אֶל פִּיהָ
יָדָהּ חוּמָה, קְטַנְטֹנֶת וְשִׁכְרָה מֵאַהֲבָה.
רָחוֹק, רָחוֹק הַלַּיְלָה. רַק אַבָּא, בַּת אוֹנִי נָאוָה,
הֵדָיו שְׁחוֹרִים יִקָּלֵט בְּנַהֲרַת־יוֹם עֲרֻמָּה.

Before his strange form terrifies you, your father shall be gone
And melt from your heart like fear — never was night.
I will heap mute sparks, your shells, until your basket's filled
And tomorrow your hands shall burn, there is work enough still.
While yet your day remains undimmed, your sky unclouded,
I shall kneel upon a northern mountain, a pauper unpitied and unknown,
I shall listen to a horse wandering in the dark, tenderness done.

IV

Black shall abound the primeval clod's tranquillity
In the corn furrow that divides after the rain.
My soul, my soul, now you can die for you have seen
The stork fluttering dew from its wing.
At dawn the farmer will bend to the grain, primal man,
Always as he touches the earth, primal man,
And the stork measures his long shadow silently.

From across the mountains spurts the mute sun,
A pine tree burdened with days, murmuring with night, quiet grows.
Suddenly a black cow will snuff you down
And all at once, disturbed, leave you alone.
My soul, my soul, you are fortunate to be abandoned so.
Beasts of the field sense in you the one wandered
Away from God, from bosom wife, from hope that comes and goes.

יָסוּף אָבִיךָ, בְּטֶרֶם זָר צַלְמוֹ יְבַהֲלֵךְ,
וּמִלְבָּךְ יִמּוֹג כְּפַחַד־לַיְלָה לֹא הָיָה.
צְדָפַיִךְ, זְקֵיוֹת אִלְּמוֹת, אֵרִי עַד מְלֹא סַלֵּךְ
וּלְמׇחֳרָת תְּלַהֵט יָדֵךְ עוֹד הַמְּלָאכָה דַּיָּהּ.
עַד לֹא יִכְהֶה יַמֵּךְ וְשַׁחֲקֵךְ לֹא יֵעָנַן,
אֶכְרַע עַל הַר צְפוֹנִי, דַּל לֹא־נִכָּר וְלֹא־חָנָּן,
אָרַח לֶחוֹ, אַקְשִׁיב לְסוּס בָּאֹפֶל יְהַלֵּךְ.

ד

שְׁחוֹרָה תִּשָּׁפַע שַׁלְוַת־הַמִּגְרָפוֹת הָעֶלְיָאִית
אַחַר הַגֶּשֶׁם בְּמַעֲנִית־תִּירֹס מִסְתָּעֲפָה.
נַפְשִׁי, נַפְשִׁי! עַתָּה תוּכְלִי לָמוּת, כִּי כֵן רָאִית
הַחֲסִידָה מִנַּעֲרָה הַטַּל מֵעַל כְּנָפָהּ.
רִאשׁוֹן אָדָם, יִגְחַן אִכָּר עִם שַׁחַר לַקָּמָה,
רִאשׁוֹן אָדָם תָּמִיד בְּמַגָּעוֹ בָּאֲדָמָה,
וַחֲסִידָה צִלּוֹ אָרֹךְ מוֹדֶדֶת חֲשָׁאִית.

מֵעֵבֶר לֶהָרִים תָּגַח הַשֶּׁמֶשׁ הַדְּמוּמָה
וְאֶרֶץ עוֹל יָמִים, הוֹמָה מִלַּיְלָה, יֵרָגַע.
פָּרָה שְׁחוֹרָה לְפֶתַע בָּךְ תְּזוֹרֵר לְפִי תֻמָּהּ
וּלְפֶתַע תִּתְעַשֵּׁת, תֵּשְׁט מֵעָלֶיךָ בִּדְאָגָה.
נַפְשִׁי, נַפְשִׁי! אַשְׁרַיִךְ כִּי הָיִית כֹּה גַלְמוּדָה,
עַד בֶּהֱמַת הָאָרֶץ בָּךְ תָּחוּשׁ אֶת הַמִּנְגָּדָה
מֵאֵל, מֵאֶשֶׁת־חֵיק וּמִתִּקְוָה נָעָה־נָדָה.

Fortunate is the man without strength to hope who hopeless is.

Fortunate is he who has been left empty that he may not be eaten by shame.

My heart belongs to the dark moist clods of the field,

Anguished with longing for extinction, with fleeing from pain,

If only as the sun's heat is lost in the lake among the reeds

I recall and do not recall the shells on the hidden shore

And the mistaken child that shall not know her father's twisting paths.

אַשְׁרֵי אִישׁ אֵין־תִּקְוָה וְאֵין־אוֹנִים גַּם מִקַוּוֹת.
אַשְׁרֵי מִי רֵיק הַצַּג וְלֹא יֹאכְלֶנּוּ הַקָּלוֹן.
לִבִּי לְמֶגְרְפוֹת שָׂדֶה, הַמַּשְׁחִירוֹת רָווֹת,
נִכְאָב מִבְּרוֹחַ מִן הַכְּאֵב, מִשְּׁאוֹף לַחִדָּלוֹן,
לוּ גַם כְּחֹם הַשֶּׁמֶשׁ בָּאֲגַם אֹבַד, בַּסּוּף,
וְאֶזְכְּרָה־לֹא־אֶזְכְּרָה צְדָפִים עַל חוֹף חָשׂוּף
וּבַת תּוֹעָה וְלֹא תֵדַע דַּרְכֵי אָב נַעֲווֹת.

SHIMON HALKIN

Seventy-five Are My Abyssed Forests

Seventy-five are my abyssed forests,
Exposed and silent under one white covering
Now in the round contracted dark. How will the gold bird*
Know to weave her twisting path in sun's blue
Down to the greyness of my forest's round contracted dark,
Under one white covering, breathing and dead?
Seventy-five are my forests that are being choked
Now under the white cover. All the days
Their sap filled and disheveled branches rustled, cried out
For this golden bird that delayed to break a path
To their imploring, that in the distances of place
And time tarried to come. In sun's blue her woven path
      was twisted to the place where
Like a harp my storming forests murmured for her.
How then shall she now, my golden bird, find her way
Into the depths of my shaken forests that expected only her:
Into the abyss of my forests that yet expect only her
Beneath the one white covering, breathing and dead?

שִׁבְעִים וַחֲמִשָּׁה יַעֲרוֹתַי הַמִּתְהָמִים

שִׁבְעִים וַחֲמִשָּׁה יַעֲרוֹתַי הַמִּתְהָמִים,
פְּרוּמִים דְּמוּמִים, מִתַּחַת לְכִסּוּי לָבָן אֶחָד
עַתָּה בַּמַּאֲפֵל מְכֻרְבָּלִים. אֵיכָה תֵּדַע
צִפּוֹר־זָהָב אֱרוֹג עִקְמָן דַּרְכָּהּ בִּתְכֵלֶת־שֶׁמֶשׁ
אֶל שֵׁיב יַעֲרוֹתַי, הַמְכֻרְבָּלִים בַּמַּאֲפֵל
מִתַּחַת לְכִסּוּי לָבָן אֶחָד, נוֹשֵׁם וָמֵת?
שִׁבְעִים וַחֲמִשָּׁה יַעֲרוֹתַי, הַמְחֻנָּקִים
עַתָּה מִתַּחַת לְכִסּוּי לָבָן, כָּל הַיָּמִים
אוֹשׁוּ שִׁוְּעוּ פַּרְעוֹת־עֲפָאֵיהֶם מִלְשָׁדוֹת
אֶל זוֹ צִפּוֹר־זָהָב, שֶׁאַחֲרָה הַבְקִיעַ דֶּרֶךְ
אֶל שַׁוְעָתָן, שֶׁבּוֹשְׁשָׁה בְּרָחֳקֵי מָקוֹם
וּזְמָן מִבּוֹא, מִשּׁוֹר דַּרְכָּהּ נִפְתָּל בִּתְכֵלֶת־שֶׁמֶשׁ
לִמְקוֹם הָמוּ שָׁם כָּעוּגָב לָהּ יְעָרַי סֹעָרוּ.
אֵיכָה תִּמְצָא עַתָּה דַּרְכָּהּ צִפּוֹר־זָהָב שֶׁלִּי
אֶל עֵמֶק יְעָרַי הַמְנֹעָרִים, רַק לָהּ פִּלֵּלוּ,
אֶל תְּהוֹם יַעֲרוֹתַי, הַמְפַלְּלִים רַק לָהּ עֲדַיִן
מִתַּחַת לְכִסּוּי לָבָן אֶחָד, נוֹשֵׁם וָמֵת?

Like This Before You

Like this before you, just as I am:
Not charming, not painted with pink and blue*
But wild and rebellious, very bad,
So do I wish to stand before you.

Thus and thus is the measure of my height,
And so my life upon earth must be.
A larger measure for my soul's ascent,
Wandering silent it escapes its captivity.

My words will not soar me up to the heights
My words melt, suddenly frightened away.
Is it so, is it so I will speak to you,
I who am dying from day to day?

From day to day, dry land and the sea
Arise and shine like visions in sleep:
Like white highways from nothing to nothing
They stretch through the blue of heights and deeps.

I shall not be, I am not already,
Across the boundary I flutter my course.

כָּזֹאת לְפָנֶיךָ, כְּמוֹת שֶׁהֻגַּנִי...

כָּזֹאת לְפָנֶיךָ, כְּמוֹת שֶׁהֻגַּנִי:
לֹא כָחָל, לֹא שָׂרָק, לֹא פִּרְכּוּס וָחֵן,
אַךְ פְּרוּעָה, סוֹרְרָה וְרָעָה מְאֹד –
וְכָךְ לְפָנֶיךָ אֲנִי רוֹצָה לַעֲמֹד.

כָּךְ וָכָךְ מִדָּה לְשִׁעוּר קוֹמָתִי,
כָּךְ וָכָךְ דּוֹרִי עַל זוֹ אַדָמָה.
מִדָּה יְתֵרָה לַעֲלַיַּת־נִשְׁמָתִי
תַּחְרֹג מִשְּׁבִיָּהּ וְתָנוּד בִּדְמָמָה.

וְלֹא יַמְרִיאֵנִי שִׂיחִי אֶל עָל –
שִׂיחִי כְּמִגְמוּג מִפַּחַד פִּתְאֹם.
הֲכָכָה, הֲכָכָה אֲדַבֵּר אֵלֶיךָ
אֲנִי הַגּוֹוַעַת מִיּוֹם אֱלֵי יוֹם?

מִיּוֹם אֱלֵי יוֹם יַבֶּשֶׁת וָיָם
עוֹלִים וְקוֹרְנִים כְּחֶזְיוֹן חֲלוֹם,
כִּדְרָכִים לְבָנִים מֵאַיִן לְאַיִן
מוֹשְׁכִים בִּתְכֵלֶת מְצוּלָה וָרוֹם.

וַאֲנִי כְּבָר לֹא אֶהְיֶה, אֵינֶנִּי מִכְּבָר,
וּמְנַפְנְפָה דַרְכִּי מֵעֵבֶר לַגְּבוּל.

Here and beyond is the sin not atoned,
The punishment, vengeance, reward and remorse?

I stand before you, just as I am.
Wild and rebellious, I bitterly cry.
Harsh and barren the weeping enfolds me.
It is for my Self who shall not be I.

הֲמִזֶּה וּבָזֶה לֹא יְכֻפַּר הַחֵטְא,
הָעֹנֶשׁ, הַנְּקָמָה, חֲרָטָה וּגְמוּל?

וְהִנְנִי לְפָנֶיךָ כְּמוֹ שֶׁאֲנִי,
פְּרוּעָה, סוֹרֲרָה וְהוֹמָה בְמִרְי.
וּסְבִיבִי מִתְעַטֵּף בְּכִי קָשֶׁה וְעָקָר
עַל עַצְמִי שֶׁלֹּא אֶהְיֶה מִמֶּנִּי אֲנִי...

The Distance Spills Itself

The distance spills itself, grows blue and shining,
Silver lights like sickles are in the field.
Who beguiles me, as if calling and answering
My heart that longs like a bird of the wild.

Sadness such sadness without reason or substance
Like mists of a river soaring aloft.
The mezuzah* of my house I will kiss and leave
Like the beggar that entered and abruptly left.

I will meet someone, he will not sense my coming.
The beasts of the field will smell me so slow.
The lanes will hum like bells toward me
And I shall whisper, one with my soul,

Oh let me, let me walk alone,
Hear the "Adoration,"* answer "Amen."
Scorched by holiness, awe, mystery and grace
I suddenly whisper, "Blessed be Your Name."

Sadness such sadness. Full distance stretches,
It reminds me of what is beyond the boundary.
I shall ask not-to-be, thus to cease
On the threshold of the boundless, atone silently.

מִשְׁתַּפֵּךְ מֶרְחָק...

מִשְׁתַּפֵּךְ מֶרְחָק, מִתְכַּחֵל וְנוֹהֵר,
אוֹרוֹת כֶּסֶף כְּמַגָּלִים בַּכָּר.
מִי מְפַתֶּה, כְּקוֹרֵא וְעוֹנֶה,
לְלִבָּבִי הוֹמֶה כְּצִפּוֹר הַבָּר?

עֶצֶב, עֶצֶב לְלֹא חֵקֶר וָשַׁחַר,
כַּאֲדֵי נָהָר מִתַּמְּרִים לָרוֹם.
מְזוּזַת בֵּיתִי הִנֵּה אֶשַּׁק וְאֵצֵא
כְּעָנִי שֶׁנִּכְנַס וְיָצָא פִּתְאֹם.

אֶפְגֹּשׁ אָדָם וְלֹא יָחוּשׁ בְּגִשְׁתִּי,
חַיַּת־שָׂדֶה תָּרִיחַ בִּי אַט,
יֶהֱמוּ שְׁבִילִים כְּזוֹגִים לִקְרָאתִי
וַאֲנִי אַחַת לְנַפְשִׁי אֶלְאַט:

תְּנוּ לִי, תְּנוּ לִי לְבַדִּי לָלֶכֶת,
לִשְׁמֹעַ „קְדֻשָּׁה", לְהַגִּיד „אָמֵן",
לִלְחֹשׁ פֶּתַע „יְהִי שִׁמְךָ מְבֹרָךְ",
צְרוּבַת קְדֻשָּׁה, סוֹד יִרְאָה וָחֵן.

עֶצֶב עֶצֶב. מְלֹא מֶרְחָק מוֹתֵחַ,
כְּזֵכֶר לְמַה שֶּׁמֵּעֵבֶר לִגְבוּל.
כָּכָה לַחְדֹּל, לֹא־לִהְיוֹת אֶשְׁאֲלָה
בְּהִתְחַטְּאוּת דְּמוּיָה עַל מִפְתָּן אֵין־גְּבוּל...

Prayer

Forgive me, you, whom we called by name,
You, the revealed, who shine out beyond.
I am not to blame, I am not to blame,
That the language of words stammers, confused.

Many is the time we tried to converse
With all of your creatures — but they did not understand.
Perhaps we were not born in the desert even then,
And was He not our father — He who was first?

For then when morning hairy and red,
The soul of night first trampled down,
Also my father, the ancient one, could
Bleat out his words like ram to ram.

The rain to grass and thunder to lamb
Spoke and listened to Abel and Cain —
What more shall we do, what shall we do
We, who speak words to the naught?

Forgive me, you, whom we called by name,
Forgive my words, my confused spirit too.
I am not to blame, I am not to blame —
Teach me to bleat to your creatures like you.

תְּפִלָּה

סְלַח לִי, אַתָּה שֶׁכִּנּוּךָ בְּשֵׁם,
אַתָּה הַנִּגְלֶה, הַזּוֹרֵם מִנֶּגֶד.
אֵינֶנִּי אָשֵׁם, אֵינֶנִּי אָשֵׁם.
כִּי שְׂפַת הַמִּלִּים נְבוֹכָה וְעִלֶּגֶת.

רַבּוֹת פְּעָמִים כְּבָר נִסִּינוּ דָבָר
אֶל כָּל יְצוּרֶיךָ – אַךְ הֵם לֹא הֵבִינוּ.
אוּלַי לֹא נוֹלַדְנוּ גַם אָז בַּמְּדַבֵּר,
וְזֶה שֶׁהָיָה הָרִאשׁוֹן – לֹא אָבִינוּ?

כִּי אָז, עֵת הַבֹּקֶר, שָׂעִיר וְאַדְמוֹן,
דָּרַס רִאשׁוֹנָה אֶת נִצְחוֹ שֶׁל הַלַּיִל,
יָדַע גַם אָבִי, גַם אֲבִי הַקַּדְמוֹן
לִגְעוֹת אֶת מִלָּיו כְּמוֹ אַיִל אֶל אַיִל.

אָז גֶּשֶׁם אֶל דֶּשֶׁא וְרַעַם אֶל שֶׂה
דִּבְּרוּ וְהִקְשִׁיבוּ אֶל הֶבֶל וָקַיִן. –
וּמַה נַּעֲשֶׂה עוֹד, מַה נַּעֲשֶׂה
אֲנַחְנוּ, דוֹבְרֵי הַמִּלִּים אֶל הָאַיִן?

סְלַח לִי, אַתָּה, שֶׁכִּנּוּךָ בְּשֵׁם,
סְלַח לְמִלַּי, לְנַפְשִׁי שֶׁנָּבוֹכָה.
אֵינֶנִּי אָשֵׁם, אֵינֶנִּי אָשֵׁם – –
עָזְרֵנִי לִגְעוֹת לִיצוּרֶיךָ, כָּמוֹךָ.

Tiller of the Soil

Camel and plow. The sharp blade
Wearies cleaving clod from clod.
Never before was the world so one,
All eternities in that moment joined.

This is hint of murder,
This is plunged blade,
This is Cain who splits the clod's unity.
Never before was the distance so small
Between man
And camel
And sky.

Shepherd

This expanse that spreads its nostrils wide.
This height that yearns to you overhead.
Light spilling the milk's white.
Fragrance of wool. Fragrance of bread.

At the feet of the sheep and man that listens,
In the water trough is the lapping tune —

עוֹבֵד אֲדָמָה

גָּמָל – וּמַחֲרֶשֶׁת. הַלַּהַב הֶחָד
הַפֶּרֶד מִתְגַּע בֵּין רֶגֶב לְרֶגֶב
מֵעוֹדוֹ לֹא הָיָה הָעוֹלָם כֹּה אֶחָד,
וְכָל הַנִּצָחִים חֲבוּקִים תּוֹךְ הָרֶגַע.

זֶה רֶמֶז לְרֶצַח.
זֶה לַהַב נִדְחָק.
זֶה קֵן אַחְדוּת־שֶׁבָּרֶגֶב־מַבְקִיעַ.
מֵעוֹלָם לֹא הָיָה כֹּה מְעַט הַמֶּרְחָק
בֵּין אָדָם –
וְגָמָל –
וְרָקִיעַ.

רוֹעֵה צֹאן

הָרֹחַב הַזֶּה, הַמְּפַשֵּׂק נְחִירָיו.
הַגֹּבַהּ הַזֶּה, הַכָּמֵהַּ אֵלֶיךָ.
הָאוֹר, הַשׁוֹפֵעַ לַבְנוּת הֶחָלָב.
וְרֵיחַ הַצֶּמֶר. וְרֵיחַ הַלֶּחֶם.

וּלְרֶגֶל הַצֹּאן וְאָדָם, הַקַּשֵּׁב
לְרֹן הַלְקְלוּק בְּתוֹךְ שֹׁקֶת הַמַּיִם, –

Barefoot,

With all his five senses bared,

Morning steps toward noon.

This morn of Creation! Wafts in the fields

Incense from dung, dew drops from grass.

From horizon to horizon: Adam and fields.

From horizon to horizon: Abel and flocks.

Jezrael

Like a caravan of nursing camels with humps in the sky —

God made the hills of Gilboa kneel,

And the fields of Jezrael like young she-camels

Cling to the nipples of those breasts.

Flow, flow, milk of rivers, flowing over the banks.

And the earth (one black pregnant mare!)

Here stretches out her neck, flares her nostrils, snuffs,

For she has smelled water.

Water! Water!

Oh, milk the holiness from your breasts, God!

יָחֵף,
בְּמַחְשׂוֹף כָּל חֲמֵשֶׁת חוּשָׁיו,
פּוֹסֵעַ הַבֹּקֶר אֶל־מוּל צָהֳרַיִם.

זֶה בֹּקֶר־בְּרֵאשִׁית! בַּשָּׂדוֹת יְאַדֶּה
טְלָלִים מִן הַדֶּשֶׁא. וּקְטֹרֶת הַזֶּבֶל.
מֵאֹפֶק עַד אֹפֶק: אָדָם – וְשָׂדֶה.
מֵאֹפֶק עַד אֹפֶק: הָעֵדֶר – וְהֶבֶל.

יִזְרְעֶאל

כְּאָרְחַת גְּמַלִּים מֵינִיקוֹת וְדַבְּשׁוֹתֵיהֶן בַּשָּׁמַיִם –
הִבְרִיךְ אֱלֹהִים אֶת הָרֵי הַגִּלְבֹּעַ
וְשַׂדְמוֹת יִזְרְעֶאל כִּבְכָרוֹת רַבּוֹת
אֶל פִּטְמוֹת שָׁדָן צָמְדוּ.

זָב, זָב חֲלֵב הַנְּחָלִים, עוֹבֵר עַל גְּדוֹתָיו.
וְהָאֲדָמָה – (הָהּ, סוּסָה שְׁחוֹרָה, הָרָה!) –
הִנֵּה תִפְשֹׁט צַוָּארָהּ, נְחִירֶיהָ תַּרְחִיב, תִּנְשֹׁף –
כִּי הֵרִיחָה מָיִם.

מָיִם! מָיִם!
הָהּ, חֲלֵב הַקֹּדֶשׁ מִשָּׁדֶיךָ, אֱלֹהִים!

But here also my udders fill with milk —
The human udders!
And my flesh — overflowing breast — protrudes high from the earth.

Oh, clodded fields of Jezrael!
Nurse! Suckle!

Come now, she-camels! horses! man! God!
And I will suckle you —
Because yours are the nipples of my breasts.

                                        *

Like hunchbacked old women here the tents hang out their tongues,
For heavy on the shoulder is the burden's girth.
Man is flesh, and he labors here in holiness,
And bread comes from the earth.

Like a limping lamb here the world is carried
Under the armpit.
Here God's curls descend in the air
Upon every human cheek, caressing it.

Who is great here, who is small
In the kingdom of work and very flesh?
The earth is unrolled here, the scroll of a new testament,
And we — we are twelve!

אַךְ הִנֵּה מָלְאוּ גַם עֲטִינֵי חָלָב –
עֲטִינֵי אָדָם!
וּבְשָׂרִי – שַׁד שׁוֹפֵעַ כֻּלּוֹ – יִגְבַּהּ מִנִּי אָרֶץ.

הָהּ, שַׂדְמוֹת יִזְרְעֶאל הָרְגוּבוֹת!
יַעֲקֹנָה! מְצֵינָה!

בֹּאנָה, בְּכָרוֹת! סוּסִים! אָדָם! אֱלֹהִים!
וְאֵינִיקֶכֶם –
כִּי לָכֶם פִּטְמוֹת שָׁדָי.

*

כִּזְקֵנוֹת גִּבְנוֹת פֹּה הִלְחִיתוּ הָאֹהָלִים,
כִּי רַב הַמַּשָּׂא עַל הַשֶּׁכֶם.
הָאָדָם בָּשָׂר הוּא, וְהוּא עָמַל פֹּה בַּקֹּדֶשׁ, –
וְלָאֲדָמָה – לֶחֶם.

כְּשֵׁיָּה צוֹלְעָה נִשָּׂא תֵּבֵל פֹּה
מִתַּחַת לְבֵית הַשֶּׁחִי.
בָּאֲוִיר יוֹרְדִים פֹּה תַּלְתַּלֵּי אֱלֹהִים
וּמְלַטְּפִים עַל כָּל לֶחִי.

מִי גָדוֹל פֹּה? מִי קָטָן
בְּמַלְכוּת הָעֲבוֹדָה וְהַבָּשָׂר?
אֲדָמָה גְלוּלָה פֹּה – מְגִלַּת בְּרִית־חֲדָשָׁה,
וְאָנוּ – שְׁנֵים־הֶעָשָׂר!

*

Sunrise lows to me from God's stable
Protruding her face and brow.
Here it is — God's image!
He she is — the lowing milk cow!

Already flocks have gone out to the ravine,
Already flocks into the field have gone.
And here my God shepherds his sheep —
And it is the sheep of man.

"Are you hungry?" "No."
"What do you seek for yourself?"
"For myself a pitcher of water and hardtack!
Oh, Brother!
I would be a kid in God's flock!"

*

The earth of Spring grew hairy — a great body.
And my flesh sprouted in its Spring.
So shall I stand naked and covet this hairy body of mine.
Here also the dawn grew hairy — and its hair blond.
Good for you that your grassy body stretches out here,
Man!

★

הַזְּרִיחָה גּוֹעָה לִי מֵרֶפֶת־אֵל
וְאֶת פַּרְצוּפָהּ מְשַׂרְבֶּבֶת. –
הִנֵּהוּ – צֶלֶם אֱלֹהִים!
הִנֵּהִי – פָּרָה גּוֹעָה וְהוֹלֶכֶת!

עֲדָרִים יָצְאוּ כְּבָר לַגַּיְא,
עֲדָרִים יָצְאוּ כְּבָר אֶל שָׁדָם.
וְאֵלִי רוֹעֶה צֹאנוֹ פֹּה –
הִיא צֹאן הָאָדָם.

– „רָעַבְתָּ?" – „לֹא!"
– „וּמַה תְּבַקֵּשׁ לָךְ?"
– כַּד מַיִם לִי וּצְנִים!
הָהּ, אָח!
אֶהִי נָא גְדִי בֵּין גְּדָיֵי אֱלֹהִים!"

★

הַשְּׂעִירָה אַדְמַת אָבִיב– גּוִיָּה גְדוֹלָה,
וּבְשָׂרִי הַדְּשִׁיא בַּאֲבִיבוֹ.
כֹּה אֶעֱמֹד עָרֹם לִי וְחוֹמֵד גּוּפִי זֶה הַשָּׂעִיר,
וְהִנֵּה הַשָּׂעִיר גַּם הַשַּׁחַר – וּשְׂעָרוֹ צָהֹב.
טוֹב לְךָ אֲשֶׁר תִּתְמוֹדֵד פֹּה גְוִיָּתְךָ הַמְדֻשָׁאָה,
אָדָם!

And goat and sheep will come to crop this tender hair

And bless you: *Meh — Meh — Meh —*

And God too will come down then like a tender kid

To graze here in your flesh, grassy in its Spring.

*

With shirt wide open, like the open temple gates,

With the toes of my feet I will caress the earth of morning.

Here will I stretch out supine, I will lie in mother's lap.

And all the rivers will come to me,

And every tree will strike its roots in me,

And the God of all the world will nestle close to me whispering with love:

— You! You!...

I will lift up my body in my palms

And beneath the mane of thick tree

On a throne of green grass I will seat —

Man God!

Behold, the sky crowns a great sun on his forehead

Like head phylacteries,*

And trickles prayer into my bosom —

Tear yourself wide open, shirt like the open temple gates.

Let the prayer of every living thing come

Before my flesh that is the good and does the good.

וּבָאוּ עֵז וָשֶׂה לְלַחֵךְ שְׂעָרְךָ זֶה הָרַעֲנָן
וּבֵרְכוּךְ: מֶה – מֶה – מֶה –
וְיָרַד אָז גַּם אֱלֹהִים כִּטְלֵה־עִזִּים רַךְ
לִרְעוֹת פֹּה בִּבְשָׂרְךָ אֲשֶׁר הִדְשִׁיא בַּאֲבִיבוֹ.

★

פְּרֹם חֻלְצָה, כְּשַׁעֲרֵי הֵיכָל פְּתוּחִים,
בְּאֶצְבְּעוֹת רַגְלַי אֲלַטְּפָה אַדְמַת בֹּקֶר.
הִנֵּה אֶתְפַּרְקֵד, אֶרְבְּצָה – חֵיק אֵם.
וְכָל הַנְּהָרוֹת יֵלְכוּ אֵלַי,
וְיַךְ שָׁרְשָׁיו בִּי כָּל אִילָן,
וּמִתְרַפֵּק עָלַי אֱלֹהֵי כָל הָעוֹלָם וְלוֹחֵשׁ לִי בְּאַהֲבָה:
– אַתָּה!... אַתָּה!...
אֶשָּׂא גוּפִי עַל כַּפַּיִם
וּמִתַּחַת לְרַעֲמַת אִילָן עָבֹת
עַל כֵּס דֶּשֶׁא יָרֹק אוֹשִׁיבֶנּוּ –
אָדָם־יְהֹוָה!
הִנֵּה עוֹטֵר הַשַּׁחַק חַמָּה גְדוֹלָה לְמִצְחוֹ
בִּתְפִלִּין שֶׁל רֹאשׁ,
וְרוֹדֵף תְּפִלָּה אֱלֵי חֵיקִי. –
הִתְפָּרְמִי, חֻלְצָה כְּשַׁעֲרֵי הֵיכָל פְּתוּחִים,
וְתָבֹא תְפִלַּת כָּל חַי
לִפְנֵי בְשָׂרִי הַטּוֹב וְהַמֵּיטִיב. –

*

At night the tents light up, great lanterns,
And mountains of Gilboa draw their breath.
Who plots there the black schemes,
Like a great beast, maw gaping death?

Long-haired Balaam,* clear-eyed in vision —
The night upon a black ass rides the land:
Beneath it crouch the mountains of Gilboa,
They sense the rustling of God's sowing hand.

With hairy hand full of stars
God sows the seed of vision well,
And black lips tremulously whisper,
— "How goodly are your tents, O Jezrael!"

Toil

We have a small hand with five fingers,
Wax fingers thin to breaking.
The pulse beats at their beginning and at their end — fingernails.
Oh, what shall we do to the fingers on the day we labor with them?

★

בַּלַּיְלָה יוּאֲרוּ אֹהָלִים – פַּנָּסִים גְּדוֹלִים,
וְנוֹשְׁמִים הָרֵי הַגִּלְבֹּעַ. –
מִי זוֹמֵם שָׁם מְזִמָּה שְׁחוֹרָה,
כְּמוֹ חַיָּה גְדוֹלָה תִּפְעַר לֵעַ? –

בִּלְעָם אֶרֶךְ־שֵׂעָר, גְּלוּי־עֵינָיִם –
לַיְל רוֹכֵב עֲלֵי אָתוֹן שְׁחוֹרָה;
אַךְ רָבְצוּ תַּחְתָּיו הָרֵי בַגִּלְבֹּעַ –
חָשׁוּ: אַוְשַׁת יַד אֱלֹהַּ זוֹרְעָה.

בְּכַף שְׂעִירָה – מְלֹא חָפְנֶיהָ הַכּוֹכָבִים –
זֶרַע־חָזוֹן יִזְרַע אֵל.
שְׂפָתַיִם שְׁחֹרוֹת לוֹחֲשׁוֹת בִּרְעָדָה:
– מַה טֹּבוּ אֹהָלֶיךָ, יִזְרְעֶאל!

עָמָל

כַּף יָד לָנוּ קְטַנָּה וְאֶצְבָּעוֹת חָמֵשׁ לָהּ,
אֶצְבָּעוֹת־שַׁעֲוָה דַּקּוֹת לְהִשָּׁבֵר,
בְּרֵאשִׁיתָן הוֹלֵם דֹּפֶק וּבְקִצֵּיהֶן – צִפָּרְנָיִם.
הָהּ, מַה נַּעַשׂ לָאֶצְבָּעוֹת בַּיּוֹם שֶׁיֵּעָבֵד בָּן?

Pound mightily, human pulse! Grow wild, fingernails!
We are going to toil!

Oh, good for you, fingers, grasping a sickle on harvest day,
Embracing the clod covered with thorn!
You tell:
What shall we do to the tender fingers?

*

Oh, Sweat!
Oh, drops of blessing falling from my high forehead
Like dew from pure skies.

Here is my flesh, pure and hairy,
And the hair, black grass.
Oh sweat! Salty sweat!
Bedew my flesh like a bristling field at dawn.
 Hallelujah!

The dawn skies sway — the tangle of a great terebinth —
And the head of Absalom, golden curled,
Is caught in the tree top —
 Sun! Sun!

הֲלֹם בְּאַדִּיר, דְּפֹק־אָדָם! גַּדְלְנָה פֶּרֶא, צִפָּרְנַיִם!
אָנוּ הוֹלְכִים אֱלֵי עָמָל!

הָה, אַשְׁרֵיכֶן, הָאֶצְבָּעוֹת, אוֹחֲזוֹת מַגָּל בְּיוֹם קָצִיר,
חוֹבְקוֹת רֶגֶב כְּסָה חָרוּל!
אִמְרוּ אַתֶּן:
מַה יֵּעָשֶׂה לָאֶצְבָּעוֹת הָעֲנוּגוֹת?

★

הָה, זֵעָה!
הָה, אֶגְלֵי בְרָכָה הַיּוֹרְדִים מִמִּצְחִי הַגָּבֹהַּ –
כַּטַּל מִשָּׁמַיִם טְהוֹרִים.

הִנֵּה בְּשָׂרִי צַח וְשָׂעִיר,
וְהַשֵּׂעָר – דֶּשֶׁא שָׁחוֹר.
הָה, זֵעָה! זֵעָה מְלוּחָה!
הַטְלִילִי נָא אֶת בְּשָׂרִי, כִּשְׂדֵה שַׁחֲרִית סָמָר.
הַלְלוּיָהּ!

יִתְנוֹפְפוּ שְׁמֵי־שַׁחֲרִית – שׁוֹבֵךְ אֵלָה גְדוֹלָה –
וְרֹאשׁ אַבְשָׁלוֹם זְהוּב תַּלְתַּלִּים
נֶאֱחָז בְּצַמַּרְתָּם –
חַמָּה! חַמָּה!

And I bend down to the sand:

From the weight of cement the dunes sigh:

— Oh, why have you come, man, to the desert

To put a bit into our mouth?

And suddenly the east wind whipped

And like flocks of camels, that knew no bit.

Stormed upon the city being built —

    Sands!

On roads, foundations their stampede hailed

And with little hoofs

Hoofs of grains of sand

They kicked at my face:

Vengeance!

And suddenly they turned about and with whistlings:

Back to the deserts! Back to the deserts!

And I turned my hand

(In my hand a spade grey with concrete)

And the twisting roads began chasing them: After them!

They flung forth their lengthened hands:

    Smash them! Smash them!

Harness the deserts!

Stretch the roads like reins!

וָאֶגְחַן אֶל הַחוֹל;
מֵעֲקַת הַבֶּטוֹן פֹּה תֵּאָנַחְנָה דִיוּנוֹת;
– הָהּ, לָמָּה בָּאתָ, אָדָם, אֶל מִדְבָּרִיּוֹת
לְהַשְׁלִיךְ רֶסֶן אֱלֵי פִּינוּ?!

וּלְפֶתַע הִצְלִיף רוּחַ קָדִים
וּכְעֶדְרֵי גְמַלִּים, אֲשֶׁר לֹא יָדְעוּ אַפְסָר,
הִשְׁתָּעֲרוּ עַל הַקִּרְיָה הַנִּבְנֵית –
חוֹלוֹת!

עֲלֵי כְבִישׁ וּמַסָּד שֶׁעֲטָטָם תֵּבְרַד
וּבְפַרְסוֹת קְטַנּוֹת, –
פַּרְסוֹת גַּרְגְּרֵי הַחוֹל,
עַל פָּנַי יְטַלְפוּ:
נְקָמוֹת!
וְהִנֵּה – הָפְכוּ פְּנֵיהֶם – וּבִשְׁרִיקוֹת:
אֶל מִדְבָּרוֹת! אֶל מִדְבָּרוֹת!

וָאַט יָדִי
(וּבְיָדִי אֶת אֲפוּרָה מִנִּי מֶלֶט) –
וַיִּדְלְקוּ כְּבִישִׁים מִתְפַּתְּלִים: אַחֲרֵיהֶם!
הֶאֱרִיכוּ כַפַּיִם:
– הַכְפִּישֵׁם! הַכְפִּישֵׁם!

רַתְּמוּ הַמִּדְבָּרוֹת!
וּכְמוֹשְׁכוֹת מַתְחוּ כְּבִישִׁים!

I ride on the driver's seat!
I am — toil! —

Like huge fists lie on the sands
Houses — Houses — Houses —

And I feel:
It is I who am caught in the morning tree top
And in my hand like a sparkling ray, the spade.
Opposite me laughs the city newly made:
    Sun! Sun!

*

Dress me, good mother, in a splendrous coat of many colors
And with dawn lead me to toil.
My land wraps in light like a prayer shawl,
Houses stand like phylacteries,
And like bands of phylacteries glide hand-laid asphalt roads.

Thus a beautiful city offers her morning prayer to her creator.
And among the creators, your son Abraham,
Poet-roadbuilder in Israel.

אֲנִי יוֹשֵׁב עַל הַדּוּכָן!
אֲנִי – הֶעָמָל! – – –

כְּאֶגְרוֹפִים גְּדוֹלִים רָבְצוּ עַל הַחוֹלוֹת:
בָּתִּים – בָּתִּים – בָּתִּים –

וַאֲנִי חָשׁ:
זֶה אֲנִי בְּצַמֶּרֶת הַשַּׁחַר נֶאֱחַזְתִּי
וּבְיָדִי כְּקֶרֶן נוֹצֶצֶת – הָאֵת.
וְצוֹחֲקָה אֶל מוּלִי הַקִּרְיָה הַנִּבְנֵית:
חַמָּה! חַמָּה!

★

הַלְבִּישִׁינִי, אִמָּא כְּשֵׁרָה, כְּתֹנֶת פַּסִּים לְתִפְאֶרֶת
וְעִם שַׁחֲרִית הוֹבִילִינִי אֱלֵי עָמָל.
עוֹטְפָה אַרְצִי אוֹר כַּטַּלִּית.
בָּתִּים נִצְּבוּ כַּטּוֹטָפוֹת.
וְכַרְצוּעוֹת תְּפִלִּין גּוֹלְשִׁים כְּבִישִׁים, סָלְלוּ כַּפַּיִם.

תְּפִלַּת־שַׁחֲרִית כֹּה תִּתְפַּלֵּל קִרְיָה נָאָה אֱלֵי בּוֹרְאָהּ.
וּבַבּוֹרְאִים – בְּנֵךְ אַבְרָהָם,
פַּיְטָן סוֹלֵל בְּיִשְׂרָאֵל.

And toward evening, at dusk, father returns from his labors
And like prayer whispers with pleasure:
A dear son of mine is Abraham:
Skin, sinew, and bones.

　　Hallelujah!

Dress me, good mother, in a splendrous coat of many colors
And at dawn lead me
　　To toil.

Morning in My City

I have seen you, my erect morning, bare chested with tree-top tousled head,
Straight footed, standing in joy upon the flat roofs of the town.
Your head, as I always pictured it, sculptured in domed pride
Like the tilted head of a violinist playing a Bach chaconne.

And I recalled that Cabbalist* — compared to you by my father
　　of blessed memory —
Who said to the scholars of the study house, removing his
　　phylacteries as morning came:
"If I had but ten young men* who thirst for the wonder like me,
I would climb with them upon the roofs to sing out the Ineffable Name!"*

Now it is poured over roofs. Every thread of my body expresses it,
With each fiber in the dewy tree, meditating upon its symbols.*

וּבָעֶרֶב בֵּין הַשְּׁמָשׁוֹת יָשׁוּב אַבָּא מִסִּבְלוֹתָיו
וְכִתְפִלָּה יִלְחַשׁ נַחַת:
הַבֵּן יַקִּיר לִי אַבְרָהָם:
עוֹר וְגִידִים וַעֲצָמוֹת –
הַלְלוּיָהּ.

הַלְבִּישִׁינִי, אִמָּא כְּשֵׁרָה, כְּתֹנֶת פַּסִּים לְתִפְאֶרֶת
וְעִם שַׁחֲרִית הוֹבִילִינִי
אֱלֵי עָמָל.

בֹּקֶר בְּעִירִי

רְאִיתִיךָ, בָּקְרֵי הַזָּקוּף, פְּרוּם־חָזֶה וּמְסֹעָף־הַצַּמֶּרֶת,
יְשַׁר־רֶגֶל מֻצָּב בְּרִנְנָה עַל גַּוּוֹת רְדוּדִים שֶׁלְּכָרֶךְ,
וְרֹאשְׁךָ־כָּךְ תֵּאַרְתִּי תָמִיד־: מִחְטָב תּוֹךְ גַּבְהוּת מְקֻמֶּרֶת,
כְּרֹאשׁוֹ הַמֻּפְשָׁל שֶׁל כַּנָּר, בְּנַגְּנוֹ אֶת שָׁקוֹנָה שֶׁל בַּאךְ.

וְזָכַרְתִּי אוֹתוֹ מְקֻבָּל, – שֶׁאָבִי ז״ל אֵלֶיךָ דָּמָהוּ, –
שֶׁחָלַץ אֶת תְּפִלָּיו עִם שַׁחֲרִית וְאָמַר לְחוֹבְשֵׁי בֵּית־מִדְרָשׁ:
„מִי יִתְּנֵנִי מִנַּעַן בַּחוּרִים, שֶׁכְּמוֹנִי לַפֶּלֶא יִכְמָהוּ, –
וְטִפַּסְתִּי עִמָּם עַל גַּוּוֹת לְרַנֵּן אֶת הַשֵּׁם הַמְפֹרָשׁ".

וְעַכְשָׁו הוּא שָׁפוּךְ עַל גַּוּוֹת, כָּל רִקְמָה בְּגוּפִי תְּבַטְאֵנוּ,
עִם כָּל סִיב בְּאִילָן מְטֻלָל יְהַגֵּנוּ בְּאוֹתִיּוֹתָיו.

Windows open in the city. Cluster upon cluster, as from a basket,
People trickle into the streets with their plucked winey smiles.

Like a cat indulging in the sun, spreading its claws at the air,
A bachelor sea stretches before you, amazing infants with its size:
As if deciding whether time had come to bristle its smooth fur...
But your hand, large and hairy, caresses, soothes "not yet!"

Your air still straightens up, stands on tiptoe straining to hear,
High heavens in priestly blessing spread their hands —
On such an intoxicating morning, how caressing to its sensing ear
This alert human stirring, this murmuring speech of man.

Soon the knobby sycamore on the construction lot strewn with nails,
Will quake hearing the sound of footsteps and the creak of scaffolds
      moving along —
Then will I see you, my upright morning, bare chested with tree-top
      tousled head;
Climbing the roofs with ten young men singing the builder's song.

חַלּוֹנוֹת נִפְתָּחִים בְּעִירִי: אֶשְׁכֹּלוֹת־אֶשְׁכֹּלוֹת, כְּמִטְמָא,
יְזַלְּפוּ בְּנֵי־אָדָם אֶל הָרְחוֹב חִיּוּכָם הַיֵּינִי הַנִּקְטָף.

כְּחָתוּל מִתְפַּנֵּק בַּחַמָּה וּמְפַשֵּׁק צִפָּרְנָיו אֶל הָרוּחַ,
יִתְמוֹדֵד מְמוּלְךָ יָם רָנָק, הַמַּפְלִיא תִּינוֹקוֹת בְּגָדְלוֹ,
כְּנִמְלְךָ, אִם הִגִּיעָה עִתּוֹ לְסַמֵּר אֶת צַמְרוֹ הַשָּׂטוּחַ...
אַךְ כַּפֵּךְ, הַשְּׂעִירָה וּגְדוֹלָה, תְּלַטְּפוּ לְהַרְגִּיעַ: עוֹד לֹא!

אֲוִירֵךְ עוֹד עוֹקֵף קוֹמָתוֹ וְעוֹמֵד עַל בְּהוֹנוֹת מֵרֹב קֶשֶׁב,
וְשָׁמַיִם גְּבוֹהִים יִפְרְשׂוּ בְּבִרְכַּת־כֹּהֲנִים אֶת יָדָם; –
בְּשַׁחֲרִית מְבֻשֶּׂמֶת כָּזֹאת מַה־לּוֹטְפָה אֶת אָזְנָם הַנִּרְגֶּשֶׁת
זוֹ אוֹשָׁה אֱנוֹשִׁית נֶעוֹרָה – הַמּוּלַת דִּבּוּרוֹ שֶׁל אָדָם.

עוֹד מְעַט וְשִׁקְמָה יַבְלוּלִית בְּכִכַּר הַבִּנְיָן הַמְסֹמֶּרֶת
תִּתְחַלְחֵל לְמִשְׁמַע קוֹל פְּסִיעוֹת וְחַרוּק פְּגוּמִים מוּנָעִים –
אָז אֶרְאֶךָ, בָּקְרִי הַזָּקוּף, פְּרוּם־חָזֶה וּמִסְעַף־הַצַּמֶּרֶת,
מְטַפֵּס עִם מִנְיַן בַּחוּרִים עַל גַּגּוֹת בִּרְנוּן בַּנָּאי.

At Evening when Flicker

At evening when flicker
Sparks on the mountain,
One goes from within me
To the landscapes of no-return.

His mantle is cloud,
His amazement like the sea.
I bend after his spirit
With grass and stillness.

I cry out without sound,
He hints without motion.
His echo distance — footsteps
Expire in me forever...

In the World's Heart Burns a Torch of Fire

In the world's heart burns a torch of fire,
In its footsteps, eternal wanderers we have gone.
Embodied light of all that transpires
It is the fire-core for everyone.

עֶרֶב בְּהִתְלַקֵּחַ...

עֶרֶב, בְּהִתְלַקֵּחַ
נִיצוֹצוֹת בָּהָר,
הוֹלֵךְ אֶחָד מִתּוֹכִי
אֶל נוֹפֵי אַל־שׁוּב.

אַדַּרְתּוֹ עֲנָנָה,
תִּמְהוֹנוֹ כַּיָּם.
אֲנִי שָׁח אַחֲרֵי רוּחוֹ
עִם דֶּשֶׁא וּדְמִי.

אֲנִי זוֹעֵק בְּאֵין הֶגֶה,
וְהוּא רוֹמֵז בְּאֵין נִיד.
וְהֵד פַּעֲמֵי מֶרְחַקָּיו
גּוֵעַ בִּי עַד...

בְּלֵב הָעוֹלָם

בְּלֵב הָעוֹלָם בּוֹעֵר לַפִּיד אֵשׁ,
וּבְעִקְבוֹתָיו תּוֹעֵי־עַד יָצָאנוּ.
הוּא הָאוֹר הַגָּלוּם בְּכָל יֵשׁ,
הוּא הַמּוֹקֵד לְכֻלָּנוּ.

We lust, building ivory spires,
We kneel silent to the secret within us alone.
And in the world's heart burns a torch of fire —
It is the fire-core for everyone ...

Suddenly We Will Wake

Suddenly we will wake from sleep at night,
Between fright and fright.
The walls are contorted, the window panes dark
And in us the light.

And for the eternals of joy our blood will listen —
And here is their voice!
And with both hands upon the tablet of the heart*
We embrace the world!

Drink Wonder

Drink wonder, my heart, drink in the wonder,
Day moves to day, night after night does not wander.
Strip off your garment, plunge into feeling and sensation,
Each shape is vision, each touch is revelation.

אָנוּ עוֹגְבִים, בּוֹנִים טִירוֹת שַׁיִשׁ.
אָנוּ כּוֹרְעִים דָּם לַסּוֹד שֶׁבָּנוּ.
וּבְלֵב הָעוֹלָם בּוֹעֵר לַפִּיד אֵשׁ –
הוּא הַמּוֹקֵד לְכֻלָּנוּ...

פִּתְאֹם נָקִיץ

פִּתְאֹם נָקִיץ מִשְּׁנָתֵנוּ בַּלֵּילוֹת,
בֵּין מוֹרָא לְמוֹרָא.
נִלְפָּתִים הַכְּתָלִים, הַשְּׁמָשׁוֹת אֲפֵלוֹת
וּבָנוּ – הָאוֹרָה.

וּלְנִצְחֵי רְנָנָה יַאֲזִינוּ דָּמֵינוּ –
וְהִנֵּה הוּא קוֹלָם!
וּבְכַפֵּינוּ הַשְּׁתַּיִם עַל לוּחַ לִבֵּנוּ –
נְחַבֵּק הָעוֹלָם!

פֶּלֶא גֶּמַע...

פֶּלֶא גֶּמַע, לִבִּי, לִבִּי, גֶּמַע הַפֶּלֶא,
יוֹם אֶל יוֹם יִשָּׂא, לֵיל עַל לֵיל לֵיל לֹא יֵלֶא.
פְּשֹׁט הַלְּבוּשׁ וְצֵלֵל בָּרַחַשׁ וּבְרֶטֶט,
כָּל מַגָּע – גָּלוּי, כָּל דְּמוּת חָזוֹן שׁוֹתֶתֶת.

Walk the path, my heart, my heart, walk the course,
Upon it man is the god, dance is the compelling force.
There where you rest, there where you wander too —
With you the mystery rests, the spirit rests with you.

Break into song, my heart, my heart, break into song,
To the infinite light,* to splendor without end.
Lift up the cup and drink to joy and to distress,
Exult toward life, exult toward death!

All Is Not So Simple

All is not so simple in the yards of the houses
From every storey the windows stare.
In pallid pavement, on walls that fade
Each hour that passes, each hour is engraved.

All is not so simple between the walls of the rooms.
There is something in the stance of the bookcase.
The heavy curtain, the made bed
Kneel under a yoke a burden of knowledge.

In every house there are dark stairs.
In the morning come down, at night go up,
Creatures who are silent, who close their doors —
For them my soul grieves, for them it implores.

אֹרַח לֵךְ, לִבִּי, לִבִּי, לֵךְ לְךָ הָאֹרַח,
בּוֹ אָדָם הָאֵל, בּוֹ מָחוֹל הַכֶּרַח.
בַּאֲשֶׁר תָּנוּד, בַּאֲשֶׁר תָּנוּחַ –
נָח עִמְּךָ הַסּוֹד, נָח עִמְּךָ הָרוּחַ.

זֶמֶר פְּצַח, לִבִּי, לִבִּי, פְּצַח הַזֶּמֶר,
לָאוֹר שֶׁאֵין לוֹ סוֹף, לַיְּקָר שֶׁאֵין לוֹ גֶּמֶר.
שָׂא הַכּוֹס וּשְׁתֵה לַגִּיל וְלָעַצֶּבֶת,
צְהַל לִקְרַאת חַיִּים וּצְהַל לִקְרַאת הַמָּוֶת!

לֹא הַכֹּל כֹּה פָשׁוּט

לֹא הַכֹּל כֹּה פָשׁוּט בְּחַצְרוֹת הַבָּתִּים,
מִכָּל הַקּוֹמוֹת חַלוֹנוֹת נִבָּטִים,
וּבְדִהֵי הַחוֹמוֹת, בְּעֵירֹם הַמִּרְצֶפֶת
תֶּחָרֵת כָּל שָׁעָה, כָּל שָׁעָה הַחוֹלֶפֶת...

לֹא הַכֹּל כֹּה פָשׁוּט בֵּין כָּתְלֵי חֲדָרִים,
יֵשׁ דָּבָר בַּמַּעֲמָד שֶׁל אֲרוֹן הַסְּפָרִים,
וְהַמָּסָךְ הַכָּבֵד וְהַמִּטָּה הַמֻּצַּעַת
כּוֹרְעִים תַּחַת עֹל. תַּחַת נֵטֶל שֶׁל דַּעַת...

וּבְכָל הַבָּתִּים מַדְרֵגוֹת אֲפֵלוֹת,
שָׁם יוֹרְדִים בַּבְּקָרִים וְעוֹלִים בַּלֵּילוֹת
יְצוּרִים שֶׁשּׁוֹתְקִים וְסוֹגְרִים אֶת הַדֶּלֶת –
נַפְשִׁי עֲלֵיהֶם, נַפְשִׁי מִתְפַּלֶּלֶת...

S. SHALOM

The Stoker

The ship sets sail, the ship is journeying
Among secret stars, among islands of basalt,
The wake is scattered, the wake is drowning
In fragments of foam, in twilight black.

The silence deepens, the silence is hoisted
Over deck and rope, over hatch and porthole:
Only from below my ear hears the echo,
From the maze of rungs life's cabin I recall.

There always stands one, his body alabaster;
He stares with glassy eyes, smoke-swarmed,
This same one always feeds the fire
Black coals with his granite arms.

Slumber is chewing, slumber is swallowing
The stars, the earth, the ship and the deep.
This flame alone never sets
And this one alone, only he does not sleep.

הַמַּסִּיק

הַסְּפִינָה מַפְלֶגֶת, הַסְּפִינָה נוֹסַעַת
בֵּין אִיֵּי בַּזֶּלֶת, בֵּין כּוֹכְבֵי מִסְתּוֹר.
הַנְּתִיבָה נִבְזֶקֶת, הַנְּתִיבָה טוֹבַעַת
בִּמְכִתּוֹת שֶׁל קֶצֶף, בִּדְמָדּוּם שָׁחוֹר.

הַדְּמָמָה תּוֹהֶמֶת, הַדְּמָמָה מוּקַעַת
עַל סִפּוּן וָחֶבֶל, בְּאֶשְׁנָב וּסְגוֹר.
רַק מִתַּחְתִּיּוֹת אָזְנֵי הַדְּהוּד שׁוֹמַעַת,
רַק בִּמְבוֹךְ שְׁלַבִּים תָּא חַיִּים אֶזְכּוֹר.

שָׁם נִצָּב תָּמִיד אֶחָד עִם גּוּף שֶׁל בַּהַט,
חַם, אָפוּף עָשָׁן, לוֹטֵשׁ עֵינֵי זְכוּכִית.
שָׁם מֵטִיל תָּמִיד אֶחָד אֶל תּוֹךְ הַלַּהַט
פֶּחָמִים שְׁחוֹרִים בִּזְרוֹעוֹת גְּרָנִיט.

תַּרְדֵּמָה כּוֹסֶסֶת, תַּרְדֵּמָה בּוֹלַעַת
כּוֹכָבִים וָאָרֶץ, אֳנִיָּה וָיָם.
הַלִּבָּה הַזֹּאת רַק הִיא אֵינָהּ שׁוֹקַעַת,
הָאֶחָד הַזֶּה רַק הִיא אֵינוֹ נִרְדָּם.

They That Sow at Night

Go slowly, go slowly, oh moon, upon your way. We are sowing by your light,
Sowing the fields of Galilee.
Enemies rise against us from all sides, the roaring human desires
    close upon us —
And we go out to sow at night,
For we want only to sow and our soul longs for grain.

Go slowly, go slowly, oh moon, upon your way.
Divided and cleft are the fields of Galilee, precious and holy
    is the seed we scatter ...
We need your light, we need your light.
Let us see our way and let them not see us.
Let our seed sprout, let not the cruel uproot it.
Make our night-sown grain grow, for the sun has surely betrayed us,
And the days are given to annihilation.

Go slowly, go slowly, oh moon, on your way, do not be alarmed
    by our moving shadows,
We are Hebrew men sowing their fields at night.
We have no voice and no sound.
There is no sound in our horses' hoofs and our wagon wheels are muffled.
Secretly, secretly we walk, the surrounding mountains do not understand us.
You, understand our deed. Let them not plunder us.
Guard us from the wandering bullet, from the knife out of the ambush.
Guard us from war's battle cry, from blood spilled on the furrows.

הַזּוֹרְעִים בַּלֵּילוֹת

לְאַט לְךָ, לְאַט לְךָ, הַסַּהַר, בְּדַרְכְּךָ, אֲנַחְנוּ זוֹרְעִים לְאוֹרְךָ,
זוֹרְעִים אֶת שַׂדְמוֹת הַגָּלִיל.
קָמוּ עָלֵינוּ אוֹיְבִים מִכָּל צַד, סָגְרוּ עָלֵינוּ מַאֲוַיֵּי־הָאָדָם הַשּׁוֹאֲגִים –
וַנֵּצֵא לִזְרֹעַ בַּלַּיְלָה,
כִּי רַק לִזְרֹעַ אָנוּ חֲפֵצִים וְנַפְשֵׁנוּ שׁוֹקֶקֶת לַבָּר.

לְאַט לְךָ, לְאַט לְךָ, הַסַּהַר בְּדַרְכְּךָ.
מֵחֲצָצִים וּמִבְּקָעִים הַשָּׂדוֹת בַּגָּלִיל, יָקָר וְקָדוֹשׁ לָנוּ הַזֶּרַע נִפְזָר –
וַאֲנַחְנוּ זְקוּקִים לְאוֹרְךָ, לְאוֹרְךָ אָנוּ זְקוּקִים.
תֶּן־נָא וְרָאִינוּ אֶת דַּרְכֵּנוּ וְרָאֹה אַל יִרְאוּנוּ הֵהֶם.
תֶּן־נָא וְנָבֵט הַזֶּרַע וְאַל יַעֲקְרוּהוּ זֵדִים.
הַצֶּמַח תְּבוּאָתֵנוּ זָרַעְנוּ בַּלַּיְלָה, כִּי בָּגוֹד בָּגְדָה בָּנוּ הַשֶּׁמֶשׁ,
וְהַיָּמִים נְתוּנִים לַכִּלָּיוֹן.

לְאַט לְךָ, לְאַט לְךָ, הַסַּהַר, בְּדַרְכְּךָ, וְאַל נָא תַּבְהֵל מִצְּלָלֵינוּ
הַנָּעִים.
אֲנָשִׁים עִבְרִים אֲנַחְנוּ, הַזּוֹרְעִים שְׂדוֹתֵיהֶם בַּלֵּילוֹת.
לֹא קוֹל לָנוּ וְלֹא הֶגֶה.
לֹא מַמָּשׁ לְפַרְסוֹת סוּסֵינוּ וְגַלְגַּלֵּי עֶגְלוֹתֵינוּ רְפוּדִים.
חֲשָׁאִים, חֲשָׁאִים נִתְהַלֵּךְ וְהֶהָרִים מִסָּבִיב לֹא יְבִינוּנוּ.
הָבֵן־נָא אַתָּה לְפָעֳלֵנוּ וְאַל תִּתְּנֵנוּ לִמְשִׁסָּה.
שָׁמְרֵנוּ מִכַּדּוּר מְתַעְתֵּעַ, מִסַּכִּין הַבָּאָה מִן הַמַּאֲרָב.
שָׁמְרֵנוּ מִתְּרוּעַת מִלְחָמָה, מִדָּם הַנִּשְׁפָּךְ עַל הַתְּלָמִים.

Guard the seed we have sown, guard it from theft and from scorching wind,
May our children eat and be satisfied. May they rise lofty and
    remember us for good.
Only for them do we sow at night, for their sake our steps are alarmed.
For we are Hebrew men, sowing our fields at night.
Go slowly, go slowly, oh moon, upon your way.

Guard Me, Oh God

Guard me, Oh God, from hating man my brother,
Guard me from recalling what, from my early youth, to me he did.
When all the stars in my sky are quenched, within me my soul's
    voice grows mute —
When I am overcome by disaster, let me not lay bare his guilt.

For he is my hidden dwelling-place, in him am I reflected again,
Like a wayfarer from the planets, beholding his face in a pool.
What use is all my struggle, to whom shall I wail out the pain —
If hollow, blemished is my distant night's moon?

When the gates are locked, darkness over the city reclining,
And emptied of love, rejected, I am bound to my rock:
Permit me to see in him a spark, only a spark still shining,
That I may know that in myself, in me, all is not yet snuffed out.

שָׁמֹר עַל הַזֶּרַע זָרַעְנוּ, שָׁמְרֵהוּ מִשֹּׁד וּמִשָּׁדָפוֹן,
יֵאָכְלוּ בָנֵינוּ וְיִשְׂבָּעוּ, יָרוּמוּ וְיִזְכְּרוּנוּ לְטוֹבָה.
כִּי רַק לְמַעֲנָם אָנוּ זוֹרְעִים בַּלֵּילוֹת וּלְמַעֲנָם צְעָדֵינוּ בְּהוֹלִים,
כִּי אֲנָשִׁים עִבְרִים אֲנַחְנוּ, הַזּוֹרְעִים שְׂדוֹתֵיהֶם בַּלֵּילוֹת.
לְאַט לְךָ, לְאַט לְךָ, הַסַּהַר, בְּדַרְכְּךָ.

שָׁמְרֵנִי, אֱלֹהִים...

שָׁמְרֵנִי, אֱלֹהִים, מִשִּׂנְאַת אָחִי הָאָדָם,
שָׁמְרֵנִי מִזְּכֹר אֵת אֲשֶׁר מֵאָבִי לִי עוֹלֵל.
בְּדַעְךָ כָּל כּוֹכְבֵי רְקִיעִי וְקוֹל הַנְּשָׁמָה בִּי נָדַם –
אַל־נָא תְּבוֹאֵנִי שׁוֹאָה עָלָיו אַשְׁמָתוֹ לְגוֹלֵל.

כִּי הוּא מְחוֹזִי הֶעָלוּם וּבוֹ אָנֹכִי מִשְׁתַּקֵּף
כְּהֵלֶךְ הַבָּא מִמֶּרְחַקִּים וְצוֹפֶה אֵת פָּנָיו בָּאֲגַם.
שֶׁלָּמָה הָיוּ נַפְתּוּלַי, וּלְמִי אֲתַנֶּה אֵת הַכְּאֵב –
אִם סַהַר לֵילִי הָרָחוֹק חָלוּל מִתּוֹכוֹ וְנִפְגָּם?

וְעֵת הַשְּׁעָרִים נְעוּלִים וְחֹשֶׁךְ רוֹבֵץ עַל הָעִיר.
וַאֲנִי מְרֻתָּק אֶל סַלְעִי, מְנֻדָּח וּמְנֹעַר אַהֲבָה –
תְּנֵנִי לִרְאוֹת בּוֹ נִיצוֹץ, רַק נִיצוֹץ שֶׁעוֹדֶנּוּ מֵאִיר,
לְמַעַן אֵדַע כִּי גַם בִּי, כִּי גַם בִּי עוֹד הַכֹּל לֹא כָבָה...

Memento of Roads

Send forth your songs like the doe and the fawn

Listen —

Yet far, far away roar

Many roads

That dug in the tunnels of the horizon,

The blue, the red,

And crossed in the stormy summer

Gliding with villages to the well,

And journeyed with rows of swaying trains

To cities and fairs.

Field roads, hill and valley roads,

Waves of their long breath . . .

Fields at moonlight in plaster masks,

Pastures, sun, and whistling.

Roads

In their expanse

White and singing.

With a rope desire dragged me!

The sound of wheel and wind and brief meetings,

A trotting horse's neigh between bell and whip,

Night flickering every jewel,

מַזְכֶּרֶת לַדְּרָכִים

שַׁלְחוּ אֶת שִׁירֵיכֶם כְּאַיָּלָה וָעֹפֶר
הַקְשִׁיבוּ –
עוֹד הָרְחֵק הַרְחֵק מְנַחֲמוֹת
הַרְבֵּה דְרָכִים.
אֲשֶׁר חָתְרוּ בִּמְנִהֲרוֹת הָאֹפֶק.
הַכְּחֻלּוֹת וְגַם הָאֲדֻמּוֹת,
וְחָצוּ בַּקַּיִץ הַסּוֹעֵר
וְגָלְשׁוּ עִם הַכְּפָרִים לַבְּאֵר
וְנָסְעוּ, בְּטוּר קְרוֹנוֹת מִתְנוֹדְדִים,
אֶל הֶעָרִים וְהַיְרִידִים.

דַּרְכֵי שָׂדֶה, דַּרְכֵי בִּקְעוֹת וְגֶבַע,
גַּלֵּי נְשִׁימָתָן הָאָרֻכָּה...
שָׂדוֹת לְאוֹר יָרֵחַ בְּמַסְווֹת הַגֶּבֶס,
כָּרֵי מִרְעֶה וָשֶׁמֶשׁ וּשְׁרִיקָה.
דְּרָכִים,
אֶל מֶרְחָבָן
הַשָּׁר וְהַלָּבָן
בְּחֶבֶל הוֹבִילַתְנִי הַתְּשׁוּקָה!

לְקוֹל גַּלְגַּל וָרוּחַ וְטִיסַת פְּגִישׁוֹת
וְנַחַר סוּס דּוֹהֵר בֵּין פַּעֲמוֹן וָשׁוֹט
וְלַיְלָה מְהַבְהֵב בְּכָל הָעֲדָיִים

And a wood huddled like a giant child
To an inn opened to greet the guests.
With pailfuls of laughter the innkeeper's daughter
Emerges beautiful in the red shawl
And the blue ice of her eyes.
Happy is he who gulped her cold milk
Somewhere along the fifty-second league.

Roads, Roads —
Rows of nights passed over them, like friars
Gone forth in throngs, lofty and fragile
As their souls of water and air expired.

Roads, with my own eyes I drew you to me,
Roads, with my own life I loved you.
Your fingernails scratch, scratch a fiery scar
On the horizon that calls and erupts.

Red Ridinghood

When our wild day is wiped like a tear
From cities and forest, from month and year,
Red Ridinghood walks on the road,
To pick a wild flower in the wood.

וְחֹרֶשׁ מְכֻוָּץ כְּיֶלֶד עֲנָקִי
וְעַד פֻּנְדָּק נִפְתָּח לִפְגֹּשׁ אֶת הַבָּאִים,
בִּמְלֹא דְלָיֵי צְחוֹקָהּ שֶׁל בַּת הַפֻּנְדָּקִי,
אֲשֶׁר תֵּצֵא יָפָה, בְּאֹדֶם הַסֻּוְדָר,
בְּקֶרַח הַתְּכַלְכַּל שֶׁלְּעֵינַיִם – –
אַשְׁרֵי אֲשֶׁר גָּמַע מֵחַלְבָּהּ הַקָּר,
אִי־שָׁמָּה, בַּפָּרָסָה הַחֲמִשִּׁים וּשְׁתַּיִם.

דְּרָכִים, דְּרָכִים – –
טוּרֵי לֵילוֹת עָבְרוּ בָּן כִּנְזִירִים אַחִים,
אֲשֶׁר יָצְאוּ בְּסָךְ גָּבֹהַּ וְשָׁבִיר,
בִּפְרֹחַ נִשְׁמָתָם שֶׁל מַיִם וַאֲוִיר.

אֲנִי אֶתְכֶן, דְּרָכִים, בְּמוֹ עֵינַי שָׁאַבְתִּי.
אֲנִי אֶתְכֶן, דְּרָכִים, בְּמוֹ חַיַּי אָהַבְתִּי.
צִפָּרְנֵיכֶן שׂוֹרְטוֹת, שׂוֹרְטוֹת צַלֶּקֶת אֵשׁ
בָּאֹפֶק הַקּוֹרֵא וְהַגּוֹעֵשׁ.

כִּפָּה אֲדֻמָּה

עֵת יוֹמְנוּ הַפֶּרֶא נִמְחָה כְּדִמְעָה
מְעָרִים וִיעָרוֹת, מִשָּׁנָה וָחֹדֶשׁ,
הוֹלֶכֶת בַּדֶּרֶךְ כִּפָּה אֲדֻמָּה,
לִלְקֹט פֶּרַח־בָּר בַּחֹרֶשׁ.

And following her is a duck and a cow,

Hobbling on a cane is a cat —

Like a tale that was lost, like a song long ago,

Like a smile that is old and forgot.

In the distance stand the coming years,

In vain our bewilderments increase,

A naked moon sucks on its thumb

As in father's lap, at the first.

And we are silent. A grassy earth

Flutters in lashes of green . . .

We closed our eyes — And suddenly look

The tree's crown is already dark.

Beyond Melody

With a violin in the alley grandfather and son disappeared.

Again the night was closed. Oh, speak, please speak!

I who grew up with all your stones,

I knew — like confession, they too would break.

Stones like tears in the lashes of the world.

How shall I set out to wipe them with a silken cloth?

וְיוֹצְאִים אַחֲרֶיהָ פָּרָה וָאֲוָז
וְחָתוּל מְדַדֶּה עַל מִשְׁעֶנֶת – –
כְּסִפּוּר שֶׁאָבַד, כְּנִגּוּן מִנִּי אָז,
כְּבַת־צְחוֹק נִשְׁכָּחָה וְנוֹשֶׁנֶת.

וְעוֹמְדוֹת מֵרָחוֹק הַשָּׁנִים הַבָּאוֹת
וְלַשָּׁוְא תְּמִיהוֹתֵינוּ כֹּה רַבּוּ
וּמוֹצֵץ לוֹ יָרֵחַ עֵירוֹם אֶצְבָּעוֹ
כְּבִימֵי בְּרֵאשִׁית, בְּחֵיק אַבָּא.

וַאֲנַחְנוּ שׁוֹתְקִים. אֲדָמָה עֲשָׂבִית
בִּירַקְרַק הָרִיסִים מְפַרְפֶּרֶת...
וְעֵינֵינוּ עָצַמְנוּ – – וּלְפֶתַע נַבִּיט
וְהִנֵּה כְּבָר חָשְׁכָה הַצַּמֶּרֶת.

מֵעֵבֶר לַמַּנְגִּינָה

בַּסִּמְטָה, עִם כִּנּוֹר, נֶעֶלְמוּ סָב וָנֶכֶד.
שׁוּב הַלַּיְלָה נִסְגַּר. הָהּ, דַּבֵּר, דַּבֵּר־נָא!
אֲנִי שֶׁגָּדַלְתִּי עִם כָּל אֲבָנֶיךָ,
יָדַעְתִּי – גַּם הֵן כְּוִדּוּי תִּשָּׁבֵרְנָה.

אֲבָנִים כִּדְמָעוֹת בְּרִיסֵי הָעוֹלָם.
אֵיךְ אֵצֵא לִמְחוֹתָן בְּמִטְפַּחַת מֶשִׁי?

Over the last song that opposite them trembles,
Silence circles like an eagle.

At times from the night we open amazed eyes,
With wisdom and folly slow, slow we shall smile.
Mother's greyness looks at our lives,
The silence of rooms where there is no child.

And we shall go out to pale roads we abandoned,
They stand erect with a cloud and a song,
They shall go rocking us in their bosom —
They shall go tall, go tender and strong.

Go and tell them
The well is filled,
The forest burns in its sovereign mantle.
But deaf and alone
Our field is tilled
By our petty, abashed pain.

It has no deliverer, it has no flags.
Dressed in mourning silence guards its cradles.
Like its big brothers it lives alone,
Like the end, the autumn, the heart.

עַל אַחֲרוֹן הַשִּׁירִים הָרוֹעֵד לְמוּלָן
חָגָה הַדְּמָמָה כְּנֶשֶׁר.

יֵשׁ נִפְקַח מִן הַלַּיְלָה עֵינַיִם תְּמֵהוֹת,
נְחַיֵּךְ אַט־לְאַט מִתְּבוּנוֹת וָאֵוֶּלֶת.
אֶל חַיֵּינוּ נִשְׁקֶפֶת שֵׁיבַת אִמָּהוֹת,
דּוּמִיַּת חֲדָרִים אֲשֶׁר אֵין בָּהֶם יֶלֶד.

יֵשׁ נֵצֵא לַדְּרָכִים הַחִוְּרוֹת שֶׁזָּנַחְנוּ,
שֶׁתִּזְקְפֶנָּה קוֹמָה בְּנִגּוּן וְעָנָן,
וְתֵלַכְנָה גְבֹהוֹת, רַכּוֹת־כֹּחַ תֵּלַכְנָה,
הָלוֹךְ וְהָגֵעַ אוֹתָנוּ בְּחֵיקָן – –

הָלוֹךְ וְדַבֵּר
שֶׁמָּלְאָה הַבְּאֵר,
שֶׁהַיַּעַר בּוֹעֵר בְּאַדְרוֹת הַמַּלְכוּת,
אַךְ בּוֹדֵד וְחֵרֵשׁ
אֶת שָׂדֵהוּ חוֹרֵשׁ
כְּאִבֵּנוּ הַנִּכְלָם וְהַפָּעוּט.

כִּי אֵין לוֹ מָשִׁיחַ וְאֵין לוֹ דְגָלִים
וּדְמָמוֹת בִּלְבוּשׁ אֵבֶל שׁוֹמְרוֹת עַרְשׂוֹתָיו.
הוּא שׁוֹכֵן לְבָדָד כְּאֶחָיו הַגְּדוֹלִים,
הַסּוֹף וְהַלֵּב וְהַסְּתָו.

It shines like light in mother's forgiveness,
In wisdom's and folly's bashful quiet —
On the lips of thresholds thirsty and wide
Its smile is stoned at our feet.

Moon

Also an old image has a moment's birth
Sky without bird
Strange and fortified
On the moonlight night opposite your window
Stands a city dipped in crickets' cry.

And as you see the road still looking to the wayfarer
And the moon
On the cypress's spear,
You say: my God, are all these still here?
May one still whisper to ask how they are?

From their pools the water looks at us.
Tranquil is the tree
In its ruby earrings,
O our God, never shall be torn from me
The sorrow of your great playthings.

הוּא זוֹרֵחַ כָּאוֹר בִּסְלִיחַת אִמָּהוֹת,
בִּשְׁתִיקָה בַּיְשָׁנִית שֶׁל תְּבוּנוֹת וְאִוֶּלֶת –
עַל שְׂפָתַי מִפְּתָנִים רְחָבוֹת וּצְמֵאוֹת
בַּת־צְחוֹקוֹ בְּרַגְלֵינוּ נִסְקֶלֶת.

יָרֵחַ

גַּם לְמַרְאֶה נוֹשָׁן יֵשׁ רֶגַע שֶׁל הֻלֶּדֶת.
שָׁמַיִם בְּלִי צִפּוֹר
זָרִים וּמְבֻצָּרִים.
בַּלַּיְלָה הַסָּהוּר מוּל חַלּוֹנְךָ עוֹמֶדֶת
עִיר טְבוּלָה בִּבְכִי הַצְּרָצָרִים.

וּבִרְאוֹתְךָ כִּי דֶּרֶךְ עוֹד צוֹפָה אֶל הֵלֶךְ
וְהַיָּרֵחַ
עַל כִּידוֹן הַבְּרוֹשׁ
אַתָּה אוֹמֵר – אֵלִי, הַעוֹד יֶשְׁנָם כָּל אֵלֶּה?
הַעוֹד מֻתָּר בְּלַחַשׁ בִּשְׁלוֹמָם לִדְרשׁ?

מֵאַגְמֵיהֶם הַמַּיִם נִבָּטִים אֵלֵינוּ.
שׁוֹקֵט הָעֵץ
בְּאֹדֶם עֲגִילִים.
לָעַד לֹא תֵעָקֵר מִמֶּנִּי, אֱלֹהֵינוּ,
תּוּגַת צַעֲצוּעֶיךָ הַגְּדוֹלִים.

The Joy of the Poor *(excerpts)*

Introduction

The joy of the poor knocked on the door,
Till then the man waited for her.
She lifted her violin, joy of the poor,
The deathly poor rejoiced in her.

> And he said: How pleasant, how good,
> The Joy of the Poor I have heard.

At night, at night — scolded and robbed
On a straw pallet he had dreamed of her:
As vengeance is dreamed, as the body pains,
And the poor man's lamb is pure.

> And he said: How pleasant, how good,
> You have come to me, Joy of the Poor.

But the joy said: No, your destroyer has come.
No, your last day has come to you.
I do not tread your olive-press or visit your home,
With the bearers-of-the-ark* I go.

> And he said: to my tormentor, my foe
> How will you return, Joy of the Poor?

And she said: I go down with you to the pit,
Ark-man you press me like a man still alive.

שִׂמְחַת עֲנִיִּים (מספר השירים)

הַקְדָּמָה

דָּפְקָה עַל הַדֶּלֶת שִׂמְחַת עֲנִיִּים.
כִּי חִכְּתָה לָהּ הָאִישׁ עַד עֵת.
וַתִּשָּׂא כְנוֹרֶיהָ שִׂמְחַת עֲנִיִּים,
וַיִּשְׂמַח בָּהּ עָנִי־כְּמֵת.

וַיֹּאמַר: מַה טּוֹב וּמַה נָּעִים,
כִּי שָׁמַעְתִּי שִׂמְחַת עֲנִיִּים.

וּבַלַּיְלָה, בַּלַּיְלָה, שָׁדוּד וְנָזוּף,
חֲלָמָהּ עַל מַצַּע הַקַּשׁ:
חֲלוּמָהּ כַּנָּקָם וְכוֹאֶבֶת כַּגּוּף
וְצַחָה כְּכִבְשַׂת הָרָשׁ.

וַיֹּאמַר: מַה טּוֹב וּמַה נָּעִים,
כִּי בָּאַתְנִי שִׂמְחַת עֲנִיִּים.

וַתֹּאמַר הַשִּׂמְחָה: לֹא, כִּי בָא מַשְׁחִיתְךָ.
לֹא, כִּי בָא לְךָ יוֹם אַחֲרוֹן.
לֹא פָּקַדְתִּי בֵּיתְךָ, לֹא דָרַכְתִּי גַּתְּךָ,
רַק אֵלֵךְ עִם נוֹשְׂאֵי־הָאָרוֹן.

וַיֹּאמַר: אֵל צָרִי וּמְעַנִּי,
אֵיךְ תָּשׁוּבִי, שִׂמְחַת הֶעָנִי?

וַתֹּאמַר: בּוֹר אֵרֵד אִתְּךָ, אִישׁ־הָאָרוֹן,
כִּי נוֹשֶׂה אַתָּה בִּי כְּמוֹ חַי.

You did not see my face until the end,
The foe too shall not see me and live.

And he said: How pleasant, how good,
That you are with me, Joy of the Poor.

1. The Song to the Wife of His Youth

My daughter, all is not vanity.
All is not vain.
My promise to silver I broke,
My days I scattered in vain.
Only you I followed, my daughter,
As the neck follows the rope.

My daughter, you wound your kerchief.
You said to me: look and see.
I vowed not to bite my crust of bread
Till your greenness blunted my teeth.
My daughter, I vowed to look at you
Till my eyes grew too dim to see.

My daughter, then sickness struck.
Poverty covered our face.

כִּי פָנַי לֹא רָאִיתָ עַד יוֹם אַחֲרוֹן
וְגַם צָר אַל יִרְאֵנִי וָחָי.

וַיֹּאמַר: מַה טּוֹב וּמַה נָּעִים,
כִּי אִתִּי אַתְּ, שִׂמְחַת עֲנִיִּים.

א. שִׁיר לְאֵשֶׁת־נְעוּרִים

לֹא הַכֹּל הֲבָלִים, בִּתִּי,
לֹא הַכֹּל הֲבָלִים וָהֶבֶל.
גַּם לַכֶּסֶף הִפְרַתִּי בְּרִיתִי,
גַּם זָרִיתִי יָמַי לַהֶבֶל.
רַק אַחֲרַיִךְ הָלַכְתִּי, בִּתִּי,
כַּצַּוָּאר אַחֲרֵי הַחֶבֶל.

כִּי עֲדִית מִטְפַּחְתֵּךְ, בִּתִּי,
כִּי אָמַרְתְּ לִי: הַבֵּט וּרְאֵנָּה,
וְאָדוֹר לֹא לִנְשׁוֹךְ פָּתִּי,
עַד שְׁנֵי מִבְּסָרֵךְ תִּקְהֶינָה.
וְאָדוֹר לִרְאוֹתֵךְ, בִּתִּי,
עַד עֵינַי מֵרְאוֹתֵךְ תִּכְהֶינָה.

וְהִכָּה הָחֳלִי, בִּתִּי,
וְהָעֹנִי כִּסָּה פָנֵינוּ.

I called sickness my home,
I called poverty our sons.
We were less than dogs, my daughter,
Dogs ran away from us.

Then iron rose up, my daughter.
It cut my head away from you.
There was nothing left except
My dust pursuing your shoes.
Iron shall be broken, my daughter,
But never my thirst for you.

There is no end to strength, my daughter,
Only the body is smashed like a shard.
Joy did not visit my house,
The earth prepared my bed.
But the day you rejoice, my daughter,
From the earth my eyes shall be glad.

My daughter, the joyful day still will come.
For us a hand and a rope remain.
You will fall to my land of promise,
With a rope they will lower you down to me.
All is not vain, my daughter,
All is not vanity.

וָאוֹמַר לַחֲלִי בֵּיתִי,
וְלָעֵנִי קָרָאתִי בְּגַנּוּ.
וַנַּדֵּל מִכְּלָבִים בִּתִּי,
וַיָּנוּסוּ כְלָבִים מִפָּנֵינוּ.

אָז עָלָה הַבַּרְזֶל, בִּתִּי,
וַיָּסִיר גַּם רֹאשִׁי מֵאֵלַיִךְ.
וְדָבָר לֹא נוֹתַר, בִּלְתִּי
עֲפָרִי הַמְרֻדָּף וְעָלַיִךְ.
כִּי בַּרְזֶל יִשָּׁבֵר, בִּתִּי,
וּצְמָאִי לֹא נִשְׁבַּר אֵלַיִךְ.

לֹא לַכֹּחַ יֵשׁ קֵץ, בִּתִּי,
רַק לַגּוּף הַנִּשְׁבָּר כַּחֶרֶס.
לֹא פָּקְדָה הַשִּׂמְחָה בֵּיתִי
וַתַּצַּע אֲדָמָה לִי עֶרֶשׂ.
אַךְ בְּיוֹם בּוֹ תָגִיל בִּתִּי
גַּם תָּגֵלְנָה עֵינַי מֵאָרֶץ.

עוֹד יָבֹא יוֹם שִׂמְחָה, בִּתִּי,
עוֹד גַּם לָנוּ בּוֹ יָד וָחֵבֶל.
וְצָנַחְתְּ עַל אַדְמַת בְּרִיתִי
וְאֵלַי יוֹרִידוּךְ בְּחֶבֶל.
לֹא הַכֹּל הֲבָלִים, בִּתִּי,
לֹא הַכֹּל הֲבָלִים וָהֶבֶל.

2. A Convert Comes to the City*

The city is beseiged, none may enter or leave,
But I shall pass through secure.
I who remember the deathly poor
Stand at the entrance over your sleep.

> I entreat with powerless hands,
> Like fire and spear I defend.
> For the appointed time I strengthen you against loss,
> I who remember, I the witness.

I pray each day that you will expire like a candle,
That the sword shall drive you to me.
Each day for your sake I beg at the door
That you shall live another eve.

> I will bring you the very last crust.
> Your name I shall call out, the first.
> The water jug to your broken mouth I guide,
> I the elder, I who provide.

For, behold, the living shall not save the living.
To cover you with love like water, I come.
It is strange to my brothers, this love unforgiving,
Revealed like rapine at noon.

ב. גֵּר בָּא לָעִיר

הָעִיר נְצוּרָה מָבוֹא וּמֶצֵאת,
וַאֲנִי אֶעֱבוֹר לָבֶטַח.
אֲנִי הַזּוֹכֵר, הֶעָנִי־כֶּמֶת,
אֶעֱמוֹד עַל שְׁנָתֵךְ בַּפֶּתַח.

וּבְאֶפֶס־כַּפּוֹת אֲחוֹנֵן,
וּכְאֵשׁ וַחֲנִית אֲגוֹנֵן,
וּבְטֶרֶם־אָבְדָן אֲאַמֶּצֵךְ לַמּוֹעֵד,
אֲנִי הַזּוֹכֵר, אֲנִי הָעֵד.

יוֹם־יוֹם אֶתְפַּלֵּל שֶׁתִּכְלִי כְּמוֹ נֵר
שְׁאֵלִי תִּרְדְּפִי בַחֶרֶב.
וְיוֹם־יוֹם בַּעֲדֵךְ עַל פְּתָחִים אֲחַזֵּר,
לְמַעַן תִּחְיִי עוֹד עֶרֶב.

פַּת לָךְ אָבִיא אַחֲרוֹנָה.
בְּשֵׁם לָךְ אֶקְרָא רִאשׁוֹנָה.
הַחֶמֶת אַגִּיעַ אֶל פִּיךְ שֶׁחָרַב,
אֲנִי הַדּוֹאֵג, אֲנִי הַשָּׁב.

כִּי הִנֵּה לֹא יוֹשִׁיעַ הַחַי אֶת הַחַי.
וָאָבוֹא כַּסּוֹתֵךְ אַהֲבָה כַּמַּיִם,
אַהֲבָה לֹא סוֹלַחַת, נָכְרִית לְאָחִי,
גְּלוּיָה כְּשֵׁד בַּצָּהֳרָיִם.

And by God you shall swear to me
To draw strength from catastrophe,
To cry out as it reaches your soul,
To me the last one of all.

For the city is beseiged, none may enter or leave
But I, secure, pass through.
The dead man said: I die at the entrance
Seventy times for you.

Like spear and fire I implore
I pour more than human strength into you.
Against loss like a candle I snuff you out,
I the stranger, I the convert.

The Abandoned

My mother left me at the foot of the fence,
Face wrinkled and silent. On my back.
As if out of a well I watched her from below —
As if from a battle she fled.
As if out of a well I watched from below,
The moon over us was a candle glow.

וְאַתְּ בֵּאלֹהִים הַשָּׁבְעִי,
כִּי אוֹנִים מִצָּרָה תִּשְׁאֲבִי,
וּבְהַגִּיעַ עַד נֶפֶשׁ, תָּרִימִי קוֹל,
אֵלַי הָאַחְרוֹן. הָאַחְרוֹן לַכֹּל.

כִּי הָעִיר נְצוּרָה מָבוֹא וּמֵצֵאת,
וַאֲנִי אֶעֱבוֹר לָבֶטַח.
בַּעֲדֵךְ, בַּעֲדֵךְ, אָמַר הַמֵּת,
שֶׁבְעָתַיִם אָמוּת בַּפֶּתַח.

וּכְאֵשׁ וַחֲנִית אֲחוֹנֵן,
וְכֹחַ לֹא-אִישׁ בָּךְ אֶתֵּן,
וּבְטֶרֶם אָבְדָן אֲכַבֵּךְ כְּמוֹ נֵר,
אֲנִי הַנָּכְרִי. אֲנִי הַגֵּר.

הָאֲסוּפִי

הִנִּיחַתְנִי אִמִּי לְרַגְלֵי הַגָּדֵר,
קְמוּט פָּנִים וְשׁוֹקֵט. עַל גַּב.
וָאַבִּיט בָּה מִלְמַטָּה, כְּמוֹ מִן הַבְּאֵר, –
עַד נוּסָהּ כְּהַנָּס מִן הַקְּרָב.
וָאַבִּיט בָּה מִלְמַטָּה, כְּמוֹ מִן הַבְּאֵר,
וְיָרֵחַ עָלֵינוּ הוּרַם כְּמוֹ נֵר.

But that night before the dawn shone,
The time had come and I slowly rose.
To her house I returned as a ball that rolls
Goes back to the kicking foot.

    I returned to her house like a ball that rolls.
    With shadowy hands I embraced her throat.

Like a leech, before the Almighty's eyes,
She tore me away from her throat.
But as night came back, I returned.
And this became our rule by rote.

    Each night, as before, to her I return
    And she bows to retribution's yoke.

The wide-open doors of her dreams I gained,
In her dream I am there alone.
Bent the love of our souls remained
Like a bow, from the day when I was born.

    Bent the love of our souls remained
    Never given or taken again.

So till the end God did not remove me
From my parent's heart that stormed.
And I torn away before I was weaned,
Was not weaned and will not be torn.

אַךְ בְּטֶרֶם הַשַּׁחַר הֵאִיר, אוֹתוֹ לֵיל,
קַמְתִּי אַט כִּי הִגִּיעָה עֵת
וָאָשׁוּב בֵּית אִמִּי כְּכַדּוּר מִתְגַּלְגֵּל
הַחוֹזֵר אֶל רַגְלֵי הַבּוֹעֵט,
וָאָשׁוּב בֵּית אִמִּי כְּכַדּוּר מִתְגַּלְגֵּל
וָאֶחְבֹּק צַוָּארָהּ בְּיָדַיִם שֶׁל צֵל.

מֵעֲלֵי צַוָּארָהּ, לְעֵינֵי כֹּל יָכוֹל,
הִיא קְרָעַתְנִי כְּמוֹ עֲלוּקָה.
אַךְ שָׁב לַיְלָה וְשַׁבְתִּי אֵלֶיהָ כִּתְמוֹל,
וַתִּהְיֶה לָנוּ זֹאת לְחֻקָּה:
בְּשׁוּב לַיְלָה וְשַׁבְתִּי אֵלֶיהָ כִּתְמוֹל
וְהִיא לַיְלָה כּוֹרַעַת לַגְּמוּל וְלָעֹל.

וְדַלְתוֹת חֲלוֹמָהּ לִי פְּתוּחוֹת לִרְוָחָה
וְאֵין אִישׁ בַּחֲלוֹם מִלְּבַדִּי.
כִּי נוֹתְרָה אַהֲבַת־נַפְשׁוֹתֵינוּ דְּרוּכָה
כְּמוֹ קֶשֶׁת, מִיּוֹם הִוָּלְדִי.
כִּי נוֹתְרָה אַהֲבַת נַפְשׁוֹתֵינוּ דְּרוּכָה
וְלָעַד לֹא נִתֶּנֶת וְלֹא לְקוּחָה.

וְעַל כֵּן עַד אַחֲרִית לֹא הֵסִיר אוֹתִי אֵל
מֵעַל לֵב הוֹרָתִי הַצּוֹעֵק
וַאֲנִי – שֶׁנִּתַּקְתִּי מִבְּלִי הִגָּמֵל –
לֹא נִגְמַלְתִּי וְלֹא אֶנָּתֵק.

And I, torn away before I was weaned,
Enter her house, lock the door.

She aged in my prison, grew thin and slight.
Her face grew as wrinkled as mine.
Then my little hands clothed her in white
As a mother dresses the living child.
    Then my little hands dressed her in white,
    I carried her off without making a sign.

I left her there at the foot of the fence,
On her back. She was watchful, subdued.
She looked at me smiling as out of a well.
We had finished our battle, we knew.
    She looked at me smiling as out of a well.
    Over us, like a candle, was the moon.

The Maid

Silent the maid with the spindle spun,
Like brightest pomegranate, scarlet thread.
"She weaves me garments, royal ones,"
The king within his own heart said.

וַאֲנִי שֶׁנִּתַּקְתִּי מִבְּלִי הַגָּמָל
נִכְנָס אֶל בֵּיתָהּ וְהַשַּׁעַר נוֹעֵל.

הִיא זְקֵנָה בִּכְלְאִי וַתְּדַל וַתִּקְטַן
וּפָנֶיהָ קָמְטוּ כְּפָנַי.
אָז יָדֵי הַקְּטַנּוֹת הִלְבִּישׁוּהָ לָבָן
כְּמוֹ אֵם אֶת הַיֶּלֶד הַחַי.
אָז יָדֵי הַקְּטַנּוֹת הִלְבִּישׁוּהָ לָבָן
וָאֶשָּׂא אוֹתָהּ בְּלִי לְהַגִּיד לָהּ לְאָן.

וָאַנִּיחַ אוֹתָהּ לְרַגְלֵי הַגָּדֵר
צוֹפִיָּה וְשׁוֹקֶטֶת, עַל גַּב.
וַתַּבִּיט בִּי שׂוֹחֶקֶת, כְּמוֹ מִן הַבְּאֵר,
וַנֵּדַע כִּי סִיַּמְנוּ הַקְּרָב.
וַתַּבִּיט בִּי שׂוֹחֶקֶת כְּמוֹ מִן הַבְּאֵר.
וְיָרֵחַ עָלֵינוּ הוּרַם כְּמוֹ נֵר.

הָעַלְמָה

דָּם טָוְתָה הָעַלְמָה בַּפֶּלֶךְ
חוּט שָׁנִי כְּרִמּוֹן שָׁחוּט.
וְאָמַר בְּלִבָבוֹ הַמֶּלֶךְ:
הִיא טֹוָה לִי בִּגְדֵי מַלְכוּת.

Silent the maid with the spindle spun,
Darkening daylight, thread so black.
In the dungeon said the highwayman:
"She spins me robes for the axman's block."

Silent the maid with the spindle spun
Golden thread like lightning's blade.
On the highway said the clown:
"She spins me costumes for the play."

Silent the maid with the spindle spun
Grey thread, source of all that is worn.
Said the dog and the beggar then:
She spins a robe for us who mourn.

Then she wove the spindled thread,
Bunched them together, put them away.
Down to the brook she stepped,
And bathed her flesh bright as day.

Then she put on the cloth of her spinning
And lovely grew forever.
Since then, she is highwayman and king
Clown and beggar.

דֹּם טָוְתָה הָעַלְמָה בַּפֶּלֶךְ
חוּט שָׁחֹר, הַמַּחְשִׁיךְ אוֹר יוֹם.
וְאָמַר הַשּׁוֹדֵד בַּכֶּלֶא:
הִיא טָוָה לִי בִּגְדֵי גַרְדּוֹם.

דֹּם טָוְתָה הָעַלְמָה בַּפֶּלֶךְ
חוּט זָהָב, כְּחַרְבוֹת בָּרָק.
וְאָמַר הַלוּלְיָן בַּדֶּרֶךְ:
הִיא טָוָה לִי בִּגְדֵי מִשְׂחָק.

דֹּם טָוְתָה הָעַלְמָה בַּפֶּלֶךְ
חוּט אֵפֶר, הוּא אֲבִי כָל כְּסוּת.
וְאָמְרוּ פּוֹשֵׁט־יָד וָכֶלֶב:
הִיא טָוָה לָנוּ בֶּגֶד בָּכוּת.

אָז אָרְגָה אֶת חוּטֵי הַפֶּלֶךְ
הָעַלְמָה, וַתִּתְגֵם בַּסָּךְ,
וַתֵּרֶד אֶל מֵי הַפֶּלֶג
וַתִּרְחַץ אֶת בְּשָׂרָהּ הַצַּח.

וַתִּלְבַּשׁ אֶת מַטְוֵה הַפֶּלֶךְ
לְשִׂמְלָה לָהּ, וַתִּיף לָעַד.
וּמֵאָז הִיא שׁוֹדֵד וָמֶלֶךְ
וְלוּלְיָן וּפוֹשֶׁטֶת־יָד.

Songs of the Stream

"A choir of small voices . . ."
Paul Verlaine

1. The Stream Sings to the Stone

Cool in its dream, I kissed the stone:
It is the quiet, I am the song,
It is the riddle, I make it known,
From one eternity we both were hewn.

I kissed the stone, its lonely flesh.
I am the betrayer, it is vowed faithfulness.
It is the constant, mystery of creation,
I am change, its revelation.

I know I touched a heart grown mute.
It is the world and I the poet.

2. The Tree Sings to the Stream

Who swept away my gilded fall,
With the falling leaves my blood did bear,
But shall see my spring return
To him in the circling of the year.

מִשִּׁירֵי הַנַּחַל

„מַקְהֵלַת קוֹלוֹת קְטַנִּים"
פּוֹל וֶרְלֶן.

א. הַנַּחַל שָׁר לָאֶבֶן

אֶת הָאֶבֶן נָשַׁקְתִּי בְּצִנַּת חֲלוֹמָהּ,
כִּי אֲנִי הַמִּזְמוֹר וְהִיא הַדְּמָמָה,
כִּי הִיא הַחִידָה וַאֲנִי הֶחָד,
כִּי שְׁנֵינוּ קְרַעֲנוּ מִנֶּצַח אֶחָד.

אֶת הָאֶבֶן נָשַׁקְתִּי, אֶת בְּשָׂרָהּ הַבּוֹדֵד.
הִיא שְׁבוּעַת אֱמוּנִים וַאֲנִי הַבּוֹגֵד,
אֲנִי הַחוֹלֵף וְהִיא הַקַּיָּם,
הִיא סוֹדוֹת הַבְּרִיאָה, וַאֲנִי – גְּלוּיִם.

וָאֵדַע כִּי נָגַעְתִּי בְּלֵב נֶאֱלָם:
אֲנִי הַמְּשׁוֹרֵר וְהִיא – הָעוֹלָם.

ב. הָעֵץ שָׁר לַנַּחַל

אֲשֶׁר נָשָׂא אֶת סְתָוַי הַזָּהוֹב,
אֶת דָּמִי בְּשַׁלֶּכֶת גָּרַף,
אֲשֶׁר יִרְאֶה אֲבִיבִי כִּי יָשׁוּב
עִם תְּקוּפַת הַשָּׁנָה אֵלָיו,

My brother the stream, forever lost,
Who is new each day, and still one thing,
My brother who flows between his shores
As I flow between fall and spring.

For I am the blossom and I am the fruit,
I am my future, my past I am.
I am the barren trunk of the tree,
And you are my season, my poem.

3. The Moon Sings to the Stream

I am unity on high,
But in the deep I am the multiple,
From the stream looks up to me
My image, my double.

I am truth on high,
I am fiction in the deep,
From the stream looks up to me
My image's foiled destiny.

Above I am wrapped in silence,
In the deep I sing and murmur,
On high I am the Lord
In the stream I am the prayer.

אָחִי הַנַּחַל, הָאוֹבֵד לָעַד,
הֶחָדָשׁ יוֹם־יוֹם וְאַחֵר וְאֶחָד,
אָחִי הַזֶּרֶם בֵּין שְׁנֵי חוֹפָיו
הַזּוֹרֵם כָּמוֹנִי בֵּין אָבִיב וּסְתָיו.

כִּי אֲנִי הַנִּצָּן וַאֲנִי הַפְּרִי,
אֲנִי עָתִידִי וַאֲנִי עֲבָרִי,
אֲנִי הַגֶּזַע הָעֲרִירִי,
וְאַתָּה – זְמַנִּי וְשִׁירִי.

ג. הַיָּרֵחַ שָׁר לַנַּחַל

אֲנִי הַיָּחוּד בַּמָּרוֹם,
אֲנִי הָרִבּוּי בַּמְּצֻלָּה.
תַּשְׁקִיף מִן הַנַּחַל אֵלַי
דְּמוּתִי, דְּמוּתִי הַכְּפוּלָה.

אֲנִי הָאֱמֶת בַּמָּרוֹם,
אֲנִי הַבִּדְיָה בַּמְּצֻלָּה,
תַּשְׁקִיף מִן הַנַּחַל אֵלַי
דְּמוּתִי בִּכְזַב גּוֹרָלָהּ.

לְמַעְלָה – עוֹטֶה דוּמִיּוֹת,
הוֹמֶה, מְזַמֵּר בַּמְּצֻלָּה.
אֲנִי בַּמָּרוֹם – הָאֵל,
בַּנַּחַל אֲנִי הַתְּפִלָּה.

4. The Girl Sings to the Stream

Where does the stream carry my small face?
Why does he widen my eyes?
Far off in the pine wood is my home
Sadly my pine trees sigh.

The stream lured me with a happy song,
Sang out and called my name.
I left my mother's house,
I followed the sound and came.

And I am her young and only child,
A cruel stream before me lies —
Where does he carry my small face?
Why does he widen my eyes?

5. The Blade of Grass Sings to the Stream

Also for little ones, just like me,
One of myriad more,
Also for children of poverty
On disappointment's shore
The stream murmurs, murmurs
Murmurs with love.

ד. הַיַּלְדָּה שָׁרָה לַנַּחַל

לְאָן יִשָּׂא הַזֶּרֶם אֶת פְּנֵי הַקְּטַנִּים?
לָמָּה הוּא קוֹרֵעַ אֶת עֵינַי?
בֵּיתִי הָרַחֵק בְּחֻרְשַׁת אֳרָנִים,
עֲצוּבָה אִשַּׁת אֳרָנַי.

פִּתַּנִי הַנַּחַל בְּזֶמֶר־גִּיל,
רָגַן וְקָרָא בִּשְׁמִי,
הָלַכְתִּי אֵלָיו אַחֲרֵי הַצְּלִיל,
נָטַשְׁתִּי אֶת בֵּית אִמִּי.

וַאֲנִי יְחִידָה לָהּ, רַכָּה בַּשָּׁנִים,
וְנַחַל אַכְזָר לְפָנַי –
לְאָן הוּא נוֹשֵׂא אֶת פְּנֵי הַקְּטַנִּים?
לָמָּה הוּא קוֹרֵעַ אֶת עֵינַי?

ה. גִּבְעוֹל הַדֶּשֶׁא שָׁר לַנַּחַל

גַּם לִקְטַנִּים כָּמוֹנִי,
אֶחָד מִנִּי רְבָבָה,
גַּם לְיַלְדֵי הָעֹנִי
עַל חוֹף הָאַכְזָבָה
הוֹמֶה, הוֹמֶה הַנַּחַל,
הוֹמֶה בְּאַהֲבָה.

The caressing sun

At times touches him.

My image, the reflected one,

Is in the water green

In the depth of the river

All of us are deep.

And my image deepening

On its way to the sea

Is swallowed and erased

On the brink of the unseen.

But with the stream's voice

The silent soul

With the stream's psalm

The world extols.

On Blossoming

(excerpts)

for Avraham Ben Yitzhak

I

Scarlet, warm and heavy in black velvet leaves

The blossoming of castor plant overnight.

Against the barbed-wire fence the row leans.

הַשֶּׁמֶשׁ הַלּוֹטֶפֶת
תִּגַּע בּוֹ לִפְרָקִים,
וְגַם דְּמוּתִי נִשְׁקֶפֶת
בְּמַיִם יְרֻקִּים
וּבְמִצְלַת הַנַּחַל
כֻּלָּנוּ עֲמֻקִּים.

דְּמוּתִי הַמִּתְעַמֶּקֶת
בַּדֶּרֶךְ אֶל הַיָּם
נִבְלַעַת וְנִמְחֶקֶת
עַל סַף הַנֶּעֱלָם.
וְעִם קוֹלוֹ שֶׁל נַחַל
הַנֶּפֶשׁ הַשּׁוֹתֶקֶת
עִם שִׁיר מִזְמוֹר הַנַּחַל
תַּגִּיד שִׁבְחֵי עוֹלָם.

עַל הַפְּרִיחָה

(מִמַּחֲרוֹזֶת הַשִּׁירִים)

לאברהם בן יצחק

א

פְּרִיחַת הַקִּיקָיוֹן אֲשֶׁר הָיְתָה בֶּן־לַיְל
שָׁנִי כָּבֵד וָחַם בִּשְׂחוֹר עֲלֵי קְטִיפָה.
שִׁדְרָה נִשְׁעֶנֶת אֶל גָּדֵר שֶׁל תַּיִל.

The sheep wearily grow quiet,

Returning to the pens. The sensuous blue

Drops from its shoulder a cloud of white.

All this, like light broken in the waterfall, somewhile will pass.

All this, in smell of grain and silence will rise anew,

And in red sunset, in tenderness of grass

As if out of the quiet of my blood it grew.

II

Old woman, blue eyed and sun burned.

In her stature's crown — greyhair, suffering persist.

The pail turns silver. From the doors of the barn

Rises the fresh and fatty mist.

Life's law in her milking hands,

As when the rope quiet sailors twist.

Docile cows. A morning without clouds.

Woman above the white that slowly spills

Plain light and the intricate secret of the ancient.

The necromancer over her spells.

הַצֹּאן אֲשֶׁר רָגְעוּ לָעֵיפָה
חוֹזְרוֹת אֶל הַדִּירִים. הַתְּכֵלֶת הָרוֹגֶשֶׁת
הִצְנִיחָה עָב צְחוֹרָה מֵעַל כְּתֵפָה.

כָּל זֶה יֹאבַד אִי־אָז כְּאוֹר נִשְׁבָּר בָּאֶשֶׁד,
כָּל זֶה יָקוּם לָעַד בְּרֵיחַ בַּר וּדְמִי
וּבַשְׁקִיעָה אָדֹם וְרַךְ הַדֶּשֶׁא

כְּאִלּוּ הוּא צֶמַח מִשֶּׁקֶט שֶׁל דָּמִי.

ב

זְקֵנָה, כְּחֻלַּת־עֵינַיִם וְנִשְׁזֶפֶת.
עֲטֶרֶת קוֹמָתָהּ – שֵׂיבָה וָסֵבֶל.
מַכְסִיף הַדְּלִי. מִשַּׁעֲרֵי הָרֶפֶת

דָּשֵׁן וְרַעֲנָן עוֹלֶה הַהֶבֶל.
דִּין שֶׁל חַיִּים – יָדֶיהָ הַחוֹלְבוֹת.
כָּךְ סַפָּנִים שְׁקֵטִים יֹאחֲזוּ בַּחֶבֶל.

כְּנִיעַת פָּרוֹת. וּבֹקֶר לֹא־עָבֹת.
אִשָּׁה מֵעַל לִלְבֶן הַשּׁוֹפֵעַ.
וְאוֹר־חֻלִּין וְסוֹד קַדְמוּת עָבֹת

וּבַעֲלַת־הָאוֹב עֲלֵי כְּשָׁפֶיהָ.

III

That death in his windows would rise

We knew: Cold and clear, like the skin

Of a grape, was his glance that cried.

And through the skin flickered and drew near

A brimming world, gold, like a sated day,

Cities and rivers, and a motleyed crowd of Springs

With a booty of blossoms burgeoning.

Loaded down he trudged to the boundary. /,

So a weary ox at wane of day

Brings the harvest to the granary.

VIII

How shall we bring our dying heart up

To a new day as the light grows?

As when the wine bubbles in the cup,

As when the sky girds on his bow,

As when morning dances in the pit

And sunset bends to the river's cheek below.

ג

כִּי מָוֶת יַעֲלֶה בְּחַלּוֹנָיו
יָדַעְנוּ: מַבָּטוֹ הַמְּשֻׁתָּוֻעַ
הָיָה שָׁקוּף וָקַר כְּזָג עֵנָב.

וּבְעַד הַזָּג הַבְּלִיחַ וְקָרַב
עוֹלָם גָּדוּשׁ, צָהֹב, כְּיוֹם שָׁבֵעַ,
עָרִים, גַּם נְהָרוֹת, גַּם עֶרֶב־רָב

שֶׁל אֲבִיבִים וּשְׁלַל פְּרִיחָה בּוֹקֵעַ.
וְהוּא הָלַךְ עָמוּס עַד קְצֵה הַגְּבוּל.
כָּךְ שׁוֹר עָיֵף עִם יוֹם שׁוֹקֵעַ

יוֹבִיל הַגֹּרְנָה אֶת הַיְבוּל.

ח

אֵיךְ אֶת לִבֵּנוּ הַגּוֹסֵס נָבִיאָה
אֶל יוֹם חָדָשׁ בְּהֵעָלוֹת הָאוֹר?
כְּאָז תּוֹסֵס הַיַּיִן בַּגָּבִיעַ,

כְּאָז רָקִיעַ אֶת קַשְׁתּוֹ יַחְגּוֹר,
כְּאָז הַבֹּקֶר מְפַזֵּז בַּשַּׁחַת
וּלְחִי־שְׁקִיעוֹת נִצְמַד לִלְחִי הַיְאוֹר.

LEAH GOLDBERG

And only we, by the terror hit,
Dream-robbed, witnesses from the fire saved,
Our blossoming land we will lift

Like a wreath of mourning unto the grave.

Dialogue

He

In your silence sank as into a deep sea
My bitter word. My love listens attentively —
From echoless distances wafts to me
The peace of your flesh without kindness and mercy.

Your body to me was exile and foreignness.
From your glance, as from a pool, I see
My image acting toward myself most cruelly,
My dark soul, from your clearness.

My beggared state — from out of abundance and loveliness.
For me you are the road to double loneliness.

וְרַק אֲנַחְנוּ, הֲלוּמֵי הַפַּחַד,
גְּזוּלֵי־חֲלוֹם, עֲדֵי הַתַּבְעֵרָה,
נִשָּׂא אֶת אַדְמָתֵנוּ הַפּוֹרַחַת

כִּגְזַר אֲבֵלוּת אֱלֵי קְבוּרָה.

דּוּ־שִׂיחַ

הוּא

בִּשְׁתִיקָתֵךְ שָׁקַע כְּבִמְצֻלָה
דִּבְרֵי הַמַּר. אַהֲבָתִי קַשֶּׁבֶת –
מִמֶּרְחָבִים אֵין־הֵד אֵלַי נוֹשֶׁבֶת
שַׁלְוַת בְּשָׂרֵךְ בְּלִי חֶסֶד וְחֶמְלָה.

גּוּפֵךְ הָיָה לִי נֵכָר וְגוֹלָה.
מִמַּבָּטֵךְ כְּמֵאֲגַם חוֹזֶרֶת
תָּמִיד אֵלַי דְּמוּתִי הַמִּתְאַכְזֶרֶת,
מִצְּלִילוּתֵךְ – נַפְשִׁי הָאֲפֵלָה.

אֶבְיוֹנוּתִי – מֻשְׁפַּע וְתִפְאֶרֶת.
אַתְּ לִי הַדֶּרֶךְ לִבְדִידוּת כְּפוּלָה.

She

> Light rushed through. It struck the pupils of my eyes,
> In its flame all other images dimmed.
> You have made me a wasteland, a blind wilderness.
> Before me you have made the fortressed wall rise.
>
> Here am I closed and enclosed within myself,
> Scorched by loneliness, toward a strange world's lands
> I carry my dust in my own hands.
> I would be glad of my own death.
>
> But woe, woe to us both if I survive
> And out of these ashes I rise new born
> Opening my eyes to see twicefold,
>
> And this time next year nothing remained
> Save the memory of your foreign form
> And the taste on my lips of bitter mold.

Remembrance of Beginnings of Things

We shall remember the wheat stalk in the greenness of her youth,
The time she stood erect with head to heaven,
Thin was her blade but straight and proud.
And now bent is her head to the ground,

הִיא

הֵגִיחַ אוֹר. הִכָּה עַל אִישׁוֹנַי,
בְּשַׁלְהַבְתּוֹ כָּבְתָה כָּל דְּמוּת אַחֶרֶת.
שָׂמַתַּנִי יְשִׁימוֹן, צִיָּה עֲוֶרֶת.
חוֹמָה בְּצוּרָה הַצַּבְתָּ בְּפָנַי.

הִנֵּה אֲנִי סֹגֶרֶת וּמִסְגֶּרֶת,
שְׂרוּפַת בְּדִידוּת, אֶל מוּל עוֹלָם נָכְרִי
נָשָׂאתִי בְּיָדַי אֶת עֲפָרִי
וּבְכִלּוֹתִי הָיִיתִי מְאֻשֶּׁרֶת.

אַךְ אוֹיָה, אוֹי לְשְׁגֵנוּ אִם הָיָה
וּמִן הָאֵפֶר קַמְתִּי לִתְחִיָּה
וְנִפְקְחוּ עֵינַי לִרְאוֹת כִּפְלַיִם,

וְלֹא נוֹתַר דָּבָר כָּעֵת חַיָּה
זוּלַת זִכְרוֹן דְּמוּתְךָ הַנָּכְרִיָּה
וְטַעַם לַעֲנָה עַל הַשְּׂפָתַיִם.

זִכְרוֹן רֵאשִׁית דְּבָרִים

נִזְכֹּר אֶת הַשִּׁבֹּלֶת בִּירַקְרַק נְעוּרֶיהָ,
עֵת כִּי עָמְדָה זְקוּפָה וְרֹאשָׁהּ לַשָּׁמַיִם,
דַּק גִּבְעוֹלָהּ אַף יָשָׁר וְגֵא הוּא.
וְעַכְשָׁיו שַׂח רֹאשָׁהּ לָאָרֶץ,

For heavy is the gold of her ripeness,

The crown of her full pregnancy.

Beautiful are her seasons.

We shall remember the tree in the middle of his spring:

His blossoms were white and pink,

Trembling sunbeams glimmered in him on the branch

And the sweet resin dropped to earth

Like the bride's tears on the day of her heart's joy.

Now he stands in the abundance of his apples

Carrying his beautiful burden motionless

Knowing the spring of things to come.

We shall surely remember these things

In the change of the year's circuit and in the passage of day and night,

How the moon was fragile

And very full, then round and died,

Yet its youth would be renewed.

We shall surely remember the beginning of our love

When she was tremulous as a fawn,

A beautiful doe lowering her eyes,

And there she has become full grown

With her open face

And her deep voice.

Beautiful are her seasons.

כִּי כָבֵד זְהַב־בַּגְרוּתָהּ,
עֲטֶרֶת הֵרְיוֹנָהּ הַמָּלֵא.
יָפוֹת עִתּוֹתֶיהָ.

נִזְכּוֹר אֶת הָאִילָן בִּדְמִי אֲבִיבוֹ:
פְּרָחָיו הָיוּ לְבָנִים וּוְרֻדִּים,
זָעוּ בּוֹ אוֹרוֹת מְרַטְּטִים בְּעֶנֶף
וְהַשָּׂרָף הַמָּתוֹק נָטַף לָאָרֶץ
כִּדְמָעוֹת כַּלָּה בְּיוֹם שִׂמְחַת־לִבָּהּ.
וְעַכְשָׁיו הוּא עוֹמֵד בִּשְׁלַל תַּפּוּחָיו
נוֹשֵׂא אֶת הָעֹל הַיָּפֶה וְלֹא יָנוּעַ,
יוֹדֵעַ אֲבִיבֵי הַבָּאוֹת.

זָכוֹר נִזְכּוֹר אֶת הַדְּבָרִים
בִּתְמוּרַת תּוֹר הַשָּׁנָה וַחֲלִיפוֹת יוֹם וָלַיְלָה,
כֵּיצַד הָיָה הַסַּהַר דַּק־לְהִשָּׁבֵר
וּמָלֵא מְאֹד וְהֶעָגִיל וְגָעַ,
וְחָדְשׁוּ נְעוּרָיו.

זָכוֹר נִזְכּוֹר רֵאשִׁית אַהֲבָתֵנוּ
בְּעוֹדָהּ רְהוּיָה כְּאַיֶּלֶת,
יַעֲלַת־חֵן מַשְׁפֶּלֶת עֵינַיִם,
וְהִנֵּה גָדְלָה מְאֹד
וּפָנֶיהָ גְּלוּיִים
וְקוֹלָהּ עָמֹק.
יָפוֹת עִתּוֹתֶיהָ.

LEAH GOLDBERG

On This Day

On this day they break bread
And gather fruit into the basket,
On this day the sons return home
And the daughters await them in the doorway. . .
On this day the clouds parade in the heavens
To bring the tidings of blessed showers to wheatfield and garden.
And in the city, in the alleyways of market places,
Rise up the fragrances of butter and oil,
Sparkle the scales of the fishes,
The wine brims.

How can you die, my soul, on this day!

That is so lovely and full,
That is so overflowing and simple,
That is light,
That is day,
That is day like all days!

How can you go down to rest.
Before his tumult abates,
How can you bid him farewell
Before his clamor grows quiet,

בְּיוֹם זֶה

בְּיוֹם זֶה פּוֹרְסִים אֶת הַלֶּחֶם
וְאוֹסְפִים אֶת הַפְּרִי אֶל הַטֶּנֶא,
בְּיוֹם זֶה חוֹזְרִים הַבָּנִים הַבַּיְתָה
וְהַבָּנוֹת מַמְתִּינוֹת בַּפֶּתַח.
בְּיוֹם זֶה הוֹלְכִים עֲנָנִים בַּשָּׁמַיִם
לְבַשֵּׂר מָטָר שֶׁל בְּרָכָה לִשְׂדֵמָה וָגָן.
וּבָעִיר, בִּמְבוֹאֵי הַשְּׁוָקִים,
עוֹלִים רֵיחוֹת שֶׁל חֶמְאָה וָשֶׁמֶן,
מַבְרִיקִים קַשְׂקַשֵּׂי הַדָּגִים,
שׁוֹצֵף הַיַּיִן.

אֵיכָה תָּמוּתִי, נַפְשִׁי, בַּיוֹם הַזֶּה!

שֶׁהוּא יָפֶה וּמָלֵא,
שֶׁהוּא גָּדוֹשׁ וּפָשׁוּט,
שֶׁהוּא אוֹר,
שֶׁהוּא יוֹם,
שֶׁהוּא יוֹם כְּכָל הַיָּמִים!

אֵיכָה תֵּרְדִי לִמְנוּחוֹת
בְּטֶרֶם יִשְׁקַע שְׁאוֹנוֹ,
אֵיכָה תֹּאמְרִי לוֹ שָׁלוֹם
בְּטֶרֶם יִדֹּם הֲמוֹנוֹ,

How can you walk mourning
Before his merriment is tarnished,

How can you visit your eternal night
Before you have kissed the first star?

Will There Yet Come

Will there yet come days of forgiveness and grace,
When you walk in the field as the innocent wayfarer walks,
And the soles of your feet the clover leaves caress,
Though stubble will sting you, sweet will be their stalks.

Or rain will overtake you its thronging drops tapping
On your shoulder, your chest, your throat, your gentle head bowed.
And you walk in the wet field, the quiet in you expanding
Like light in the hem of a cloud.

And you will breathe the odor of furrow, breathing and quiet,
And you will see mirrored in the gold puddle the sun above,
And simple will be these things and life, permitted to touch,
Permitted, permitted to love.

Slowly you will walk in the field. Alone. Unscorched by flame
Of conflagrations on roads that bristled with horror and blood. Again
You will be peaceful in heart, humble and bending
Like one of the grasses, like one of man.

אֵיכָה תֵּלְכִי אֲבֵלָה
בְּטֶרֶם יוּעַם שְׂשׂוֹנוֹ,

אֵיכָה תִּפְקְדִי לֵילֵךְ הַנִּצְחִי
בְּטֶרֶם נָשַׁקְתְּ לְכוֹכָב רִאשׁוֹן?

הַאָמְנָם עוֹד יָבוֹאוּ

הַאָמְנָם עוֹד יָבוֹאוּ יָמִים בִּסְלִיחָה וּבְחֶסֶד,
וְתֵלְכִי בַּשָּׂדֶה, וְתֵלְכִי בּוֹ כַּהֵלֶךְ הַתָּם,
וּמַחֲשׂוֹף כַּף־רַגְלֵךְ יִלָּטֵף בַּעֲלֵי הָאַסְפֶּסֶת,
אוֹ שְׁלָפֵי־שִׁבֳּלִים יִדְקְרוּךְ וְתִמְתַּק דְּקִירָתָם.

אוֹ מָטָר יַשִּׂיגֵךְ בַּעֲדַת טִפּוֹתָיו הַדּוֹפֶקֶת
עַל כְּתֵפַיִךְ, חָזֵךְ, צַוָּארֵךְ, וְרֹאשֵׁךְ רַעֲנָן,
וְתֵלְכִי בַּשָּׂדֶה הָרָטֹב וְיִרְחַב בָּךְ הַשֶּׁקֶט
כָּאוֹר בְּשׁוּלֵי הֶעָנָן.

וְנָשַׁמְתְּ אֶת רֵיחוֹ שֶׁל הַתֶּלֶם נָשׁוֹם וְרָגוֹעַ,
וְרָאִית אֶת הַשֶּׁמֶשׁ בִּרְאִי־הַשְּׁלוּלִית הַזָּהֹב,
וּפְשׁוּטִים הַדְּבָרִים וְחַיִּים, וּמֻתָּר בָּם לִנְגוֹעַ,
וּמֻתָּר, וּמֻתָּר לֶאֱהֹב.

אַתְּ תֵּלְכִי בַּשָּׂדֶה. לְבַדֵּךְ. לֹא נִצְרֶבֶת בְּלַהַט
הַשְּׂרֵפוֹת, בַּדְּרָכִים שֶׁסָּמְרוּ מֵאֵימָה וּמִדָּם.
וּבִישֶׁר־לֵבָב שׁוּב תִּהְיִי עֲנָוָה וְנִכְנַעַת
כְּאַחַד הַדְּשָׁאִים, כְּאַחַד הָאָדָם.

IV

The Younger Poets

המשוררים הצעירים

Birth

The rain has passed.

And yet from roofs and trees
It sings in my ears
And covers my head
With a bluish bridal-veil.

Good for you, my God,
In your net the child has been caught.
Now I shall bring leaf close to leaf
Watch how leaf covers leaf
And the drops join,
Then I will call the swallows
To betrothal from my sky.
And crown my windows with flower pots.

Good for you, my God,
In your net the child has been caught.
I open my eyes —
My earth is very wide
And all a beaten work
Of knobby buds,
Green.

Oh my God, how embraced we have been.

הַיֶּלֶד

הַגֶּשֶׁם חָלַף.

וְהוּא עוֹד מִגַּגּוֹת וּמֵעֵצִים
מְזַמֵּר בְּאָזְנַי
וּמְכַסֶּה עַל רֹאשִׁי
בְּהַנּוּמָה כְּחַלְחֵלֶת.

אַשְׁרֶיךָ, אֱלֹהַי,
בְּרִשְׁתְּךָ נָצוֹד הַיֶּלֶד.
הִנֵּה אַקְרִיב עָלֶה אֶל עָלֶה
וְאֶרְאֶה אֵיךְ מְכַסֶּה עָלֶה עַל עָלֶה
וּמִתְמַזְּגִים הָרְסִיסִים.
וְאֶקְרָא לִכְלוּלוֹת מִשָּׁמַי
אֶת הַסִּיסִים.
וְכָל חַלּוֹנַי אֲעַטֵּר עֲצִיצִים.

אַשְׁרֶיךָ, אֱלֹהַי,
בְּרִשְׁתְּךָ נָצוֹד הַיֶּלֶד.
אֲנִי פּוֹקֵחַ אֶת עֵינַי –
אַדְמָתִי רְחָבָה מְאֹד
וְכֻלָּהּ מִקְשָׁה
שֶׁל פְּטוּרֵי צִיצִים
יְרֻקִּים.

הוֹ, אֱלֹהַי, אֵיךְ הָיִינוּ חֲבוּקִים!

Against the Wind

As we stood on the edge of the crag

A great wind began blowing

And all drew back disheveled,

But I grasped the sledge hammer,

Preserved here from a generation past,

And began to strike the rock

And the wind answered, Amen, Amen.

In Darkness

I stretched my hand out in front of me, into the darkness,

And my fingers sought light,

Trembling from the horror of uncertainty.

Therefore I gathered the fingers

Inward into the palm

And they opened up with a warm whimpering

Like puppies at the teats of the bitch.

So there was no end to the security

In the community of the closed fist.

Afterward the sun rose.

מוּל הָרוּחַ

כְּשֶׁעָמַדְנוּ עַל שְׂפַת הַצּוּק
הִתְחִילָה רוּחַ גְּדוֹלָה נוֹשֶׁבֶת
וְהַכֹּל מָשְׁכוּ אֶת בְּדוּרָם לְאָחוֹר
אַךְ אֲנִי תָּפַסְתִּי בַּמַּקֶּבֶת
הַשְּׁמוּרָה כָּאן מִלִּפְנֵי דוֹר
וְהִתְחַלְתִּי מַכֶּה בַּסֶּלַע

וְעָנְתָה הָרוּחַ אָמֵן סֶלָה.

בַּחֹשֶׁךְ

שָׁלַחְתִּי אֶת יָדַי לְפָנַי, אֶל תּוֹךְ הַחֹשֶׁךְ
וְהָאֶצְבָּעוֹת בִּקְשׁוּ אוֹר
רוֹעֲדוֹת מֵאֵימַת אִי הַוַּדָּאוּת.

אָסַפְתִּי, לָכֵן, אֶת הָאֶצְבָּעוֹת
פְּנִימָה אֶל תּוֹךְ הַכַּף
וּפָתְחוּ הֵן בִּנְהִימָה חֲמִימָה
כְּגוּרֵי כַלְבָּה עַל הַדַּדִּים
וְקֵץ לֹא הָיָה לְבִטְחוֹנָן
בְּצִנַּת הָאֶגְרוֹף הַקָּמוּץ.

אַחַר כָּךְ עָלָה הַשַּׁחַר.

AMIR GILBOA

Isaac

Toward morning the sun strolled in the forest
Together with me and with father,
My right hand was in his left.

Like lightning flash, a knife between the trees
And I fear the terror of my eyes opposite the blood on the leaves.

Father, Father, come quickly and save Isaac
That no one may be missing at the noon meal.

It is I who am slaughtered, my son,
And my blood is already on the leaves.
Father's voice choked.
His face grew pale.

And I wanted to scream, writhing not to believe
And I opened my eyes wide.
And I awoke.

Bloodless was my right hand.

יִצְחָק

לִפְנוֹת בֹּקֶר טִיְּלָה שֶׁמֶשׁ בְּתוֹךְ הַיַּעַר
יַחַד עִמִּי וְעִם אַבָּא
וִימִינִי בִשְׂמֹאלוֹ.

כִּבְרָק לָהֲבָה מַאֲכֶלֶת בֵּין הָעֵצִים.
וַאֲנִי יָרֵא כָּל־כָּךְ אֶת פַּחַד עֵינַי מוּל דָּם עַל הֶעָלִים.

אַבָּא אַבָּא מַהֵר וְהַצִּילָה אֶת יִצְחָק
וְלֹא יֶחְסַר אִישׁ בִּסְעֻדַּת הַצָּהֳרַיִם.

זֶה אֲנִי הַנִּשְׁחָט, בְּנִי,
וּכְבָר דָּמִי עַל הֶעָלִים.
וְאַבָּא נִסְתַּם קוֹלוֹ.
וּפָנָיו חִוְּרִים

וְרָצִיתִי לִצְעֹק, מְפַרְפֵּר לֹא לְהַאֲמִין
וְקוֹרֵעַ הָעֵינַיִם.
וְנִתְעוֹרַרְתִּי.

וְאָזְלַת־דָּם הָיְתָה יַד יָמִין

AMIR GILBOA

Moses

I approached Moses and said to him:
Arrange the camps thus and so.
He looked at me
Arranged them as I bid.

And who did not see my honor then!
Sarah was there from childhood,
In her name I drafted plans for building a city.
There was the long-legged one from the girls' farm
There was Melvina from Rabat on Malta.
Dinah from the Italo-Yugoslav border.
And Ria from the northern lowland.

And very proud I turned to Moses
To teach him the correct way
But suddenly it became clear to me
That she who in my name
Was carved and fixed —
Was not there.

Moses, Moses, lead on the people.
See, I am so tired and still want to sleep,
I am still a young boy.

מֹשֶׁה

נִגַּשְׁתִּי אֶל מֹשֶׁה וְאָמַרְתִּי לוֹ:
עֲרֹךְ אֶת הַמַּחֲנוֹת כָּךְ וְכָךְ.
הוּא הִסְתַּכֵּל בִּי
וְעָרַךְ לְפִי שֶׁאָמַרְתִּי.

וּמִי לֹא רָאָה אָז בִּכְבוֹדִי!
הָיְתָה שָׁם שָׂרָה מִן הַיַּלְדוּת
שֶׁעַל שְׁמָהּ תִּכַּנְתִּי לִבְנוֹת עִיר.
הָיְתָה שָׁם אֲרֶכַת־הָרַגְלַיִם מֶחַוַּת־הַפּוֹעֲלוֹת.
הָיְתָה מְלְוִינָה מֶרַבַּת אֲשֶׁר בְּמַלְטָה.
דִּינָה מֵהַגְּבוּל הָאִיטַלְקִי־הַיּוּגוֹסְלָבִי.
וְרִיָּה מֵהַשְּׁפֵלָה שֶׁבַּצָּפוֹן.

וְגֵאֶה מְאֹד מִהַרְתִּי אֶל מֹשֶׁה
לְהוֹרוֹתוֹ הַדֶּרֶךְ הַנְּכוֹנָה
וְהָחְוַר לִי לְפִתְאֹם
כִּי זוֹ אֲשֶׁר בְּתוֹךְ שְׁמִי
חֲרוּתָה וּנְכוֹנָה –
אֵינֶנָּה.

מֹשֶׁה מֹשֶׁה הַנְחֵה אֶת הָעָם,
רְאֵה, אֲנִי כָּל־כָּךְ עָיֵף וְרוֹצֶה לִישֹׁן עוֹד
אֲנִי עוֹדֶנִּי נַעַר.

A Song of Blue and Red

As if in snow you walked. And you walked in snow.
Bears rose against you! Papa bear. Mama bear. Baby bear.
You ran with all your strength. You imagined you were tumbling,
And in your eyes the terror of myriad years.

Now here you are. Years have passed. Passed.
The beautiful bears are gone. Gone. Will they ever reappear?
Tonight in our park the branches were broken.
And the trees still trickle blood and tears.

So that's how it is. We are young.
Yet, in memory, thousands of years.
See, all the imagined shapes arrayed outside your window
In a single straight line. Yet none is far, none is near.

On a Recollected Road

Today on a sandy road
Swirled by wind
Golden with sun
And remembered from past generations,
From the time I was among my predecessors,

שִׁיר כָּחֹל וְאָדֹם

כְּמוֹ בַּשֶּׁלֶג הָלַכְתְּ. וְאַתְּ הָלַכְתְּ בַּשֶּׁלֶג.
וּדְבָרִים עָלַיִךְ קָמוּ. דֹב. דֻבָּה. וְדֻבּוֹן.
וְרַצְתְּ בְּכָל כֹּחֵךְ. דָּמִית – הִנֵּה כּוֹשֶׁלֶת.
וְכָל רֶגַע בְּעֵינַיִךְ – פַּחַד שָׁנִים רִבּוֹא.

וְהִנֵּה כָּאן הִנֵּךְ. שָׁנִים עָבְרוּ. עָבְרוּ.
הָלְכוּ דְבָרִים יָפִים. הָלְכוּ. הַאִם יָשׁוּבוּ?
בְּגִנֵּנוּ הַלַּיְלָה בַּדֵּי הָאֳרָנִים נִשְׁבָּרוּ.
וְהָאִילָנוֹת – דְּמָעוֹת וָדָם יָזוּבוּ.

הִנֵּה כִּי כֵן. צְעִירִים אֲנַחְנוּ.
וְאַלְפֵי שָׁנִים בַּזִּכָּרוֹן.
רְאִי, כָּל הַדְּמֻיּוֹת מוּל חַלּוֹנֵךְ תֵּעָרַכְנָה
שׁוּרָה אַחַת. וְאֵין רָחוֹק וְאֵין קָרוֹב.

בְּדֶרֶךְ זְכוּרָה

הַיּוֹם בְּדֶרֶךְ חוֹלִית
סְעוּרָה מֵרוּחַ
זְהֻבָּה מִשֶּׁמֶשׁ
וּזְכוּרָה מִדּוֹרוֹת
מֵהְיוֹתִי בֵּין קוֹדְמַי

There came toward me many acquaintances.

Silent they looked into my eyes

As children look

Into the eyes of their begetter

And they passed along the road

Each one carrying under his arm

A volume...

Perhaps written there were

Conclusions.

Perhaps fanciful imaginings.

Perhaps laws of construction.

Perhaps the breaking down of every fence

So that there might be no barrier.

Perhaps calculations

For explosive material.

Perhaps the description of things

In a translucent language

Cold as mirrors.

Perhaps pictures of song

In a valley oozing droplets

And the words —

Crystals of heat and frost —

None stop trembling.

On a sandy road —

בָּאוּ מוּלַי רַבִּים מִמַּכָּרַי
שׁוֹתְקִים הִבִּיטוּ בְּעֵינַי
כְּהַבִּיט צֶאֱצָאִים
בְּעֵינֵי הַמּוֹלִיד
וְעָבְרוּ לַדֶּרֶךְ
כָּל אֶחָד נוֹשֵׂא תַּחַת בֵּית־שֶׁחְיוֹ
כֶּרֶךְ –
אֶפְשָׁר בָּם כְּתוּבִים
תּוֹלְדֵי מַחֲשָׁבָה.
אֶפְשָׁר דִּמְיוֹנֵי הַזַּיָה.
אֶפְשָׁר תּוֹרוֹת הַבִּנְיָן.
אֶפְשָׁר הֲרִיסַת כָּל גָּדֵר
שֶׁלֹּא יִהְיֶה חוֹצֵץ.
אֶפְשָׁר סִפְרוֹת הַחִשּׁוּב
לַחֹמֶר הַמְפוֹצֵץ.
אֶפְשָׁר תֵּאוּר הַדְּבָרִים
בְּלָשׁוֹן שְׁקוּפָה
וְקָרָה כַּמַּרְאוֹת.
אֶפְשָׁר מַרְאוֹת שֶׁל שִׁיר
בְּבִקְעָה נְטוּפָה
וְהַמִּלִּים –
גְּבִישֵׁי חֹם וּכְפוֹר –
אֵין חַדְלוֹת בָּן לִרְעֹד.

בְּדֶרֶךְ חוֹלִית –

Golden with sun remembered from past generations,
From the time I was among my predecessors —
Forever I shall walk, so will I walk
Ancient and young and begetting.

Evening of the Whirlwind

And still the sun rosies the fronts of houses
With the light of children's smiles,
With the flags of youth,
With holiday proclamations,
With the light of few voices,
In the mass of the oppressive silence
Before the lightning strikes again.

The Circle of Weeping

I heard the weeping of the newly born in its mother's bosom
And, as I returned, the weeping of the mother over her young.
And I did not stop to try to speak
And I did not ask who did her wrong
For this was the closed circle of weeping —
    the fixed song
That circles between the mother and her young.

זְהֻבָּה מִשֶּׁמֶשׁ וּזְכוּרָה מִדּוֹרוֹת
מִהְיוֹתִי בֵּין קוֹדְמַי –
לְעוֹלָם אֵלֵךְ כָּךְ וְאֵלֵךְ
עַתִּיק וְצָעִיר וּמוֹלִיד.

עֶרֶב סוּפָה

וְעוֹד הַשֶּׁמֶשׁ מוֹרִיד אֶת חֲזִיתוֹת הַבָּתִּים
בְּאוֹר שֶׁל חִיּוּכֵי יְלָדִים
שֶׁל דִּגְלֵי נֹעַר
שֶׁל כְּרָזוֹת חַג
בְּאוֹר שֶׁל קוֹלוֹת מְעֻטִּים
בְּתוֹךְ חַשְׁרַת דְּמָמָה מְעִיקָה
טֶרֶם שׁוּב יַכֶּה הַבָּרָק.

סְגוֹר הַבְּכִי

שָׁמַעְתִּי בְּכִי הַנּוֹלָד בְּחֵיק אִמּוֹ
וּבְשׁוּבִי בְּכִי הָאֵם עַל עוֹלָלָהּ
וְלֹא עָמַדְתִּי לָשֵׂאת דְּבָרַי לֵאמֹר
וְלֹא שָׁאַלְתִּי מִי עוֹלֵל לָהּ
כִּי הָיָה זֶה סְגוֹר הַבְּכִי –
מִזְמוֹר חֹק
הַהוֹלֵךְ־סוֹבֵב בֵּין אֵם וְתִינוֹק.

If They Show Me a Stone and I Say Stone

If they show me a stone and I say stone they will say stone,
And if they show me a tree and I say tree they will say tree.
But if they show me blood and I say blood they will say color.
If they show me blood and I say blood they will say color.

From All Sides Laughter Shall Strike Them

All those who, over the sorrows of strangers, led their spirits to
    dance and to delight
At the sunsets in the day's noon,
They are destined to know no victory. Their laughter from all sides
Shall strike them, echoing the fragments of a battle day's void
Where no victors and no vanquished are.

AND THE WORLD IS DESTROYED.

בָּעֲלֶטֶת

אִם יַרְאוּנִי אֶבֶן וְאֹמַר אֶבֶן יֹאמְרוּ אֶבֶן.
אִם יַרְאוּנִי עֵץ וְאֹמַר עֵץ יֹאמְרוּ עֵץ.
אַךְ אִם יַרְאוּנִי דָם וְאֹמַר דָם יֹאמְרוּ צֶבַע.
אִ ם יַ רְ א וּ נִ י דָ ם וְ אֹ מַ ר דָ ם יֹ א מְ ר וּ צֶ בַ ע.

צְחוֹקָם מֵעֲבָרִים יִתְקְפֵּם

כָּל שֶׁהִלְּכוּ רוּחָם לִהְיוֹת שְׂמֵחִים וְרוֹקְדִים עַל עַצְבוֹנוֹת זָרִים
עַל שְׁקִיעוֹת יוֹם בְּצָהֳרָיו
סוֹפָם לֹא יֵדְעוּ נִצָּחוֹן וּצְחוֹקָם מֵעֲבָרִים
יִתְקְפֵּם מְהַדְהֵד שִׁבְרֵי יוֹם קְרָב
בּוֹ אֵין מְנַצְּחִים וּמְנֻצָּחִים.

וְעוֹלָם נֶחֱרָב.

AMIR GILBOA

Song Yet Song

Happy are those of simple ways who still bless the light
of candles shining in the dark.
Hidden in their palaces, in their magnificent machines,
the others profane
All that is good and shining and make loathsome to the point of scorn
their faith written on the proclamation received from their fathers.
Should anyone walk out into the street he will find the sons who
are legitimate by virtue of their spirit, yet who are illegitimate upon
this earth that so loves them and there are none like who so love her.

Make gleeful, oh earth, your face to them
for there is yet song for them within you.

שִׁיר עוֹד שִׁיר

אַשְׁרֵי תְמִימֵי דֶרֶךְ וְעוֹד יְבָרְכוּ עַל אוֹר נֵרוֹת
מְאִירִים בָּעֲלָטָה.
סְפוּנִים בְּאַרְמוֹנֵיהֶם, בִּמְכוֹנִיּוֹתֵיהֶם הַמְהֻדָּרוֹת
יְפַגְּלוּ הָאֲחֵרִים
כָּל טוֹב וּמֵאִיר וְיַבְחִילוּ עַד בּוּז אֱמוּנָתָם הַכְּתוּבָה עֲלֵי־כְּרוּז קִבְּלוּ
מֵאֲבוֹתֵיהֶם.
אִם יֵצֵא מִי לָרְחוֹבוֹת וְיִמְצָא אֶת הַבָּנִים הַחֲקֻקִּים־מִכֹּחַ־
רוּחָם וְהֵם בִּלְתִּי־חֲקֻקִּים עַל הָאֲדָמָה הַזֹּאת שֶׁכֹּה אֲהַבְתָּם וְאֵין
כְּמוֹתָם לְאַהֲבָה.

הַצְהִילִי, אֶרֶץ, פָּנַיִךְ אֲלֵיהֶם
כִּי עוֹד שִׁיר לָהֶם בָּךְ.

DAVID ROKEAH

Beyond Imagination

As my imagination rises
To spheres above the earth,
I refine my ear to your word
As to existing reality
Beyond imagination.

From the watchtower of my dreaming, on the shore,
I call to you
As the ship calls dry land
Waving flags of longing

The messages of your love,
Purple waves at the edge of sunrise
For him who wakens at dawn.

Whirlwind

With fiery-lashing
Lightning will traverse the nights of our silence.
Illusion's mass will crumble
In the light of swords on mountain peaks.

מֵעֵבֶר לַדִּמְיוֹן

בִּנְסֹק דִּמְיוֹנִי
אֶל סְפִירוֹת־עַל־אָרֶץ
אֶלְטֹשׁ אָזְנִי אֶל דְּבָרֵךְ
כְּאֶל מַמָּשׁוּת קַיֶּמֶת
מֵעֵבֶר לַדִּמְיוֹן.

מִמִּצְפֶּה־חֲלוֹמִי, בְּחוֹף יָם
אֶקְרָאֵךְ
כִּקְרֹא סְפִינָה לַיַּבֶּשֶׁת
בַּהֲנִיפָה דִּגְלֵי־עֶרְגָּה.

אַשְׁדְּרוֹת־יְדִידוֹתֵךְ –
גַּלֵּי־אַרְגָּמָן בְּפַאֲתֵי־זְרִיחָה
לַגְּעוֹר עִם־שַׁחַר.

סוּפָה

בִּצְלִיפַת־אֵשׁ
יֵחָצֶה הַבָּרָק לֵיל־דּוּמִיָתֵנוּ.
חַשְׁרַת־אַשְׁלָיוֹת תִּתְפָּרֵק
לְאוֹר־חֲרָבוֹת, בְּרֹאשׁ־הֶהָרִים.

DAVID ROKEAH

With downpour of morning rain

    Wisdom's dream will sprout

    Our day's desire charged

    By poles of passion in abandoned night.

Hands Full of Sun

Hands full of sun are in spring's longing for you —
Tulips raised early their flame on the hills.
Yellow-petaled daisies,
Clappers of *izdarac** sway in the wind
Within my windows' spacious vista.

In spring's rush to you — the weary yearning of dusk.
From reed stalks, the flutter of ducks
Startled by stars falling into the. mirror of your river.
Night moisture. Fragrant essence of rain
In dew drops upon vine twigs.
God spreads gossamer silence over troughs of spices
Before our white-faced dream strengthens
On buds of late almond.

בְּהִנָּתֵךְ גֶּשֶׁם־שַׁחֲרִית
יָנִיב חֲלוֹם־בִּינוֹת
חֹשְׁקֵי יוֹמֵנוּ הַמִּתְחַשְׁמֵל
מִקַּקְטְבֵי־אַהַב, בַּעֲזוּבַת־לֵיל.

מְלֹא־חָפְנַיִם שֶׁמֶשׁ

מְלֹא־חָפְנַיִם שֶׁמֶשׁ בִּכְמִיהַת־אָבִיב אֵלַיִךְ –
צִבְעוֹנִים הִשְׁכִּימוּ לַהַטָּם עֲלֵי גְבָעוֹת
קַחְוָנִים צִהֲבֵי־הָעֱלִי
עִנְבְּלֵי־אֹזְדָּרֶכֶת הַנִּשְׁקָלִים בָּרוּחַ
לְרֹחַב־הַתַּצְפִּית שֶׁל חַלּוֹנִי.

בִּנְהִירַת אָבִיב אֵלַיִךְ – עֶרְגָּה לֵאָה שֶׁל עַרְבַּיִם.
רַחַשׁ אַוְזֵי־בָר מֵעַם קְנֵי־הַסּוּף
מִשְׁתָּאִים לִצְנִיחַת־כּוֹכָבִים אֶל רְאִי־נְהָרַיִךְ.
טַחַב־לֵיל. רֵיחַ־תַּמְצִית שֶׁל גֶּשֶׁם
בְּאֶגְלֵי־טַל עַל זַלְזַלֵּי־גֶפֶן.
דַּק־דְּמָמָה פּוֹרֵשׂ אֱלֹהִים עַל רַהֲטֵי־בַּשָּׁמַיִם
טֶרֶם יִתְעַצֵּם חֲלוֹמֵנוּ לִבֶן־הַסֵּבֶר
עַל כַּפְתּוֹרֵי שָׁקֵד אֲפִילִים.

Solar Years

Count the transmutations of solar years

In the folds of dreams on masts

In the branching of olive slips

In seasonal rings on birch trunks

In disintegrating roadstones

In mussel shells masking the sea's retreat from the shore

In layers of rust on struts of the pier

In the dimensions of minerals in the dark ground.

Count the desires

Sailboats that refused to return to anchor.

Open-Eyed Angel

On life and extinction with sea wind changes.

Morning's flood on crags.

Sunset's song beating

On cliffs of night.

When the rolling wave halts, a sunbeam shatters.

A cloud passes in the form of an open-eyed angel.

The moon embalms death's shadow. A blind snake at the house door.

שְׁנוֹת־שֶׁמֶשׁ

מְנֵה עִרְעוּרֵי שְׁנוֹת־שֶׁמֶשׁ
בְּקִפּוּלֵי־חַלּוֹם בַּתְּרָנִים
בְּסַעֲפוֹת גְּרוּפִיּוֹת הַזַּיִת
בִּפְצָלוֹת־עוֹנָה עַל גֶּזַע־לְבָנִים
בְּחִסְפּוּסֵי־פֵּרוּק שֶׁל אַבְנֵי־אֹרַח
בִּצְדָפִים הַמַּסְרִים נְסִיגַת־יָם מִן הַיַּבֶּשֶׁת
בְּרָבְדֵי־חַלְדָּה עַל אַלְכְסוֹנֵי־מֶזַח
בְּמֶמֶד־הַבְּצָרִים בְּקַרְקַע אֲמוּשָׁה.

מְנֵה אֲוֵי־כְּבָר
סִירוֹת־מִפְרָשׂ מֵאֲנוּ חֲזֹר לַמַּעֲגָן.

מַלְאָךְ שְׁתוּם־עֵנָיִם

עֲלֵי חַיִּים וְחַדְלוֹנָם בַּחֲלִיפוֹת רוּחַ־יָם.
גֵּאוּת שַׁחַר עֲלֵי צוּקִים.
שִׁיר דָּכְיָן שֶׁל שְׁקִיעוֹת
בְּשׁוּנִיּוֹת הַלֵּיל.

כִּי יֵעָצֵר גַּל בַּזֶּרֶם – קֶרֶן שֶׁמֶשׁ תִּשְׁתַּבֵּר.
יַחֲלֹף עָנָן בִּדְמוּת־מַלְאָךְ שְׁתוּם־עֵנָיִם.
צַלְמָוֶת יַחֲנֹט סַהַר. נָחָשׁ סוּם לְפֶתַח־בָּיִת.

Until blue prayer is kindled in a sky of longing
     As lakes are still in the heatwave before dusk.

Rest, sea, in twilight pause between day and night,
     The lament of shores waving a requiem for illusions
     Heart's scaffold in its solitude. Disconsolate song,
        The whistling of border wind.

Like the ocean floor
     Midnight will gather the anguish of daggers
Unsheathed from soul's bitterness at blinding noon.
On beds of quicksand night will thicken
        Dream torn and scheming.

                    Jerusalem

          Your stones I shall polish into a mirror
          For in them is my yearning,
          Pines' loftiness and their hearts' resin.

          In dawns' topazes
          I shall store
          The reflection of your day
          Rising early on the city wall

עַד יִדְלֶק כֹּחַל־תְּפִלָּה בְּשַׁפְרִיר־הָאֲוִיּים
כְּדוּמִיַּת־אֲגַמִּים בִּשְׁרַב־טְרוֹם־עַרְבָּיִם.

שָׂפָה, יָם, בְּדִמְדוּמֵי־הָעֲצֶרֶת בֵּין יוֹם וָלַיְל –
אֱלִיַּת־חוֹפִים בְּהִתְאַדּוּ לְאַשְׁכָּבַת־הָאַשְׁלָיוֹת.
גְּרַדְּם־לֵבָב   בִּבְדִידוּתוֹ.   שִׁיר־לֹא־נֻחַם
בִּשְׁרֵקַת רוּחַ־סְפָר.

כְּקַרְקָעִית אֹקְיָנוֹס
תֶּאֱסֹף חֲצוֹת יְגוֹן פְּגִיוֹנוֹת
הַנִּשְׁלָפִים מִמְּרִי־נֶפֶשׁ בְּסַנְוְרֵי־צָהֳרָיִם.
עַל יְצוּעַ־חוֹלוֹת־נַד יַחֲשִׁיר לַיְל
פְּרוּם־חֲלוֹמוֹת וְזוֹמֵם.

יְרוּשָׁלַיִם

אֲבָנַיִךְ אֶלַטֵּשׁ עַד אַסְפַּקְלָר
תְּשׁוּקָתִי בָּךְ
גֵּאוּת־אֲרָנִים וּשְׂרָף־לִבָּם.

בִּגְבִישֵׁי־שַׁחֲרִית
אֶאֱצֹר
בְּבוֹאַת יוֹמֵךְ
הַמַּשְׁכִּים עַל חוֹמַת עִיר

Like a stream of light
On a slope of flint
In a bronze mortar sheath.

Your stones I shall polish until my dreams course in you
Like a flow smashing your rocks —
Your yearning, wanderer.

Negev

Again the flutter of desert,
Beat of eagle wings
Among wilderness crags.
Light of noon skies
In primal blindness,
God manifest
On copper mountains
In green rust.

Be uplifted mountains, for vision.
A wayfarer prophesies in the valley.
Yearning will materialize
In the glow of red clay.

כְּשִׁבֹּלֶת־אוֹר
עַל אַשְׁדַּת־שָׁמִיר
בִּנְדָן מַכְתֵּשׁ־עֲרָד.

אֲבָנַיִךְ אֲלַטֵּשׁ עַד יָרוּץ חֲלוֹמִי בָּךְ
כְּיוּבַל עוֹרֵךְ טְרָשַׁיִךְ –
תְּשׁוּקָתֵךְ, נַוַּד.

נֶ גֶ ב

וְשׁוּב תְּנוּפַת מִדְבָּר
מַשַּׁק כַּנְפֵי נֶשֶׁר
בֵּין צוּקֵי־צִיָּה.
אוֹר שְׁמֵי־צָהֳרַיִם
בְּסַנְוֵור הַיּוֹלִי
הִתְגַּלּוּת־אֱלֹהִים
עַל הָרֵי־נְחֹשֶׁת
בִּירַק הַחַלְדָּה.

הִנָּשְׂאוּ הָרִים, כִּי חָזוֹן.
הֵלֶךְ מִתְנַבֵּא בַּגַּיְא.
יִתְגַּלֵּם הַכֶּסֶף
בִּזְרִיחַת חַרְסִית.

DAVID ROKEAH

Light will materialize
In flint crystals,
The wanderer's desire
In gleaming isolation.

Sun will pulverize stones,
Road dust like song
In the nomad's longing.

Silence will flame like a lover's expectation
Lonely in its hope.
Wilderness will carry the ardor of his blood
To deposits of sulphur — a gift.

Tremble, earth convulsed in Khamsin.
Your day, appointed, is sand in the fire-core.
In my yearning's burden your thirst is weighed.
Beneath vaults of immortality
Catapult-stones of lust.

יִתְגַּלֵּם הָאוֹר
בִּגְבִישֵׁי־הַצּוּר
תְּשׁוּקַת־נַוְד
בִּבְדִידוּת זְהָרָה.

שֶׁמֶשׁ אֲבָנִים תָּדֵק.
אֲבַק־דְּרָכִים כְּזֶמֶר
בְּנַעֲגוּעֵי־צֹעַן.

יִלְהַט הַדְּמִי כְּצִפִּיַּת אֹהֶב
עֲרִירִי בְּסִבְרוֹ.
קִנְאַת דָּמוֹ יִשָּׂא מִדְבָּר
אֶל רִבְצֵי־גָפְרִית – דוֹרוֹן.

גּוּרִי, אֶרֶץ, עֲוִיַּת־חַמְסִין.
יוֹמֵךְ בְּהִפָּקֵד חוֹל בַּמּוֹקֵד.
בְּמַשְּׂאוֹי עֶרְגָּתִי יִשָּׁקֵל צִמְאוֹנֵךְ.
תַּחַת קִמְרוֹנֵי־אַלְמָוֶת
בְּלִיסְטְרָאוֹת־חֶמְדָּה.

DAVID ROKEAH

Zealots of Yearning

For the expectant is the glory,
For the future is theirs.
Who stand against the mountain without recoil
Shall ascend its summit.

So hopes the river, pushing to the sea,
For the freeing of its desires in the roar of ocean.
So hopes the tree, sending a branch toward the sky
To touch the palm of the sun some day.

Therefore we love dawn as certainty of sunrise,
The nightingale's love-song as longings of motherhood,
The bubbling of fountains as beat of dreams becoming real.
Streams pulsing channels for rivers of the future
And not growing weary.
And all who join in the covenant of hope with the universe —
They are the zealots of yearning.

Therefore, forge the future's desires,
As the waves beat out the rocks of the shore,
As the smith forms the white-heated steel to his will.
Form dreams of faithfulness.
The desolation will not vanish from the Negev before it
        vanishes from the heart . . .

קַנָּאֵי עֶרְגָּה

לַמְצַפִּים הַתְּהִלָּה,
כִּי לָהֶם הֶעָתִיד.
הָעוֹמְדִים מוּל הָהָר וְאֵינָם נִרְתָּעִים
יַעֲלוּ אֶל פִּסְגָּתוֹ.

כָּךְ קוֹוֶה הַנָּהָר הַחוֹתֵר אֱלֵי יָם
לְפָרְקֵן מַאֲוַיָּיו בְּדִכְיֵי־הָאוֹקְיָנוֹס.
כָּךְ מְיַחֵל אִילָן בְּשָׁלְחוֹ פֶּארָה לָרָקִיעַ
כִּי תִגַּע בָּה כַּף־שֶׁמֶשׁ בְּיוֹם מִן הַיָּמִים.

עַל־כֵּן נֹאהַב אֶת הַשַּׁחַר כְּוַדָּאוּת שֶׁל זְרִיחָה.
שִׁירַת־דּוֹדִים שֶׁל זָמִיר כְּכִסּוּפֵי־אִמָּהוֹת.
פִּכּוּי־עֵינוֹת כִּפְעִימַת חֲלוֹם מִתְמַמֵּשׁ.
פְּלָגִים הַפּוֹלְסִים עֲרוּצִים לִנְהָרוֹת־הֶעָתִיד
וְלֹא יִלְאוּ.
וְכָל הַבָּאִים בִּבְרִית־תּוֹחֶלֶת עִם הַיְקוּם –
וְהֵם קַנָּאֵי־עֶרְגָּה.

וְעַל־כֵּן חִשְּׁלוּ אֶת מַשְׂאַת־הֶעָתִיד,
כַּאֲשֶׁר מְחַשְּׁלִים הַגַּלִּים אֶת סַלְעֵי־הַחוֹף.
וּכְבַרְזֶל מֻלְבָּן אֲשֶׁר הַנַּפָּח יְצוּרוֹ כִרְצוֹנוֹ
צוֹרְרוּ אֶת חֲלוֹמוֹת־הָאֻמֶּן.
לֹא תָגֹז הַשַּׁמָּה מִנֶּגֶב בְּטֶרֶם תָּגֹז מִלְּבָבוֹת...

HAYYIM GURI

The Silent Words

(of the woman, the poem, the mother, and death)

I did not cry, my good mother, the song in my hand burst in tears.
I did not kill, my good mother, his blood in my hand I spilled.
His lives carried me to the block, like a blazing star he rose,
For he set his hand to my throat, touched my tongue with a burning coal.

He accompanied me like a shadow, he was to me judge and God,
Within my flesh he was sealed, his paths on my forehead paced,
When weary I fell at his feet, he stopped his ears: not to forgive.
When I remained speechless, alone, my head in his hands he embraced.

He soared in myriad bloomings, in the many hues of the bow.
He wandered with my sleep across heavens high and cold.
With my heart he pounded heavy strokes, in the streets of the noisy town.
He shrieked like white-heated iron at the cruel hammer's blow.

I could not hold his face, his eyes that were touching mine.
His spirit lost in the distance, his days immersed in flame.
When I slept dead on the floor, the lamp before him still shone.
He stirred my life with his hand, the *shamir** upon stone.

And here he lies. Is it you? Or my body here outstretched?
Is the dagger plunged in your chest or my body anguished and pained?

הַדְּבָרִים הַשּׁוֹתְקִים

(על האשה, השיר, האם והמות)

ג

לֹא בָּכִיתִי, אִמִּי הַטּוֹבָה, רַק הַשִּׁיר בְּיָדִי הִתְיַפֵּחַ.
לֹא רָצַחְתִּי, אִמִּי הַטּוֹבָה, רַק שָׁפַכְתִּי דָמוֹ בְּכַפִּי.
אֶל גַּרְדֹּם נְשָׂאוּנִי חַיָּיו, כִּי עָלָה כְּכוֹכָב מִתְלַקֵּחַ,
כִּי שָׁלַח אֶת יָדוֹ אֶל צַוָּאר, כִּי נָגַע בָּרִצְפָּה בְּמוֹ פִּי.

הוּא לִוַּנִי כַּצֵּל, הוּא הָיָה לִי שׁוֹפֵט וֶאֱלֹהַּ,
הוּא נֶחְתַּם בִּבְשָׂרִי, עַל מִצְחִי רִחֲפוּ אֹרְחוֹתָיו.
עֵת נָפַלְתִּי עָיֵף לְרַגְלָיו, הוּא אָטַם אֶת אָזְנָיו: לֹא לִסְלֹחַ.
עֵת נוֹתַרְתִּי יָחִיד וְאֵין קוֹל, הוּא חִבֵּק אֶת רֹאשִׁי בְּיָדָיו.

הוּא פָּרַח בְּאַלְפֵי תִפְרָחוֹת, בַּגְּוָנִים הָרַבִּים שֶׁל הַקֶּשֶׁת.
הוּא נָדַד עִם שְׁנָתִי מוּל שָׁמַיִם גְּבוֹהִים וְקָרִים.
הוּא הָלַם חֲזָקוֹת עִם לִבִּי, בְּחוּצוֹת הַקִּרְיָה הָרוֹעֶשֶׁת.
הוּא נָאַק כְּבַרְזֶל מְלֻבָּן, מוּל מַפַּץ פַּטִּישִׁים אַכְזָרִי.

לֹא יָכֹלְתִּי כַּלְכֵּל אֶת פָּנָיו, אֶת עֵינָיו הַנּוּגוֹת בְּעֵינַי,
אֶת רוּחוֹ הָאוֹבֵד בַּמֶּרְחָק, אֶת יָמָיו הַטּוֹבְלִים בַּשַּׁלְהֶבֶת.
עֵת נִרְדַּמְתִּי הָרוּג עַל רִצְפָּה, עוֹד דָּלְקָה הַמְּנוֹרָה לְפָנָיו
וְיָדוֹ אֶת חַיֵּי דוֹבְבָה בְּצִפֹּרֶן שָׁמִיר עַל הָאֶבֶן.

וְהִנֵּה הוּא מוּטָל, הַאַתָּה? אוֹ גוּפִי פֹּה צוֹנֵחַ?
הַפִּגְיוֹן בְּחָזְךָ אוֹ גוּפִי מְיֻגָּן וְנִכְאָב?

On my face a great stream of water... silence... the moon's crescent
And his head upon my knees and my lips move over his face.

Requiescat

For my dear H.B.D.

Lay wreaths upon the stone. Wreaths
About his amazed, listening face arrange.
He was yours, but you were like strangers:
No ray of light on the cobwebs in the eaves,
He looks at you out of mist, curtains of rain.

To my memory from childhood rises
The picture of his face innocent, aglisten.
Youth blue-heated the iron of his life
Struck by the fire from the pupils of his eyes.
As a man, he came to anguish and cognition.

But what between his walls was mute,
And what outside of them was choked,
To the conflagration of his nights he took.
And with his best friends did not lock
What he carried to his grave and to his book.

זֶרֶם מַיִם אַדִּיר עַל פָּנַי... דּוּמִיָּה... חֶרְמֵשׁוֹ שֶׁל יָרֵחַ...
וְרֹאשׁוֹ עַל בִּרְכַּי, וּשְׂפָתַי מְהַלְּכוֹת עַל פָּנָיו.

נִשְׁמַת

לְיַקִּירִי, ח. ב. ד.

זֵרִים תַּנִּיחַ עַל הָאֶבֶן. וְזֵרִים
תַּקִּיף פָּנָיו תְּמוּהֵי הַקֶּשֶׁב.
וְהוּא הָיָה שֶׁלְּךָ, אֲבָל הֱיִיתֶם כְּזָרִים
בְּאֵין קַו אוֹר עַל הַזַּוִּית וְהַקּוּרִים,
וְהוּא צוֹפֶה בְּךָ מִתּוֹךְ הָעֲרָפֶל וּמַסְכֵי הַגֶּשֶׁם.

מִן הַיַּלְדוּת עוֹלָה תְּמוּנַת פָּנָיו
אֶל זִכְרוֹנִי, תְּמִימָה וּמְהַבְהֶבֶת.
וּבִנְעוּרִים הִכְחִיל בַּרְזֶל חַיָּיו
מִכֶּה בָּאֵשׁ אֲשֶׁר פָּרְחָה מֵאִישׁוֹנָיו.
וְגֶבֶר בָּא אֶל הַיָּגוֹן וְהַמַּחֲשֶׁבֶת.

אֲבָל אֶת שֶׁשָּׁתַק בֵּין קִירוֹתָיו,
וְאֶת אֲשֶׁר נֶחְנַק מֵעֵבֶר – – –
גָּרַר עִמּוֹ אֶל דְּלֵקָתָם שֶׁל לֵילוֹתָיו.
וְלֹא הִסְגִּיר לַטּוֹב בִּידִידָיו
אֶת שֶׁנָּשָׂא עִמּוֹ לַסֵּפֶר, וְלַקֶּבֶר.

This is the book of facts. Like a cruel scroll

His heart and his confessions on my deafness strike.

I beg pardon for the grudge that passes by,

For the error that recurs eternally.

But he just smiled to me from beyond his life.

His Mother

Long ago at the end of Deborah's song

I heard the silence of Sisera's chariots that were late.

I looked at Sisera's mother gazing through the window there,

A woman with a streak of silver in her hair.

Maidens saw "a spoil of varicolored embroidery,

Of varicolored embroidered cloth on the captive's neck."*

He lay as if asleep in the tent then.

His hands were very empty.

Traces of milk, butter and blood on his chin.

The silence lay unbroken by horse or chariot.

The maidens kept silent one by one.

My silence touched their own.

After a while the sun went down,

The setting rays went out.

זֶה סֵפֶר הַדְּבָרִים. כִּמְגִלָּה אַכְזֶרֶת
עַל חֲרָשׁוּתִי מַכִּים לִבּוֹ וּוִדּוּיָיו.
בַּקַּשְׁתִּי שֶׁיִּסָּלַח עַל טִינָה עוֹבֶרֶת,
עַל דְּבַר טָעוּת שֶׁלְּעוֹלָם חוֹזֶרֶת.
אַךְ הוּא חִיֵּךְ אֵלַי מֵעֵבֶר לְחַיָּיו.

אִמּוֹ

לִפְנֵי שָׁנִים, בְּסוֹף שִׁירַת דְּבוֹרָה,
שָׁמַעְתִּי אֶת דּוּמִיַּת רֶכֶב סִיסְרָא אֲשֶׁר בּוֹשֵׁשׁ לָבוֹא,
מַבִּיט בְּאִמּוֹ שֶׁל סִיסְרָא הַנִּשְׁקֶפֶת בַּחַלּוֹן,
אִשָּׁה שֶׁפַּס כֶּסֶף בִּשְׂעָרָהּ.

שְׁלַל צְבָעִים רִקְמָה,
צֶבַע רִקְמָתַיִם לְצַוְּארֵי שָׁלָל, רָאוּ הַנְּעָרוֹת.
אוֹתָהּ שָׁעָה שָׁכַב בָּאֹהֶל כְּנִרְדָּם.
יָדָיו רֵיקוֹת מְאֹד.
עַל סַנְטֵרוֹ עִקְּבוֹת חָלָב חֶמְאָה וָדָם.

הַדּוּמִיָּה לֹא נִשְׁבְּרָה אֶל הַסּוּסִים וְאֶל הַמֶּרְכָּבוֹת,
גַּם הַנְּעָרוֹת שָׁתְקוּ אַחַת אַחַר אַחַת.
שְׁתִיקָתִי נָגְעָה בִּשְׁתִיקָתָן
אַחַר זְמַן־מָה שָׁקְעָה הַשֶּׁמֶשׁ.
אַחַר זְמַן־מָה כָּבוּ הַדִּמְדּוּמִים.

For forty years the land was stilled, forty years

Horses did not race. Dead riders did not pierce with glassy eyes.

But she died shortly after her son was killed.

Pictures of the Jews

For Ezra

My quiet prison guards, much tried. My beloved.

Their glance strokes my face till the end.

I am there.

Dungeon. Stones, iron, and twilight.

They do not come to me now by inheritance.

I see them:

Half of them alive and half of them dead,

Free men.

Easy smugglers, of subtle grasp.

Who know by heart the approaches to the sky

And it is there they wander, as if to a familiar country.

And their faces are like the faces of the weary sages.

And they return, in hours of weak-mindedness, to strange earth,

To look about and to meditate.

They return like renters.

After a short time their faces are in blood.

אַרְבָּעִים שָׁנָה שָׁקְטָה הָאָרֶץ. אַרְבָּעִים שָׁנָה
לֹא דָהֲרוּ סוּסִים וּפָרָשִׁים מֵתִים לֹא נָעֲצוּ עֵינֵי זְכוּכִית.
אֲבָל הִיא מֵתָה, זְמַן קָצָר אַחַר מוֹת בְּנָהּ.

תְּמוּנוֹת הַיְּהוּדִים

לעזרא

סוֹחֲרֵי הַשְּׁקָטִים, הַמְנֻסִּים מְאֹד, אוֹהֲבַי.
מַבָּטָם מְלַטֵּף אֶת פָּנַי עַד סוֹף.
אֲנִי שָׁם.
כֶּלֶא. אֲבָנִים, בַּרְזֶל וּבֵין עַרְבַּיִם.
הֵם אֵינָם בָּאִים אֵלַי כָּעֵת בִּירֻשָּׁה.

אֲנִי רוֹאֶה אוֹתָם:
מַחֲצִיתָם חַיִּים וּמֵתִים מַחֲצִיתָם,
בְּנֵי חוֹרִין.
מַבְרִיחִים קַלִּים, דַּקֵּי תְּפִיסָה,
הַיּוֹדְעִים בְּעַל־פֶּה אֶת מְבוֹאוֹת הַשָּׁמַיִם
וּלְשָׁם נָעִים כְּמוֹ לְאֶרֶץ מַכָּרָה.
וּפְנֵיהֶם כִּפְנֵי הַחֲכָמִים הָעֲיֵפִים.

וְהֵם שָׁבִים, בִּשְׁעוֹת חֻלְשַׁת־דַּעַת, אֶל אֲדָמָה זָרָה,
לְהָצִיץ וּלְהַרְהֵר.
שָׁבִים כְּמוֹ שׂוֹכְרֵי־דִירָה.
וּלְאַחַר זְמַן מָה פְּנֵיהֶם בַּדָּם.

And they wander, wander and scatter in the wind,

Wind that erases footprints,

Wind that carries the smell of the dead,

Like an agent traveling and weary, black and white,

Who sells wind and trembling.

And his beard grows on the way,

And his house is far away, high up, beyond the silence.

They come to me,

Their footstep close to quiet

And fearful like mortal danger. They come here.

Attack me, achieve a sad victory

And retreat in me silently to the royal city ancient and far.

They come to me, out of the sickness.

From beyond forests and lands and water.

Their faces return from the tear that salted the sea.

Their faces are the smile of the sages,

Above stones and metals and dark pitch

I dream them.

The inhabitants of the city sense them suddenly:

Thieves on ladders to the clouds.

וְהֵם נָעִים, נָעִים וּמִתְפַּזְּרִים בָּרוּחַ,
רוּחַ הַמּוֹחֶקֶת עֲקֵבוֹת,
רוּחַ הַנּוֹשֵׂאת אֶת רֵיחַ הַמֵּתִים.
כְּמוֹ סוֹכֵן נוֹסֵעַ וְעָיֵף, שָׁחוֹר־לָבָן,
הַמּוֹכֵר רוּחַ וָרַעַד,

וּזְקָנוֹ צוֹמֵחַ בַּדֶּרֶךְ,
וּבֵיתוֹ רָחוֹק, לְמַעְלָה, מֵעֵבֶר לַדּוּמִיָּה.

בָּאִים אֵלַי.
צַעֲדָם קָרוֹב לַשֶּׁקֶט
וְחָרֵד כְּמוֹ פִּקּוּחַ נֶפֶשׁ. בָּאִים לְכָאן.
פּוֹשְׁטִים עָלַי, מוֹתִירִים נִצָּחוֹן עָצוּב
וּנְסוֹגִים בִּי חֶרֶשׁ אֶל עִיר מֶלֶךְ עַתִּיקָה וּרְחוֹקָה.

בָּאִים אֵלַי, מִן הַמַּחֲלָה.
מֵעֵבֶר לִיעָרוֹת וַאֲדָמוֹת וּמַיִם
וּפְנֵיהֶם שָׁבוֹת מִן הַדִּמְעָה אֲשֶׁר הִמְלִיחָה אֶת הַיָּם.

וּפְנֵיהֶם חִיּוּךְ הַחֲכָמִים.
מֵעַל לָאֲבָנִים וּמַתָּכוֹת וְזֶפֶת אֲפֵלָה.
אֲנִי חוֹלֵם אוֹתָם.

אַנְשֵׁי הָעִיר חָשִׁים בָּהֶם פִּתְאֹם:
גַּנָּב עַל סֻלָּמוֹת לָעֲנָנִים.

When they shoot at them,
Half their outcry falls with them.
Half rises to the skies, accustomed to them,
To be received,
To become the song of the angels.

And tonight they return to attack me with prolonged attacks,
Footprints in blood.

I do not move now.
I continue, as if enchanted, their movements,
And they go on and are murdered within me like father.
And they are alone.
And only God is with them.

Odysseus

And when he returned to his birthplace he found sea
And various fishes and grass floating on slow waves
And sun weakened in the rims of the sky.

An error forever recurs, said Odysseus in his tired heart,
And returned to the cross-roads close to the neighboring city
To find the road to his birthplace that was not water.

כְּשִׁיּוּרִים בָּהֶם,
מַחֲצִית צַעֲקָתָם נוֹפֶלֶת עִמָּהֶם.
מַחֲצִית עוֹלָה אֶל הַשָּׁמַיִם, הָרְגִילִים לָהֶם,
לְהִתְקַבֵּל,
לִהְיוֹת שִׁירַת הַמַּלְאָכִים.

וְהַלַּיְלָה, שָׁבִים לִתְקוֹף אוֹתִי בְּהַתְקָפוֹת מְמֻשָּׁכוֹת,
עֲקֵבוֹת מִדָּם.

אֵינֶנִּי נָע כָּעֵת.
אֲנִי מַמְשִׁיךְ כְּמוֹ מְכַשֵּׁף אֶת תְּנוּעָתָם
וְהֵם הוֹלְכִים וְנִרְצָחִים בִּי כְּמוֹ אָב,
וְהֵם לְבַדָּם.
וְרַק אֱלֹהִים עִמָּהֶם.

אוֹדִיסֵס

וּבְשׁוּבוֹ אֶל עִיר מוֹלַדְתּוֹ מָצָא יָם
וְדָגִים שׁוֹנִים וְעֵשֶׂב צָף עַל הַגַּלִּים אִטִּיִּים
וְשֶׁמֶשׁ נֶחֱלֶשֶׁת בְּשׁוּלֵי שָׁמַיִם.

טָעוּת לְעוֹלָם חוֹזֶרֶת, אָמַר אוֹדִיסֵס בְּלִבּוֹ הֶעָיֵף
וְחָזַר עַד פָּרָשַׁת־הַדְּרָכִים הַסְּמוּכָה לָעִיר הַשְּׁכֵנָה,
לִמְצֹא אֶת הַדֶּרֶךְ אֶל עִיר מוֹלַדְתּוֹ שֶׁלֹּא הָיְתָה מַיִם.

A wayfarer weary as a dreamer yearning much
Between people who spoke another Greek.
The words he had taken as provision for his travels had meanwhile perished.

For a moment he thought he had slumbered many days
And had returned to people who were not amazed to see him
And did not open their eyes wide.

He questioned them with motions and they tried to understand him
From a distance.
The scarlet turned violet and faded in the rims of those skies.

The adults arose and took the children standing about him in a circle
And drew them away.
And light after light yellowed in house after house.

The dew came and fell upon his head.
The wind came and kissed his lips.
Water came and washed his feet like old Eurycleia.*
And it did not see the scar and continued down the slope like water.

הָלַךְ עָיֵף כְּחוֹלֵם וּמִתְגַּעְגֵּעַ מְאֹד
בֵּין אֲנָשִׁים שֶׁדִּבְּרוּ יְוָנִית אַחֶרֶת.
הַמִּלִּים שֶׁנָּטַל עִמּוֹ כְּצֵידָה לַדֶּרֶךְ הַמַּסָּעוֹת, גָּוְעוּ בֵּינְתַיִם.

רֶגַע חָשַׁב כִּי נִרְדַּם לְיָמִים רַבִּים
וְחָזַר אֶל אֲנָשִׁים שֶׁלֹּא תָמְהוּ בִּרְאוֹתָם אוֹתוֹ
וְלֹא קָרְעוּ עֵינַיִם.

הוּא שָׁאַל אוֹתָם בִּתְנוּעוֹת וְהֵם נִסּוּ לְהָבִין אוֹתוֹ
מִתּוֹךְ הַמֶּרְחַקִּים.
הָאַרְגָּמָן הִסְגִּיל וְהָלַךְ בְּשׁוּלֵי אוֹתָם שָׁמַיִם.

קָמוּ הַמְבֻגָּרִים וְנָטְלוּ אֶת הַיְלָדִים שֶׁעָמְדוּ סְבִיבוֹ בְּמַעְגָּל
וּמָשְׁכוּ אוֹתָם.
וְאוֹר אַחַר אוֹר הִצְהִיב בְּבַיִת אַחַר בַּיִת.

בָּא טַל וְיָרַד עַל רֹאשׁוֹ.
בָּאָה רוּחַ וְנָשְׁקָה לִשְׂפָתָיו.
בָּאוּ מַיִם וְשָׁטְפוּ רַגְלָיו כְּאֶבְרֵיקְלֵיָּה הַזְּקֵנָה.
וְלֹא רָאוּ אֶת הַצַּלֶּקֶת וְהִמְשִׁיכוּ בַּמּוֹרָד כְּדֶרֶךְ הַמַּיִם.

Piyyut for Rosh Hashana*

for Aharon Meyerovitz

For this is not the road against which stand enemy lines, or foreign languages
Or muteness.
Neither I nor my voice is tied by the conditions set on these distances.
I walk and I am not murdered.
I come at last to the house. I stop. I knock at the door.

All men who forgive say. What has been has been. I repeat.
All women who forgive stand on the porches sooner or later.
There is a window which is not black. There is a letter which is not
        lost on the way.
And if it did not arrive yesterday it will certainly arrive tomorrow.

All the cities are open tonight. None is besieged or embalmed.
Guests will arrive tonight and I am one of them.
In all the windows branches of regret are opening one after the other.
Many words come up in pilgrimage from lands of silence and death.

The curtains billow and the doors move on their hinges.

אין

<h1 style="text-align:center">פִּיּוּט לְרֹאשׁ הַשָּׁנָה</h1>

לאהרן מאירוביץ

הֲלֹא אֵין זוֹ דֶּרֶךְ שֶׁנִּצָּבִים לָהּ קַוֵּי הָאוֹיְבִים אוֹ הַשָּׂפוֹת הַזָּרוֹת
אוֹ הָאִלֵּם.
לֹא אֲנִי וְלֹא קוֹלִי אֵינֶנּוּ קְשׁוּרִים בְּהַסְכָּמַת הַמֶּרְחַקִּים הָאֵלֶּה.
אֲנִי הוֹלֵךְ וְאֵינֶנִּי נִרְצָח.
אֲנִי בָּא לִכְסוֹף אֶל בַּיִת. אֲנִי נֶעֱצָר. אֲנִי דוֹפֵק בַּדֶּלֶת.

כָּל הַסּוֹלְחִים אוֹמְרִים, מַה שֶּׁהָיָה הָיָה. אֲנִי שָׁב וְחוֹזֵר.
כָּל הַסּוֹלְחוֹת נִצָּבוֹת עַל מִרְפָּסוֹת בְּמֻקְדָּם אוֹ בִּמְאֻחָר.
יֵשׁ חַלּוֹן שֶׁאֵינֶנּוּ שָׁחוֹר. יֵשׁ אִגֶּרֶת שֶׁאֵינֶנָּה אוֹבֶדֶת בַּדֶּרֶךְ.
וְאִם לֹא הִגִּיעָה אֶתְמוֹל וַדַּאי תַּגִּיעַ מָחָר.

כָּל הֶעָרִים פְּתוּחוֹת הַלַּיְלָה. אֵין נְצוּרָה וְאֵין חֲנוּטָה.
אוֹרְחִים יָבוֹאוּ הַלַּיְלָה וַאֲנִי אֶחָד מֵהֶם.
בְּכָל הַחַלּוֹנוֹת הוֹלְכִים וְנִפְתָּחִים אֶחָד אַחַר אֶחָד סְנִיפֵי הַחֲרָטָה.
מִלִּים רַבּוֹת עוֹלוֹת לְרֶגֶל מֵאַרְצוֹת דּוּמָה וְצַלְמוֹתָהּ.

הַוִּילוֹנוֹת פּוֹרְחִים וְהַדְּלָתוֹת נָעוֹת עַל צִירֵיהֶן.

Here We Loved

(from the sonnet sequence)

I

My father was four years at their war
And did not hate or love his enemies.
But I know that he, already there,
Formed me daily out of his tranquillities,

They were so very few that he could pick
Between the bombs and smoke
And put them in his tattered sack
With the remains of mother's hardening cake.

Nameless dead he gathered in his eyes,
Numerous dead he gathered for me so
That I might love them, in his glances recognized,

And not die like them by terror taken ...
He filled his eyes with them, he was mistaken:
To all my battles I must go.

אָהַבְנוּ כָּאן

(מתוך מחזור סונטות)

א

אָבִי הָיָה אַרְבַּע שָׁנִים בְּמִלְחַמְתָּם,
וְלֹא שָׂנֵא אוֹיְבָיו וְלֹא אָהַב.
אֲבָל אֲנִי יוֹדֵעַ, כִּי כְּבָר שָׁם
בָּנָה אוֹתִי יוֹם־יוֹם מִשַּׁלְווֹתָיו.

הַמְעַטוֹת כָּל־כָּךְ, אֲשֶׁר לָקַט
אוֹתָן בֵּין פְּצָצוֹת וּבֵין עָשָׁן,
וְשָׂם אוֹתָן בְּתַרְמִילוֹ הַמְמָרְטָט
עִם שְׁאֵרִית עוּגַת־אִמּוֹ הַמִּתְקַשָּׁה.

וּבְעֵינָיו אָסַף מֵתִים בְּלִי שֵׁם,
מֵתִים רַבִּים אָסַף לְמַעֲנִי,
שֶׁאַכִּירֵם בְּמַבָּטָיו וְאוֹהֲבֵם

וְלֹא אָמוּת כְּמוֹהֶם בַּזְּוָעָה...
הוּא מִלֵּא עֵינָיו בָּהֶם וְהוּא טָעָה:
אֶל כָּל מִלְחֲמוֹתַי יוֹצֵא אֲנִי.

On My Birthday

Thirty-two times I went forth to my life
Each time it pained my mother less,
Pained others less,
And me more.

Thirty-two times I put on the world
And still it does not fit me.
It burdens me,
Unlike my overcoat whose shape is now
The shape of my body, comfortable
And growing worn.

Thirty-two times I went over the account
Without finding the error.
I began the story
And was not allowed to finish it.

Thirty-two years I carry with me my father's qualities
And most of them I dropped by the roadside
To ease the burden for myself.
Grass in my mouth. I wonder,
And the beam I am unable to remove from my eyes
Begins to flower with the trees in springtime.

לְיוֹם הֻלַּדְתִּי

שְׁלֹשִׁים וּשְׁתַּיִם פַּעַם יָצָאתִי אֶל חַיַּי
וּבְכָל פַּעַם מַכְאִיב פָּחוֹת לְאִמִּי,
פָּחוֹת לָאֲחֵרִים,
יוֹתֵר לְעַצְמִי.

שְׁלֹשִׁים וּשְׁתַּיִם פַּעַם אֲנִי לוֹבֵשׁ אֶת הָעוֹלָם
וְטֶרֶם הָתְאַם לִי.
הוּא מֵעִיק עָלַי,
שֶׁלֹּא כַּמְּעִיל, שֶׁצּוּרָתוֹ עַכְשָׁו צוּרַת גּוּפִי
וְהוּא נוֹחַ
וְיִתְבַּלֶּה.

שְׁלֹשִׁים וּשְׁתַּיִם פַּעַם עָבַרְתִּי עַל הַחֶשְׁבּוֹן
בְּלִי לִמְצֹא אֶת הַטָּעוּת,
הִתְחַלְתִּי אֶת הַסִּפּוּר
וְלֹא נָתְנוּ לִי לְסַיְּמוֹ.

שְׁלֹשִׁים וּשְׁתַּיִם שָׁנָה אֲנִי נוֹשֵׂא עִמִּי תְּכוּנוֹת אָבִי
וְאֶת רְבָן הִשְׁאַרְתִּי לְאֹרֶךְ הַדֶּרֶךְ,
כְּדֵי לְהָקֵל מֵעָלַי אֶת הַמַּשָּׂא.
וּבְפִי עֲשָׂבִים. וַאֲנִי תוֹהֶה,
וְהַקּוֹרָה בֵּין עֵינַי, שֶׁלֹּא אוּכַל אוֹתָהּ, לִטֹּל,
הֻחְלָה לִפְרוֹחַ בָּאֲבִיבִים עִם אִילָנוֹת.

My deeds grow fewer,
Progressively fewer,
But commentaries about them have increased:
Just as the Talmud* grows difficult
Concentrated on a page,
And Rashi* and the Tosaphists*
Enclose it on every side.

And now for the thirty-second time, :
After the thirty-second year,
I am still a parable
With no chance of a moral.
I stand without camouflage before enemy eyes,
With obsolete maps in my hands,
With growing opposition and amidst towers,
Alone without recommendations
In the great wilderness.

Leaves Without Trees

Leaves without trees
Must wander.
Blood without a body
Will not return to the basic elements,

וּמַעֲשַׂי מִתְמַעֲטִים
הָלֹךְ וְהִתְמַעֵט. אֲבָל
הַפֵּרוּשִׁים גָּדְלוּ סְבִיבָם, כְּמוֹ,
כְּשֶׁהַתַּלְמוּד נַעֲשֶׂה קָשֶׁה
וּמְצֻטְצָם בַּדַּף,
וְרַשִׁ"י וְתוֹסָפוֹת
סוֹגְרִים עָלָיו מִכָּל צַד.

וְעַכְשָׁו, אַחַר שְׁלֹשִׁים וּשְׁתַּיִם פַּעַם,
אַחַר שְׁלֹשִׁים וּשְׁתַּיִם שָׁנָה,
אֲנִי עֲדַיִן מָשָׁל,
בְּלִי סִכּוּיִים לִהְיוֹת נִמְשָׁל.
וְעוֹמֵד בְּלִי הַסְוָאָה מוּל עֵינֵי אוֹיֵב
וּמַפּוֹת מְיֻשָּׁנוֹת בְּיָדִי
בְּהִתְנַגְּדוּת הַגּוֹבֶרֶת וּבֵין מִגְדָּלִים,
וּלְבַדִּי, בְּלִי הַמְלָצוֹת
בַּמִּדְבָּר הַגָּדוֹל.

עָלִים בְּלִי אִילָנוֹת

עָלִים בְּלִי אִילָנוֹת
צְרִיכִים לִנְדוֹד.
דָּם בְּלִי גוּף,
לֹא יָשׁוּב לַגּוּפִים,

It will dry on every road.

And all words must be weaned

From the mouths

To find new ones.

The earth must be cured

Of history

And the stones need to sleep

Even that one*

That which killed Goliath must sleep, dark.

But I

Like a garage

Turned into a synagogue,

And again abandoned.

And I

Like the surveyors

Must drive sharpened hopes

With black and white sticks

Far into the desolate plain

Before me.

יִיבַשׁ בְּכָל דֶּרֶךְ,
וְכָל הַמִּלִּים צְרִיכוֹת לְהִגָּמֵל,
מִן הַפִּיּוֹת
וְלִמְצוֹא לָהֶן חֲדָשִׁים.
וּלְהַחְלִים צְרִיכָה הָאֲדָמָה
מִדִּבְרֵי הַיָּמִים.
וְלִישֹׁן צְרִיכוֹת הָאֲבָנִים
וְגַם זוֹ,
שֶׁהָרְגָה אֶת גָּלְיַת, תִּישַׁן שְׁחוֹרָה.

אֲבָל אֲנִי
כְּמוּסָךְ,
שֶׁהָפְכוּ אוֹתוֹ לְבֵית־כְּנֶסֶת,
עַכְשָׁו שׁוּב נָטוּשׁ.

אֲבָל אֲנִי,
כַּמּוֹדְדִים,
צָרִיךְ לִתְקֹעַ תִּקְווֹת מְחֻדָּדוֹת,
בְּמַקְלוֹת – שָׁחוֹר־לָבָן,
הַרְחֵק אֶל תּוֹךְ הַמִּישׁוֹר הַשּׁוֹמֵם
אֲשֶׁר לְפָנַי.

The Green Refrain

Rain comes and goes
                    The earth
Licks up abundant dew drops. Green refrain
Gushes from her throat: tree foliage, grain,
Bushes, wild grass. By the law

Of cycle following cycle, after many cycles.
And again returns the yellow summer,
Returns and rests, like locust swarm
Upon the dust.
                    Endless dance,

Eternal saraband.
                    Breakers, indifferent smash
On cliffs of existence barnacled with charm.
And profusion of sandsilt ranges stratified
Forms mounds, forms mountains.
                    Indeed,

Our most solid thoughts will not escape
The stalest conclusion rooted in
Our spastic lives. Our captive lives.
Sing your song, sing your song, bird in the net.

פִּזְמוֹן יָרֹק

גֶּשֶׁם בָּא וְהוֹלֵךְ.
הָאֲדָמָה
לוֹחֶכֶת אֶת הָרִי. פִּזְמוֹן יָרֹק
גָּח מִגְּרוֹנָהּ: עֲלְוַת־אִילָן, קָמָה,
שִׂיחִים וְעֵשֶׂב־בָּר. כְּחֹק

דּוֹר אַחַר דּוֹר אַחַר דּוֹרוֹת הַרְבֵּה.
וְשׁוּב חוֹזֵר הַקַּיִץ הַצָּהֹב,
חוֹזֵר וְנָח, כְּלַהֲקַת־אַרְבֶּה
עַל הֶעָפָר.
רִקּוּד שֶׁאֵין לוֹ סוֹף.

מָחוֹל נִצְחִי.
מִשְׁבַּר־הַסְּתָם חוֹבֵט
אֶת שׁוּנִיּוֹת־הַיֵּשׁ הַמִּצְדָּפוֹת בְּחֵן,
וְשֶׁפַע חוֹל־הַסַּחַף מִתְרַבֵּד
וְצָר גְּבָעוֹת וְצָר הָרִים.
אָכֵן,

לֹא יִמָּלְטוּ כָּל הַגִּיגֵינוּ הַשְּׁפוּיִּים
מִמַּסְקָנַת הַתֵּפֶל הַמְשֹׁרֶשֶׁת
בְּתוֹךְ עֶוֵית חַיֵּינוּ. הַשְּׁבוּיִּים.
שִׁירֵי שִׁירֵךְ, שִׁירֵי שִׁירֵךְ, צִפּוֹר בָּרֶשֶׁת!

AVRAHAM HUSS

The Command

for Shimon Halkin with esteem

Neither the paths determine, nor the goal.
The command of our being (which may strike
Among myriads of possibilities) alone creates —
Alone is able to create — the lesion

On the body of the habitual, which daily forces
The morrow into a mold, known
Beyond escape,
                          A scar which making pulse
With sharpness of unaccustomed pain, until spasm

Both chambers of the heart.
                          And then — Perhaps! —
The song may gush. Who then can ordain:
"This path of mine example is; my footsteps
Follow!" (or also: "Don't!?").
                          Far

From each known certainty the command forms
This riddle of the blessed or barren womb.
Why ever solve it disappointingly?
The paths do not determine, nor the goal.

הַצַּו

לשׁ. הלקין בהוקרה

לֹא הַדְּרָכִים קוֹבְעוֹת וְלֹא הַמַּטָּרָה.
צַו הֱוָיָתֵנוּ (זוֹ הַמִּתְחַבֶּטֶת
בֵּין רְבָבוֹת אֶפְשָׁרָיוֹת) רַק הוּא יִבְרָא –
רַק הוּא יוּכַל לִבְרֹא! – אֶת הַשָּׁרֶטֶת

בְּגוּף הַהֶרְגֵּלִים הָאֵלֶּה הַכּוֹפִים
יוֹם יוֹם אֶת הַמָּחָר אֶל דְּפוּס יָדוּעַ
עַד אֵין מוֹצָא.
שָׁרֶטֶת שֶׁתַּפְעִים,
בְּחַדְיוֹת כְּאֵב־הַלֹּא־מְרֻגָּל, עֲדֵי קִרְטוּעַ,

אֶת שְׁנֵי חַדְרֵי הַלֵּב.
וְאָז־אוּלַי! –
יִקְּלַח הַשִּׁיר. וּמִי יוּכַל לִפְסֹק:
"שְׁבִילִי שֶׁלִּי מוּפָת. בִּשְׁעָלַי
לֵךְ!" (אוֹ גַם: "אַל תֵּלֵךְ!?").
רָחוֹק

מִכָּל וַדַּאי מוּדָע נִרְקָם הַצַּו.
וְזוֹ חִידַת בְּרוּכַת־הָרֶחֶם וְהָעֲקָרָה
מַה לָּנוּ לְפָתְרָה פִּתְרוֹן אַכְזָב?
לֹא הַדְּרָכִים קוֹבְעוֹת וְלֹא הַמַּטָּרָה.

Canaan

Canaan, oh Canaan!

In Shechem, in Bethlehem

The olives murmured.

But here, my God,

The great cities storm,

Here the serpents nest.

Seven highways go up to Rome

And seven roads to the heart

But one and only one the pathway home.

Be it tranquil or storm.

Therefore, when foxes wail to every wind

We too go up to the mountain top.

Release countless circles of smoke

And opposite Beersheba's road — we watch.

Of Those Who Go, Not to Return

Not the dead today shall praise you, God!*

The pierced shall drip one by one.

And even if it is the same for us — thus, or so —

They are the ones who go and shall not return.

כְּנַעַן

כְּנַעַן, הוֹ כְּנַעַן!
בִּשְׁכֶם, בְּבֵית־לֶחֶם,
הָיוּ הַזֵּיתִים רוֹחֲשִׁים.
אַךְ כָּאן, אֱלֹהַי,
כָּאן כְּרָכִים סוֹעֲרִים,
כָּאן קְנֵי נְחָשִׁים.
שִׁבְעִים דַּרְכֵי־מֶלֶךְ עוֹלוֹת לָעִיר רוֹמָא
וְשֶׁבַע דְּרָכִים יֵשׁ לַלֵּב.
אַךְ חַד הוּא, רַק חַד הוּא הָאֹרַח הַבַּיְתָה.
יְהִי נָא סוֹעֵר, יְהִי נָא שָׁלֵו!

עַל כֵּן בְּיַלֵּל שׁוּעָלִים לְכָל רוּחַ –
אַף אָנוּ עוֹלִים לְראֹשׁ גֶּבַע,
פּוֹלְטִים טַבָּעוֹת־שֶׁל־עָשָׁן לְאֵין סְפוֹר
וְצוֹפִים – לְמוּל דֶּרֶךְ בְּאֵר־שֶׁבַע.

עַל הַהוֹלְכִים שֶׁלֹּא יָשׁוּבוּ

לֹא הַמֵּתִים הַיּוֹם יְהַלְלוּךְ, יָהּ!
אֶחָד־אֶחָד מְדַקָּרִים יָזוּבוּ.
וְאַף כִּי הֵינוּ־הַךְ הוּא לָנוּ – כָּךְ, אוֹ כָּךְ –
הֵן הֵמָּה הַהוֹלְכִים שֶׁלֹּא יָשׁוּבוּ.

Their name is covered now by darkness, Lord, my God!
They did not arrive, but one by one they went.
To his dust the murdered boy returned,
By a forest of roots his mouth was rent.

Also, our memory is poor. We shall not see far.
All who have gone — a whisper shall not bring them back.
What more, what more shall we do that we have not done to you?
What more, our brother, by deceit trapped?

For not forever shall your girl there weep many tears
And not forever shall she look down.
In the village where you were born the bells hum
As if you had not come and had not gone.

And man's soul? Does it live forever?
Who shall tell us so, in kindness or angry pain?
Better the live dog than the dead lion,*
For life will not be given us again.

שָׁמָם יְכַסֶּה עַתָּה בַחֹשֶׁךְ, יָהּ־אֵלִי!
אֶחָד־אֶחָד הָלְכוּ וְלֹא הִגִּיעוּ.
חָזַר לַעֲפָרוֹ הַנַּעַר הֶהָרוּג
וְיַעַר שָׁרָשִׁים נָחַר אֶל פִּיהוּ.

אַף זִכְרוֹנֵנוּ דַל. וְלֹא נַרְחִיק רְאוֹת.
כָּל מִי אֲשֶׁר הָלַךְ – לֹא יַחְזִירֶנּוּ לַחַשׁ.
מָה עוֹד, מַה נְּעוֹלֵל – וְלֹא עוֹלַלְנוּ לָךְ?
מָה עוֹד, אָחִינוּ, נִסְבְּךְ בְּכַחַשׁ?

כִּי לֹא לָעַד שָׁם תֵּבְךְ נַעֲרָתְךָ, רַב בְּכִי
וְלֹא לָעַד תַּשְׁפֵּל עֵינֶיהָ מַטָּה.
בִּכְפַר מוֹלַדְתְּךָ, – הוֹמִים פַּעֲמוֹנִים
כְּאִלּוּ לֹא הָלַכְתָּ, אַף לֹא בָאתָ.

וְנֶפֶשׁ הָאָדָם? הַהִיא הוֹיָה לָעַד?
מִי יַגִּידֶנּוּ כֵּן, לְחֶסֶד אוֹ לְזַעַם?
כֹּה טוֹב לְכֶלֶב חַי מִן הָאֲרִי הַמֵּת,
כִּי הַחַיִּים לֹא יִנָּתְנוּ עוֹד פָּעַם.

TUVIA RIVNER

The Fire in the Stone

Y.L.

Also in sleep I see you, comprehend,
And my fear streams to the joy
As I myself stream to your hand.

As the rainbow leans on the cloud,
The wind on the trunk of the tree,
The head upon the shoulder, you lean on me.

In your heart, returned as in the ark,
I crossed alive the water's terrored dark.

Shaken free of all, endless, you dwell in me alone
As I dwell in my bones.

As within stone the fire rests,
As within nothingness being nests.

In me your voice speaks, love wrought.
We have become one in thought.

הָאֵשׁ אֲשֶׁר בָּאֶבֶן

י. ל.

גַּם בַּשֵּׁנָה אֲנִי רוֹאֶה אוֹתְךָ
וּפַחֲדִי זוֹרֵם אֶל הַשִּׂמְחָה
כָּמוֹנִי הַזּוֹרֵם אֶל תּוֹךְ יָדְךָ.

כְּהִשָּׁעֵן הַקֶּשֶׁת עַל עָנָן,
הָרוּחַ עַל גּוּפוֹ שֶׁל הָאִילָן,
רֹאשׁ עַל כָּתֵף, אַתָּה עָלַי נִשְׁעָן.

וּבְלִבְּךָ יָשׁוּב כְּמוֹ בַתֵּבָה
עָבַרְתִּי חַי אֶת מֵי הַזַּעֲוָה.

נָעוּר מִכֹּל – תָּגוּר בִּי עַד־אֵין־דַּי
כְּמוֹ אֲנִי אָגוּר בְּעַצְמוֹתַי.

כְּמוֹ בָּאֶבֶן תִּתְגּוֹרֵר הָאֵשׁ.
כְּמוֹ בָּאַיִן מְקַנֵּן הַיֵּשׁ

קוֹלְךָ בִּי מְדַבֵּר בְּאַהֲבָה.
הָיִינוּ לְאֶחָד בַּמַּחֲשָׁבָה.

Lullaby

The nocturnal, my panther, has eyes that spark,
His teeth flash in the dark, in dark,
His claw is sharp as the razor blade,
Sleep, my child, in the forest glade!

If you sleep and nap, my God's pity prevails,
And you shall not see mother draw in a pail
The blue eyes of the light
To water the creator of night.

Close your eyelids, sleep as you are,
In the sky hangs a merciful star,
On mother's forehead a star again,
My panther is lurking in vain
At night, at night in the forest glade,
In dream at your throat like a razor blade.

The Wicked Clamor

The wicked clamor, my ear grows deaf.
They sit six days in my soul,
When shall the Sabbath free my captivity

שִׁיר עֶרֶשׂ

הַלֵּילִי, נְמֵרִי, לוֹ עֵינַיִם דּוֹלְקוֹת,
בַּחֹשֶׁךְ בַּחֹשֶׁךְ שִׁנָּיו בּוֹרְקוֹת,
צִפֹּרֶן חַדָּה־לוֹ כַּתַּעַר,
נוּמָה, יַלְדִּי, בַּיַּעַר!

אִם תִּישַׁן, אִם תָּנוּם, יְרַחֵם אֵלִי,
לֹא תִרְאֶה אֶת אִמְּךָ שׁוֹאֶבֶת בִּדְלִי
אֶת עֵינֵי־הָאוֹרָה הַתְּכֵלוֹת
לְהַשְׁקוֹת אֶת בּוֹרֵא־הַלֵּילוֹת.

סְגֹר עַפְעַפֶּיךָ וְנוּם,
בַּשָּׁמַיִם כּוֹכָב רַחוּם,
עַל מֵצַח־אִמְּךָ כּוֹכָב.
נְמֵרִי אוֹרֵב לַשָּׁוְא
בַּחֹשֶׁךְ בַּחֹשֶׁךְ, בַּיַּעַר,
בַּחֲלוֹם עַל גְּרוֹנְךָ כְּמוֹ תָעַר.

הָרְשָׁעִים רוֹעֲשִׁים

הָרְשָׁעִים רוֹעֲשִׁים, אָזְנִי חֵרְשָׁה,
הֵם יוֹשְׁבִים בְּנַפְשִׁי יָמִים שִׁשָּׁה,
מָתַי תָּשִׁיב שַׁבָּת שְׁבוּתִי

And I provide again for my household,

Break with hands the whole

Daily bread of mercy, crusted gold?

And in silence also hear water's sound,

And my despair not bark again?

I shall be able to touch you then!

Sunflower

Fiery wheel without beginning,

Fiery wheel without an end.

The revolving sword of flame.

In dance the wings of cherubim

About an eye dark and flickering

About a heart dark and dumb.

וְאֶעֱשֶׂה־שׁוּב לְבֵיתִי
וּבְיָדִי אֶבְצַע, תָּמִים,
אֶת לֶחֶם־חָק־הָרַחֲמִים
זְהוּב־הַגּוּף? וְגַם אֶשְׁמַע
אֶת קוֹל־הַמַּיִם בַּדְּמָמָה
וְיֵאוּשִׁי לֹא עוֹד יֻנְבַּח
וְשׁוּב אוּכַל לָגַעַת בָּךְ!

חַמָּנִית

גַּלְגַּל הָאוֹר לְלֹא רֵאשִׁית,
גַּלְגַּל הָאוֹר לְלֹא אַחֲרִית,
חֶרֶב הָאֵשׁ הַמִּתְהַפֶּכֶת,
כַּנְפֵי כְּרוּבִים בִּמְחוֹלָם
סְבִיב עַיִן אֲפֵלָה, דּוֹעֶכֶת,
סְבִיב לֵב אָפֵל וְנֶאֱלָם.

OMER HILLEL

Sun

A thousand years I was sick with darkness,

And my veins whispered darkness instead of blood.

The sun rose and set — I did not see it.

    For I was very sick with darkness,

    The night shut its gates around me.

Then I was as one who walks on clouds and, behold, they are not clouds

        but thoughts —

Then whipped I crouched to shout lightning, to weep rainstorms.

    But no wind came to me.

    Only death gnawed at my throat,

And my heart, paralyzed and impotent, would not bear me life and blood.

Nightmare frightened me to escape myself,

I fled from earth's end to the ends of earth.

    My feet shouted distances — distances,

Deceived into believing that in distances is the end of all darkness,

That everything there is radiant!

And, behold, there, knives of darkness sparkled against me,

    night's gates were high.

My feet fell away from me, terrible terrible stumbling.

My soul saddened to know the sun outside weeps toward my flesh,

The sun outside weeps toward my eyes — the weeping of awful light.

שֶׁמֶשׁ

אֶלֶף שָׁנָה חָלִיתִי חֹשֶׁךְ
וְעוֹרְקַי לָחֲשׁוּ חֹשֶׁךְ תַּחַת דָּם.
וְהַשֶּׁמֶשׁ יָצְאָה וּבָאָה – וַאֲנִי לֹא רְאִיתִיהָ.
כִּי חָלִיתִי חֹשֶׁךְ מְאֹד,
וְלַיְלָה סָגַר עָלַי שְׁעָרִים.
אָז הָיִיתִי כְּמִתְהַלֵּךְ עַל עֲנָנִים, וְהִנֵּה לֹא עֲנָנִים, כִּי
מַחֲשָׁבוֹת –
אָז שַׁחוֹתִי צָלוּף – לִצְעֹק בָּרָק, אוֹ לִבְכּוֹת סוּפוֹת
הַגְּשָׁמִים.

וְרוּחַ לֹא בָּאָה אֵלַי.
רַק הַמָּוֶת כִּרְסֵם גְּרוֹנִי,
וְהִנֵּה לִבִּי שָׁתוּק וְעָקָר לֹא יוֹלִיד לִי חַיִּים וָדָם.

וְהַבַּלָּהָה אֲחָזַתְנִי לִבְרֹחַ מִפָּנַי,
וָאָנוּס מִיַּרְכְּתֵי תֵבֵל עַד יַרְכְּתֶיהָ.
וְרַגְלַי צוֹעֲקוֹת מֶרְחַקִּים־מֶרְחַקִּים,
כַּאֲשֶׁר נִפְתְּחוּ הָיוּ לְהַאֲמִין בִּי בַּמֶּרְחַקִּים קֵץ כָּל חֹשֶׁךְ,
שֵׂכֶל אֲשֶׁר שָׁם – הוּא הַמֵּאִיר!
וְהִנֵּה סָבִיב נוֹצְצוֹת עָלַי סַכִּינֵי הַחֹשֶׁךְ, וְשַׁעֲרֵי הַלַּיְלָה
גְּבֹהִים.

וְרַגְלַי נָפְלוּ מִמֶּנִּי. אֵימוֹת־אֵימוֹת־כִּשָּׁלוֹן.
וְנַפְשִׁי עָצְבָה לָדַעַת, כִּי הַשֶּׁמֶשׁ בַּחוּץ בּוֹכָה אֶל בְּשָׂרִי,
כִּי הַשֶּׁמֶשׁ בַּחוּץ בּוֹכָה אֶל עֵינַי – בְּכִי־נוֹרָא־אוֹר.

And, alas, I am cast dark within myself

And deep are the anguishes of darkness in my chambers.

In the darkness I despaired of morning and I said it would not come.

    Morning will not come within me for it paces, paces outside,

And I am cast — And I am dark within myself.

But suddenly I shouted

    Sun!

    For you I shall be morning!

At once I was utterly shattered, from within the soul's rose blossomed in me.

    Or a woman's hand touched my soul,

    Or a bird sang above its chords.

Inanimate the gates of night fell about me.

Here in the place of my being's darkness, I stormed whirlwind of light

And my flesh, white out of darkness, was not flesh but sun!

Sun!

I said, I shall sing aloud, and I spoke light!

When I trampled my thought clouds, I grew suddenly light as wind,

    My body bereft of thought

    Struck waves of light, seas upon seas.

Then I laughed at fleeing darkness,

Not as a foe whose rear guard is captured, but like he whom death's fear seized,

    Whose feet wind grasped.

וַאֲנִי אֻלְלַי־אֻלְלַי. מֻטָּל חָשֵׁךְ בְּתוֹכִי
וַעֲמֻקִים יִסּוּרֵי־הַחֹשֶׁךְ בַּחֲדָרָי.
וּבַחֹשֶׁךְ נוֹאַשְׁתִּי מִן הַבֹּקֶר וְאָמַרְתִּי בִּי לֹא יָבוֹא.
לֹא יָבוֹא בִּי עוֹד הַבֹּקֶר כִּי יִתְהַלֵּךְ־יִתְהַלֵּךְ בַּחוּץ,
וַאֲנִי מֻטָּל – וְהִנֵּה חָשֵׁךְ בְּתוֹכִי.

אַךְ פִּתְאֹם צָעַקְתִּי:
שֶׁמֶשׁ!
אֲנִי אֱהִי לָךְ בֹּקֶר!
וּלְפֶתַע נִשְׁבַּרְתִּי כֵּלִי וּפָקַע בִּי שׁוֹשַׁן הַנֶּפֶשׁ מִבִּפְנִים.
אוֹ נָגְעָה בְּנַפְשִׁי יַד־אִשָּׁה,
אוֹ צִפּוֹר שׁוֹרְרָה עַל מֵיתָרֶיהָ.
דּוֹמְמִים נָפְלוּ שַׁעֲרֵי הַלַּיְלָה סָבִיב.
וְהִנֵּה תַּחַת חֹשֶׁךְ־עוֹרְקַי סָעַרְתִּי סוּפַת הָאוֹר
וּבְשָׂרִי הַלָּבָן מֵחֹשֶׁךְ הָיָה לֹא־בָשָׂר – כִּי שֶׁמֶשׁ!

שֶׁמֶשׁ!
אָמַרְתִּי, אָשִׁירָה בְּקוֹלִי וְהִנֵּה דִּבַּרְתִּי אוֹר!
וְכִי דָרַכְתִּי עַנְגֵי־מַחְשְׁבוֹתַי, קַלּוֹתִי פֶּתַע כָּרוּחַ,
וְגוּפִי חֲסַר מַחֲשָׁבוֹת –
מֻכֶּה גַלֵּי־אוֹר יָמִים־יָמִים.

אָז צָחַקְתִּי לַחֹשֶׁךְ הַנָּס,
לֹא כַּצַּר הַנִּמְלָט יְזַנֵּב לַשְּׁבִי, כִּי כְמִי אֲחָזוֹ פַחַד־מָוֶת
וְרַגְלָיו לָפְתָה רוּחַ.

Silent I laughed the wondrous joy,

Silent I sang within myself choirs of light.

My soul still recalled deep anguish of darkness, its chambers fell,

    I did not dream to ascend all the pinnacles of light

    For transcending my soul's understanding, sky above sky.

Then I laughed at the folly of sciences. They say the sun is round,

    Circles in its orbit.

Why, it has neither form nor path

    Save the being of eternal light!

Light!

My soul laughed light,

My flesh spoke sun instead of blood —

For I did not wait for the morning to come to me from outside —

    But I shouted, I shall be sun!

Then from within the soul's rose blossomed in me,

Or a woman's hand touched my soul,

Or a bird sang above its chords.

And I awoke radiating the suddenly-forever.

    And I radiated the morning from my flesh.

דּוּמָם צָחַקְתִּי נִפְלָא־אֹשֶׁר,

דּוּמָם נִגַּנְתִּי בִּי מִקְהֲלוֹת הָאוֹר,

וּבְעוֹד נִזְכְּרָה נַפְשִׁי עֹמֶק יְסוּרֵי הַחֹשֶׁךְ, רָדוּ חֲדָרֶיהָ,

לֹא חָלַמְתִּי עֲלוֹת כָּל גָּבְהֵי הָאוֹר,

כִּי גָּבְהוּ מִבִּינַת נַפְשִׁי שָׁמַיִם עַל שָׁמַיִם.

אָז צָחַקְתִּי אִוֶּלֶת הַמַּדָּעִים. הַגִּידוּ עֶגְלָה הַשֶּׁמֶשׁ,

הוֹלֶכֶת־סוֹבֶבֶת בִּמְסִלָּתָהּ.

הֲלֹא אֵין צוּרָה לָהּ וָדֶרֶךְ

כִּי הָיִיתָ אוֹר־עוֹלָם!

אוֹר,

אוֹר צָחֲקָה נַפְשִׁי

וּבְשָׂרִי דִּבֶּר שֶׁמֶשׁ תַּחַת דָּם –

כִּי לֹא חִכִּיתִי לַבֹּקֶר – יָבוֹא אֵלַי מִבַּחוּץ –

כִּי צָעַקְתִּי אֱהִי שֶׁמֶשׁ!

וּפָקַע בִּי שׁוֹשַׁן הַנֶּפֶשׁ מִבִּפְנִים

אוֹ נָגְעָה בְּנַפְשִׁי יַד אִשָּׁה,

אוֹ צִפּוֹר שׁוֹרְרָה עַל מֵיתָרֶיהָ,

וָאִיקַץ וָאָאוֹר פִּתְאֹם־עוֹלָמִים,

וְזָרַחְתִּי הַבֹּקֶר מִבְּשָׂרִי!

T. CARMI

René's Songs*

First Song

Bright-haired am I, my face and body white.
Bright as my mother's hair;
White as my father's silence;
The day he ascended in the smoky chariots,*
Why did Lo-Imi* whisper in the frosty light that hour!
        — René, you are the black flower.

In my lungs, the blood lurks
For the frost's white, the sheet's white,
Decay gnaws my teeth —
        Is that why?

My bread is not moldy now,
Against my hunger
Again no one connives;
But night after night the corn bread
Still heaped under my mattress,
Lurks,
Humped,
For my midnight hunger.
        Is that why?

שִׁירוֹ שֶׁל רָנֵי

שיר ראשון

בְּהִיר־שֵׂעָר, לְבֶן־פָּנִים־וָגֵו אֲנִי.
בָּהִיר כְּשַׂעֲרוֹת אִמִּי;
לָבָן כִּדְמוּמַיַּת אָבִי,
יוֹם בּוֹ עָלָה בְּמַרְכְּבוֹת־עָשָׁן,
וְלָמָּה לָאֲטָה לִי לֹא־אִמִּי לְאוֹר־הַכְּפוֹר:
– רָנֵי, אַתָּה הַפֶּרַח הַשָּׁחוֹר.

בִּרְאוֹתַי אוֹרֵב הַדָּם
לְלֹבֶן כְּפוֹר, סָדִין,
וּבְשֹׁנֵי כּוֹסֵס הַמַּק –
הֲמִשּׁוּם כָּךְ?

לַחְמִי אֵינוֹ עָבֵשׁ עַתָּה;
שׁוּב אֵין זוֹמֵם לְהַעֲרִים
עַל רַעֲבוֹנִי;
אַךְ לַיְלָה־לַיְלָה־לַיְלָה לֶחֶם־הַתִּירָס
עוֹד נֶעֱרָם מִתַּחַת מִזְרָנִי,
אוֹרֵב,
קְמוּר־גַּב,
לְרַעֲבוֹן־חֲצוֹת שֶׁלִּי –
הֲמִשּׁוּם כָּךְ?

I said to her:

> Jacques' nose is scarred;
>
> My brother was clear faced.
>
> Marcel's eyes are vengeful;
>
> My father's eyes are only haunted.
>
> Jeannine's hands are sticky;
>
> My sister's hands, frost on the forehead —
>
> > Is that why?

I said to her:

> And you
>
> With the warm, soft brown hair,
>
> You are not
>
> My mother —
>
> Brown hair,
>
> > Is that why?

What did she see and hear in the frost's light that hour

That she whispered so:

> — René, you are the black flower?

Second Song

My brothers are big, so much bigger than I.

All of them sit on the branches high.

אָמַרְתִּי לָהּ:

אֵפוֹ שֶׁל זַ׳קוֹ מְצֻלָּק;

אָחִי הָיָה טְהָר־פָּנִים.

עֵינֵי מַרְסֶל נוֹקְמָנִיּוֹת;

עֵינֵי אָבִי – רַק מְרֻדָּפוֹת.

יָדֵי זַ׳נִין שַׁמְנוּנִיּוֹת;

יַד אֲחוֹתִי – כִּכְפוֹר עַל מֵצַח –

הֲמִשּׁוּם כָּךְ?

אָמַרְתִּי לָהּ:

וְאַתְּ,

חוֹמַת שֵׂעָר חָמִים וָרַךְ,

אַתְּ לֹא –

אִמִּי,

חוֹמַת־שֵׂעָר –

הֲמִשּׁוּם כָּךְ?

מָה רָאֲתָה וּמַה שָׁמְעָה לְאוֹר־הַכְּפוֹר

שֶׁכָּךְ תִּלְאַט:

– רְנֵי, אַתָּה הַפֶּרַח הַשָּׁחוֹר?

שִׁיר שֵׁנִי

אַחַי גְּדוֹלִים הֵם, כֹּה גְדוֹלִים מִמֶּנִּי.

כֻּלָּם יוֹשְׁבִים בֵּין אַמִּירִים.

My father's voice rises from the sky.
It whispers to mother, returning birds fly.

My brothers are big, so much bigger than I.
They rejoice with the wind at a star's touch.
My father barks from the heights of the night.
To me mother murmurs: "Now, René, come up."

My brothers, blood lurks for each cough.
With each loaf of bread the mouth kisses pain.
Father, tomorrow the spring will soar at you.
Mother, tomorrow my spellbound voice will be changed.

Third Song

Lo-Imi, Lo-Imi!
From the garden I call you
I stand by the bamboo tree.
Come please to the veranda to see the wonder,
To caress the bud.

For I woke at midnight to pay my night's debt
I stretched my hand into darkness;
As always, into darkness —
But my midnight hunger did not take it;

וְקוֹל אָבִי עוֹלֶה מִן הַשָּׁמַיִם.
לָאֵם לוֹאֵט עַל שׁוּב הַצִּפֳּרִים.

אַחַי גְּדוֹלִים הֵם, כֹּה גְּדוֹלִים מִמֶּנִּי.
כֻּלָּם שָׂשִׂים עִם רוּחַ אֵל מַגַּע כּוֹכָב.
אָבִי נוֹבֵחַ מִגָּבְהֵי־הַלַּיְלָה.
אִמִּי לוֹאֶטֶת לִי: עֲלֵה, רְנִי, עַכְשָׁיו.

עַל כָּל שָׁעוּל אוֹרֵב הַדָּם, אַחַי,
עִם כָּל כִּכָּר הַפֶּה נוֹשֵׁק מַכְאוֹב.
מָחָר, אָבִי, אָבִיב־יַמְרִיא עָלֶיךָ.
אִמִּי, מָחָר יֹאבַד קוֹלִי־מֵאוֹב.

שיר שלישי

לֹא־אִמִּי, לֹא־אִמִּי!
אֲנִי קוֹרֵא לָךְ מֵהַגָּן.
אֲנִי עוֹמֵד לְיַד עֵץ הַבַּמְבּוּק.
צְאִי־נָא לַגְּזוּזְטְרָה לַחֲזוֹת בַּפֶּלֶא,
לְלַטֵּף נִצָּן.

כִּי קַמְתִּי בַּחֲצוֹת לִפְרֹעַ חוֹב־לֵילִי.
שָׁלַחְתִּי אֶת יָדִי לָאֲפֵלָה,
כְּמוֹ תָמִיד, לָאֲפֵלָה –
וְרַעֲבוֹן־חֲצוֹת שֶׁלִּי לֹא נִטְלָה;

In vain I sought the humped backs —
They were gone.

Then I heard at midnight
(song dearest of songs)
How the wind is piping in the bamboo:
      Melted the frost-frozen hours.
      There are no black flowers.

I called out:
      Marcel, merciful eyed,
      Jacques, pure faced,
      Jeannine, soft hands,
      Awake,
      Waken, embrace me in the dance of pipes...

Then I saw at midnight
Clouds pregnant with moon
Swell in the ripe aura
And a silver thread fastening their edges.

Then I saw at midnight
How an almond tree
Glides suddenly to your window
Like the scented snow;

לַשָּׁוְא בִּקַּשְׁתִּי אֶת קְמוּרֵי הַגַּב —
אֵינָם.

וְאָז שָׁמַעְתִּי בַּחֲצוֹת
(שִׁיר יָקָר לִי מִשִּׁירִים)
כֵּיצַד הָרוּחַ בַּבַּמְבּוּק מְחַלְּלָה:
נָמַסּוּ הַכְּפוֹרִים.
אֵין פְּרָחִים שְׁחוֹרִים.

קָרָאתִי:
מַרְסֵל חֲנוּן־עֵינַיִם,
זַ'קוֹ טְהוֹר־פָּנִים,
זַ'נִין רַכַּת־יָדַיִם,
עוּרוּ,
עוּרוּ וְחַבְּקוּנִי בִּמְחוֹל־הַחֲלִילִים...

וְאָז רָאִיתִי בַּחֲצוֹת
עָבִים הֲרֵי־לְבָנָה
תּוֹפְחִים בַּגֹּגַּה הַבָּשֵׁל
וְחוּט־הַכֶּסֶף שׁוּלֵיהֶם הוֹדֵק.

וְאָז רָאִיתִי בַּחֲצוֹת
כֵּיצַד גּוֹלְשָׁה לְפֶתַע
שְׁקֵדִיָּה אֶל חַלּוֹנֵךְ
בַּשֶּׁלֶג הַבָּשׂוּם;

Breaks into your room
With stunning abundance;
Breaks through to your heart
With white blossoms ashower —

There are no black flowers.

Lo-Imi, my mother!
Please come to the veranda
Look at me here in the garden.
Listen to the fragrance of the tiding.

When the pipes break forth
From the tender bamboo trunk
Swaying in the wind;
When the Chevreaux valley
Sparkles like a many-colored vase;

When the shining bud sings
I fasten my mouth
To the pipe
And spring melodies break forth and rise
Out of this damaged lung of mine
From between my decaying teeth —

פּוֹרֶצֶת אֶל הַדֶּרֶךְ
בַּשֶּׁפַע הַהוֹמֶם;
הוֹרֶסֶת אֶל לִבֵּךְ
בְּנִצָּנֶיהָ הַצְּחוֹרִים –

אֵין פְּרָחִים שְׁחוֹרִים.

לֹא־אִמִּי, אִמִּי!
צְאִי־נָא לַגְּזוּזְטְרָה.
רְאִינִי כָּאן, בַּגַּן.
הַקְשִׁיבִי בְּשֵׁם־הַבְּשׂוֹרָה:

בִּבְקַע חֲלִילִים
מִגֶּזַע הַבַּמְבּוּק הָרַךְ,
הַנָּע לָרוּחַ;
בִּבְהֹק גֵּיא־הַשֶּׁוְרוּו
כַּאֲגַרְטֵל רְוֵה־גָּנָן;

בְּרֹן נִצָּן זָהוּר –
מַצְמִיד אֲנִי אֶת פִּי
אֶל הֶחָלִיל
וּמַנְגִּינַת אָבִיב בּוֹקַעַת וְעוֹלָה
מִתּוֹךְ זוֹ רְאָתִי פְּגוּמָה,
מִבֵּין שְׁנֵי הַנְּמַקוֹת –

My mother, my mother!
Like the almond tree I burst in Spring's heart,
Into the heart of Springtime with lively pipes.

There are no black flowers!

She Sleeps

She sleeps: yet is her hand awake
More than the surgeon's palm
To breathe, to pulse, to smell,
To murmur of the dirge that hidden breaks.

She sleeps: but cocked remain her ears
For the chill metal's clink, the glide
Of heavy eyelid. Always she bides
For sudden silence and malaise.

She sleeps: still her eye she keeps
On you, on falling leaves, on rushing Spring,
On the next to die, on the soul of living things,
Peace to her dream. She sleeps.

Yet cuts her faithful fingering
Till sunset in the living flesh.

אִמִּי, אִמִּי!
אֶל לֵב־אָבִיב אֲנִי פּוֹרֵץ כַּשְּׁקֵדִיָּה,
אֶל לֵב־אָבִיב בַּחֲלִילִים עֵרִים –

אֵין פְּרָחִים שְׁחוֹרִים!

הִיא יְשֵׁנָה

הִיא יְשֵׁנָה; אֲבָל יָדָהּ עֵרָה
יוֹתֵר מִכַּף־יָדוֹ שֶׁל הַמְנַתֵּחַ
לָרוּחַ וְלַדֹּפֶק וְלָרֵיחַ,
לְרַחַשׁ הַקִּינָה הַמִּסְתָּרָה.

הִיא יְשֵׁנָה; אֲבָל אָזְנָהּ פְּקוּחָה
לְקִישׁ מַתֶּכֶת קְרִירָה וְנִיד
עַפְעַף כָּבֵד. הִיא עֲרוּכָה תָּמִיד
לְדוּמִיַּת־פִּתְאֹם וְלַמְּבוּכָה.

הִיא יְשֵׁנָה; אֲבָל בָּךְ עֵינָהּ,
בְּפַחַז הָאָבִיב וּבַשַּׁלֶּכֶת,
בַּמֵּת הַבָּא, וּבְנִשְׁמַת־כָּל־חַי...
שָׁלוֹם לַחֲלוֹמָהּ. הִיא יְשֵׁנָה.

אֲבָל יָדָהּ הָאֱמוּנָה חוֹתֶכֶת
עַד בּוֹא הַשֶּׁמֶשׁ בַּבָּשָׂר הַחַי.

Cat in the Dovecote

He climbed, devoured. In her mouth
Nothing will remain,
And she will not return to the ark.*

Satisfied and tranquil
He glides on velvet paws,
His knives padded,
Until he finds a resting place
And picks the bones.

A drizzle.
Only a drizzle.
There will be no deluge again.

חָתוּל בַּשּׂוֹבָךְ

עָלָה, טָרַף. בְּפִיהָ
לֹא יִהְיֶה עוֹד דָּבָר,
וְלֹא תוֹסִיף לָשׁוּב אֶל הַתֵּבָה.

הַשְׁלֵים וּבְשָׁלוֹם
יַחְלִיק עַל קְטִיפוֹתָיו,
סַכִּינָיו מְרֻפָּדוֹת.
עַד יִמָּצֵא מָנוֹחַ לְרַגְלָיו,
וִיגָרֵם.

זַרְזִיף.
זַרְזִיף בִּלְבַד.
מַבּוּל לֹא יִהְיֶה עוֹד.

Sunbeams

Do not allow the sun to dim.

Out of paper, friendship, smiles,

Cut many suns

As one cuts cookies with the glass's rim.

Let it be round,

Rays extending from it

(They'll say: make believe!)

Two lines like two hands,

Outspread with a fistful of seeds,

Two lines like two feet,

Tracing love on the ground,

Give it many rays —

Don't be grudging —

As many as will stretch

From you to the people around.

קַרְנַיִם

אַל תִּתֵּן לַשֶּׁמֶשׁ לִכְבּוֹת.
מִנְּיָר, מֵאַהֲוָה, חִיּוּכִים,
גְּזֹר שְׁמָשׁוֹת לָרֹב
בְּפִי הַכּוֹס, כְּמַעֲשֵׂה עוּגוֹת.

תֵּן לָהּ לִהְיוֹת עָגוֹל,
וְקַוִּים יוֹצְאִים מִמֶּנּוּ
(יֹאמְרוּ: בְּדָיָה!):
שְׁנֵי קַוִּים כִּשְׁתֵּי יָדַיִם
פְּשׁוּטוֹת עִם חֹפֶן הַזֶּרַע,
שְׁנֵי קַוִּים: כִּשְׁתֵּי רַגְלַיִם
הַכּוֹתְבוֹת אַהֲבָה לָאָרֶץ,
וְתֵן לָהּ הַרְבֵּה קַוִּים –
אַל תַּחְסֹךְ –
כַּמִּסְפָּר הַנִּתָּן לְהִמָּתַח
מִמְּךָ אֶל הָאֲנָשִׁים סָבִיב.

YEHIEL MAR

Handfuls of Wind

All that I have —
Handfuls of wind,*
A gift for the kingdom of birds.

All the silences —
A throatful — small silences,
A present
For the stone and the doe.

All the illumination —
Flask of illumination,
For the sea of rising dawn
An offering.

With all one's heart
With all one's might
As both innocent and guilty.

And my eyes shall not see
The ocean overflowing
Its banks...

מְלֹא חָפְנַיִם רוּחַ

כָּל מַה שֶּׁיֵּשׁ לִי –
מְלֹא חָפְנַיִם רוּחַ,
שַׁי לְמַמְלֶכֶת צִפֳּרִים.

כָּל הַשְּׁתִיקוֹת –
מְלֹא הַגָּרוֹן מְעַט שְׁתִיקוֹת
מַתָּת
לָאֶבֶן וְלָאַיָּלָה.

כָּל הַמָּאוֹר –
צְלוֹחִית הַמָּאוֹר.
לְיָם הַשַּׁחַר הָעוֹלֶה
מַשְּׂאֵת.

בְּלֵב שָׁלֵם
בְּכָל הַמְּאֹד
כְּזוֹכֶה וְחַיָּב.

וְעֵינַי לֹא תֶחֱזֶינָה
בַּעֲבֹר הַיָּם
עַל גְּדוֹתָיו...

NOTES ON THE POEMS

(All biblical citations and quotations are from
Holy Scriptures according to the Masoretic text
[Jewish Publication Society of America, 1962].)

BIALIK
The Pool, pp. 2–19

PRESENCE. The visual presence of God (Shekinah) manifested
as light or illumination. In Cabbala the feminine principle,
the emanation through which the natural world is created.
According to legend, the Shekinah took upon herself the state
of exile so that she might accompany the Jewish people in
their suffering and be their comforter.

ELIJAH. The prophet who was taken to heaven alive in the
fiery chariot. According to legend, he wanders the earth to
reveal himself as a bearer of good tidings. It is said that he will
bring the tidings of the coming of the Messiah and go before
him.

And If the Angel Should Ask, pp. 24–29

GEMARA. The Passages of Talmud which deal with *halakah* or
law. The subject of exegesis based on biblical text as codified
in the Mishnah.

FRINGES *(zizit)*. They were worn at the four corners of the
prayer shawl, and were a reminder of the duties toward the
holy law and of God's love for Israel. Made according to
certain specifications, they were considered defective when
they became torn or altered and had to be replaced.

SMALL PRAYER SHAWL. Although a large prayer shawl was
used during devotional services, in daily life it was customary
for young boys and pious men to wear a small prayer shawl
with their clothing.

I Have a Garden, pp. 28–35

BRIDAL CANOPY. It is customary for a Jewish wedding to be
performed under a velvet canopy supported by four poles.

347

TCHERNICHOVSKY

To the Sun, pp. 38–45

The dedication to the sonnet sequence is taken from the second Order of Mishnah called *Moed,* and a Tractate called *Sukkah* deals with the Feast of Tabernacles.

IRIS AND THE ANEMONE. In the Hebrew text the iris and the anemone are called "Hyacinthus and Adonis." These words denote the mythical flower springing from the spilled blood of these two, beloved of Venus. The poet uses this allusion not only in the specific Greek sense but also in the broader Mediterranean connotation of nature worship.

SHEBA'S TRADERS. The merchants who brought gold dust and spices from Ethiopia, the land of the legendary queen.

THE IMAGE-KINGDOM'S IDOL OF THE GENERATION PAST. After enumerating the various deities of Greek and Mediterranean origin, in addition to his own, which drew him through history, Tchernichovsky, the poet-physician, designates Science the deity of the generation preceding his. "The image-kingdom's idol" is thus exemplified by the Theory of Evolution as developed by Darwin.

Levivot, pp. 44–67

In contemporary Hebrew, *levivot* means pancakes. In this poem, however, the poet refers to a dough filled with cheese, then boiled in hot water and washed with buttermilk.

TZENA URENA. A collection of Midrash (imaginative stories interpreting verses of the Bible) which were written in Yiddish for women.

SUPPLICATIONS OF SARA BAT-TUVIM. A book of prayers used particularly by women.

UNCLEAN BLEMISH. Books in a foreign language were considered dangerous by the extremely pious, who feared their contamination.

THE FORTRESS OF PETER AND PAUL. In Czarist Russia political prisoners and those active in revolutionary movements were confined here.

The Bells, pp. 66–71

THUNDER OF BELLS. In Russia and Poland the ringing of church bells often aroused the mob during a pogrom.

HAIDAMAKS. Armed bands of rebellious peasants headed by

Cossack leaders in the first half of the eighteenth century.

TORAH SCROLL. The parchment scrolls upon which the books of the Bible are inscribed and kept in the Ark in synagogues.

"THIRTY-SIX JUST." According to legend and folklore, there are thirty-six righteous men in each generation who live anonymous, humble lives. Their acts of humane piety and simple human kindness merit for the world the divine grace that prevents its destruction.

PRAYER FOR THE DEAD. The Kaddish is the traditional prayer that glorifies and sanctifies the name of God, thereby affirming the immortality of the soul. The first part of the "Lord's Prayer" is derived from this prayer.

THE WATCH OF THE MIDNIGHT HOUR. The watch called *Tikkun Hazot* (an act of mending) when the pious rise at midnight to mourn the destruction of the temple and the dispersion of the people. In legend it was the possible moment of miracle.

They Say There Is a Country, pp. 70–73

SEVEN PILLARS. The seven pillars of wisdom.

SEVEN WANDERING STARS. The ancient term for the planets that moved through the firmament.

AKIBA. The Rabbinic teacher who was burned alive by the Romans because he encouraged the rebellion against Rome in the first century.

MACCÁBEE. The popular name given the Hasmonean family who led the revolt against the Selucid dynasty of Syria in the second century, B.C.E. Emperor Antiochus Epiphanes attempted the forcible conversion of the Jews to the Greek religion. The Syrian Greeks were driven from the country and Hebrew sovereignty reëstablished. Maccábee means *hammer*, and it is also the acrostic in Hebrew of the first letters of a motto, "Who Is Like Thee Oh God." In modern Hebrew *Maccábee* is a symbolic term for those who oppose tyranny.

SCHNEOUR

The Middle Ages Draw Near, pp. 90–95

Schneour wrote this poem in 1913 while traveling in Germany. He defined the spirit of the twentieth century not as modern but as a reversion to the spirit of the middle ages at the time of the Great Inquisitors.

The Fruited Month, pp. 98–101

THE FRUITED MONTH. The eighth month of the Hebrew lunar calendar, called *Iyar;* it usually falls toward the end of April and the beginning of May.

NARGILEH. Oriental water pipe.

Poppies, pp. 100–101

THE GREEN IS NOT CONSUMED. From Exodus 3:2— "... the bush burns with fire, and the bush is not consumed."

HAMEIRI

Passover in Jerusalem, pp. 102–103

KING MESSIAH. The traditional concept of the Redeemer, a man born out of the house of David who would restore a peaceful kingdom to the earth and bring unity and fulfillment to the Jewish people and to all mankind.

KARNI

Put Me into the Breach, pp. 108–109

THE MESSIAH'S ADVENT. According to Hebrew legend, the Messiah would enter the city of Jerusalem through the Shaar Harahamim, the Mercy Gate in the old wall of the city.

BLUWSTEIN

Aftergrowth, pp. 112–113

AFTERGROWTH. The kernels that fall to the ground from stalks, as they are harvested, to sprout the following year.

GREENBERG

By the Waters of the Sava, pp. 116–117

THE SAVA. A river in Yugoslavia where Austrian and Russian troops met in battle during World War I, and where Greenberg fought as a young soldier.

IN THE MYSTERY OF FEAR *(pahad).* While the literal meaning of *pahad* in Hebrew is fear, it is also one of the designated names of God. "... except the God of my father, the God of Abraham and the Fear of Isaac ..." (Genesis 31:42).

A Penny for You, pp. 116–119

The Hebrew word *Asimon* is translated as *penny.* It means literally an old minted coin without any imprint, of the least valuable denomination.

At Your Feet, Jerusalem, pp. 120–125

HORA. A popular pioneer folk dance derived from Slavic and

Hassidic origins.

GOD WILL BUILD THE DESOLATION. An early Zionist song asks "Who will build Galilee?" It answers "We will build Galilee, God will build Galilee." Greenberg uses the last half of the phrase with a satirical twist.

Lord You Saved Me from Ur-Germany, pp. 126–129

UR-GERMANY. Ur-Chaldea was the birthplace of Abraham, the patriarchal father of the Jewish people. According to legend, when King Nimrod cast him into the fiery furnace, the furnace was transformed into a green country where Abraham walked unharmed.

LAKE-OF-WEEPING. In modern Hebrew, Lake Galilee is called Kinneret, because it is shaped like a harp. The poet uses the term "Kinneret of Weeping" in the Hebrew to structure his poem about this major image.

LAMDAN

In the Khamsin, pp. 130–135

KHAMSIN. This word, Arabic for a foehn wind or sirocco, has become part of the modern Hebrew vocabulary.

BASKET OF CHILDHOOD. The phrase refers to the basket containing the infant Moses as described in Exodus.

IKVAH. A stream in the forest of the Ukraine near Lamdan's birthplace.

YELLOW BADGE. The yellow mark Jews were compelled to wear in the Middle Ages which the Nazis revived.

HAGAR AND ISHMAEL. Genesis 21:20–21.

Israel, pp. 136–137

LIMPING UPON MY THIGH. Genesis 32:25.

HALKIN

Reward, pp. 138–141

THRONE OF GLORY. The mystic throne, or seat of God, seen in the vision of Isaiah 6 and Ezekiel 1.

PRAYER'S LADDER. A comparison with Jacob's ladder upon which angels ascended and descended. Genesis 28:12.

To Tarshish, pp. 144–157

TARSHISH. The city to which the Prophet Jonah fled from God, who then sent him to Nineveh instead. Jonah 1:3.

SIVAN. The ninth month of the Hebrew lunar calendar, usually around June or July.

RETURNED ATOMS OF THE GOD BECOME UNITIES. "In the mystic concept of creation according to Isaac Luria and his school the first configuration of divine light flows from the essence of the infinite One into primal space. At first these lights were coalesced in a totality or form without differentiation.... The light coming from the eyes of this primal form (Adam Kadmon) emanated in atomized form. . . . This world of punctiform lights is also called the world of confusion or disorder. Since the divine scheme of things involved the creation of finite beings and forms. . . it was necessary that the isolated lights be caught and preserved in special receptacles created or rather emanated for this particular purpose. When the lower six emanations could not bear the impact of the light they broke and shattered. . . . The Breaking of the vessels is compared to the break-through of birth, the deepest convulsion of the living organism. . . . At any rate the breaking of the Vessels in the literature of the Lurian Kabbalah is the decisive turning point in the cosmological process. Taken as a whole it is the cause of the inner deficiency inherent in everything that exists. Conversely the restoration of ideal order which forms the original aim of creation is also the secret purpose of existence. Salvation means actually nothing but restitution, reintegration of the original whole or Tikkun to use the Hebrew term. . . ." — Gershon G. Scholem, *Major Trends in Jewish Mysticism* (Jerusalem: Schocken, 1951), pp. 265–268.

Seventy-five Are My Abyssed Forests, pp. 158–159
THE GOLD BIRD. The beloved — a reference to *tzipor hanefesh,* the bird of the soul.

BAT-MIRIAM
Like This Before You, pp. 160–163
NOT CHARMING, NOT PAINTED WITH PINK AND BLUE. In the Talmudic tractate Ketubot (marriage agreements), there is a discussion of a Mishnah dealing with laws concerning the divorced woman (Chap. II, p. 15, col. 2). Into this discussion are injected extraneous, spontaneous questions. The first asks what is customary praise to speak to a bride. The school of Hillel says all brides are to be pronounced beautiful and wise, but the school of Shammai says that a bride must be praised for her own qualities, just as she is. The second

question (p. 17, col. 1) asks what may be sung to the bride as she is carried upon a litter to her wedding. The answer is given to Rabbi Dimi in a formula: ". . . without blue paint upon her eyes, pink powder upon her face and without elaborate coiffure, she is still charming as a gazelle." The poet adapts this text to her psychological state. Feeling herself divorced and rejected, she takes for herself, nevertheless, the bride's prerogative — to be accepted as she is. The "You" she addresses may be a husband or lover, but she is also speaking to God.

The Distance Spills Itself, pp. 164-165

MEZUZAH. The name of a small receptacle of wood or metal containing a parchment with the prayer "Hear, Oh Israel, the Lord Is One." Fastened to the doorposts of the Jewish home, it is traditionally kissed as one enters or leaves the house.

"ADORATION." The prayer sanctifying God's name in the liturgy. It is taken from Isaiah 6:3 — "Holy Holy Holy is the Lord of Hosts, the whole world fills with his glory."

SHLONSKY

Jezrael, pp. 170–179

PHYLACTERIES. Two small leather boxes, each containing four scriptural passages, fixed to looped leather squares. The arm phylactery is bound to the right arm, and the head phylactery is bound to the forehead. Put on by men with the prayer shawl before the morning service, they are a reminder of the binding covenant between the Jew and his God. According to Maimonides, their purpose was to direct man's meditation toward truth and righteousness.

BALAAM. See Numbers 23–24.

Morning in My City, pp. 186–189

CABBALIST. A student and practitioner of mysticism.

TEN YOUNG MEN. Although it is permitted to pray and study alone, communal prayer requires a congregation of a minyan, or ten.

INEFFABLE NAME. The Tetragrammaton YHWY is the distinctive personal name of the God of Israel which is customarily Anglicized as Jehovah. Used by the High Priest in temple services in Jerusalem until the year 30, C.E., it was then forbidden to be pronounced, and the term *Adonai Elohim* or Lord

God was substituted in prayer. It continued to form an important part of mystic teaching and practice. Cabbalists believed that the sounding of this name under proper circumstances held great power and could accomplish miracles. EVERY THREAD OF MY BODY EXPRESSES IT, WITH EACH FIBER IN THE DEWY TREE, MEDITATING UPON ITS SYMBOLS. According to Cabbalist symbolism, the Sephirot (ten spheres of creation) form two corresponding configurations: the body of a man *(Adam Kadmon)* and/or the figure of a tree; thus the body of the poet and the tree on the construction lot symbolize the miracle of creation in contemporary terms and times.

SHALOM
Suddenly We Will Wake, pp. 192–193

TABLET OF THE HEART. Proverbs 3:3. "Let not mercy and truth forsake thee... write them upon the tablet of thine heart."

Drink Wonder, pp. 192–195

INFINITE LIGHT *(ein sof).* "The impersonal character of this aspect of the hidden God... signifies 'the infinite' not as He who is infinite, but that which is infinite" (Scholem, *op. cit.,* p. 12).

ALTERMAN
The Joy of the Poor, pp. 212–221

BEARERS-OF-THE-ARK. In biblical usage the word ark *(aron)* signifies the *ark of the covenant.* In modern Hebrew *aron* also means a coffin. In biblical usage the bearers of the ark were the priests. In Alterman's use of this phrase, the bearers of the ark are pallbearers.

CONVERT. One who has changed from the religion of life to that of death.

ROKEAH
Hands Full of Sun, pp. 272–273

IZDARAC. A flowering shrub of Israel.

GURI
The Silent Words, pp. 284–287

SHAMIR. A Hebrew word for the legendary worm described

in the legends of King Solomon which had the power to cut and shape the hardest substance at touch. It was used to build the Temple where metal tools (instruments used for war) were forbidden.

His Mother, pp. 288–291

Lines 5–6 are from Judges 5:30.

Odysseus, pp. 294–297

EURYCLEIA. The old nurse of Odysseus who recognized him by his childhood scar as she washed his feet when he returned as a stranger to his home.

Piyyut for Rosh Hashana, pp. 298–299

Before the Hebrew New Year it is customary to recite a group of hymns *(piyyutim)* called *Selihot* which ask forgiveness. Yet tradition holds that before one can be forgiven, one must also forgive. See also Introduction.

AMIHAI

On My Birthday, pp. 302–305

TALMUD. A page of Talmud is composed of a portion of Mishnah expanded by both legal exegesis and legend which is in turn surrounded by many commentaries upon the passage. In the printed text the commentary on the page therefore surrounds and encloses a fragment of text with many columns and lines. See also Introduction.

RASHI. The name refers to Rabbi Solomon Bar Isaac (1040–1105), a Hebrew scholar of Troyes, France, who wrote an important commentary on the Bible and the Talmud noted for its clarity and insight.

TOSAPHISTS. A critical explanatory gloss on the Talmud given in the margins of texts opposite Rashi's notes. The Tosaphists began to compose their commentary in the immediate period after Rashi, and they followed his style.

Leaves Without Trees, pp. 304–307

EVEN THAT ONE. The phrase refers to the small stone in David's sling which killed Goliath (I Samuel 17:49). In contemporary metaphor it means the small Israeli force that defeated the seven Arab armies that attempted to prevent the establishment of Israel in 1948.

GALAI

Of Those Who Go, Not to Return, pp. 312–315

NOT THE DEAD TODAY SHALL PRAISE YOU, GOD! Compare Psalms 115:17: "Not the dead shall praise the Lord."
BETTER THE LIVE DOG THAN THE DEAD LION. Ecclesiastes 9:4.

CARMI
René's Songs, pp. 328–339

In 1946 Carmi worked in France in refugee orphanages. The orphaned children mentioned in *"Réne's Songs"* are drawn from this experience. The orphanage was set in a dilapidated chateau which, incongruously, had bamboo trees in a grotto. "René's Songs" occur at various places throughout the book *There Are No Black Flowers* (Carmi's first volume of poetry). The title of the volume of poetry, which is also the refrain in the poems, is a quotation from "On Style" (from Marx and Engels, *Literature and Art* [International Publishers], p. 60): ". . . the essential form of the spirit is gaiety and light, and you make shadows its only manifestation; it must be dressed only in black and yet there are no black flowers. . ." (Karl Marx).

SMOKY CHARIOTS. Elijah's chariot of fire that carried him to heaven; the crematorium of the concentration camp whose smokestacks René remembers.

LO-IMI (*"Not My Mother"*). This term of rejection is derived from the book of Hosea, where the prophet names his child symbolically *Lo Ami* (Not My People) (Hosea 1:9). In the poem *Lo-Imi* is the name René gives the directress of the orphanage.

TRAININ
Cat in the Dovecote, pp. 340–341

ARK. This usage refers to Genesis 8:11, which tells of the dove bringing an olive leaf on her return to the ark.

MAR
Handfuls of Wind, pp. 344–345

WIND. This is a translation of the Hebrew word *Ruah* which means *wind*, but also *spirit*.

SELECTED READINGS

IN ENGLISH

Buber, Martin. *Tales of the Hassidim*. New York: Schocken, 1948.
———. *Hassidism and Modern Man*. New York: Horizon, 1958.
Chomsky, William. *The Eternal Language*. Philadelphia: Jewish Publication Society, 1957.
Halkin, Simon. *Modern Hebrew Literature*. New York: Schocken, 1950.
Scholem, Gershon. *Major Trends in Jewish Mysticism*. Jerusalem: Schocken, 1951.
Spiegel, Shalom. *Hebrew Reborn*. New York: Macmillan, 1930.
Waxman, Meyer. *A History of Modern Hebrew Literature*. New York: Bloch, 1938.

IN HEBREW

Ben-Or, Aharon. *Toldot Sifrut Haivrit Bedorenu*. Tel Aviv: Yizrael, 1955.
Bialik, H. N., and H. Ravnitzki. *Sefer Haggadah*. Jerusalem: Dvir, 1956.
Fichman, Yakov. *Amat Habinyan*. Jerusalem: Mosad Bialik, 1951.
———. *Shirat Bialik*. Jerusalem: Mosad Bialik, 1946.
Klausner, Joseph. *Meshorerey Dorenu*. Jerusalem: Dvir, 1949.
Luzzatto, Moshe Hayyim. *Shirim*. Jerusalem: Mosad Bialik, 1948.
Shirman, Hayyim. *Shirat Yemey Habenayim*. Jerusalem, Tel Aviv: Mosad Bialik–Dvir, 1954–1956.
Tishbi, Yeshiah. *Mishnat Hazohar*. Jerusalem: Mosad Bialik, 1957–1961.
Toren, H., and M. Robinson. *Sifrutenu Hayafa*. Jerusalem: Ahiasaf, 1954.

357

NOTES ON THE POETS

BIALIK, HAYYIM NAHMAN (1873–1934)
Born in Volhynia, Russia. He received a traditional Hebrew
education. At the age of eleven he began to read the medieval
Hebrew literature; at sixteen he studied at the Talmudic Academy
of Voloshin and began to read widely in secular modern Hebrew
literature and Russian literature. He wrote his first poetry in
Voloshin. In 1891 he came to Odessa and succeeded in publishing
his first poem. Returning home, he became a teacher and began
to write the poetry and the short stories that brought him
recognition. In 1901 he was invited to return to Odessa, the active
Hebrew literary center, where he published his first volume of
poetry and became literary editor of *Hashiloach*. Together with
Ravnitzki and Benzion he founded the Moriah Publishing
Company. With Ravnitzki he reëdited for modern readers *Sefer
Ha'aggada* (1908–1910) and collaborated in the publication of
works of medieval Hebrew poets (Ibn Gabirol and Moshe Ibn
Ezra). In 1924 he settled in Palestine and established the Dvir
Publishing Company, of which he was editor. In Palestine he
became an animating spirit of cultural activity and was chairman
of the Hebrew Language Committee. He went to America in
1926 and to Poland and Lithuania in 1931 on cultural missions.
After his death a prize in belle-lettres bearing his name was
established by the city of Tel Aviv, and Mosad Bialik, a publishing
house for fostering Hebrew literature, was founded by the Jewish
Agency in Jerusalem. Among his translations are Cervantes'
Don Quixote, Schiller's *Wilhelm Tell*, and S. Ansky's *The Dybbuk*.
His poems have been translated into Russian, German, English,
French, and Italian.
  Prose works: *Devorim Shebeal Peh* (2 vols.; Tel Aviv: Dvir,
1935), *Vayehi Hayom* (Tel Aviv: Dvir, 1934) [translated by H.
Danby as *Stories about King David and King Solomon* (1938)],
Safiah (Tel Aviv: Dvir, 1934) [translated by I. M. Lask as *After-
growth and Other Stories* (1939)], *Divrey Aggadah* (Tel Aviv:
Dvir, 1934), and *Igrot* (4 vols.; Tel Aviv: Dvir, 1935).

Poetic works: *Shirim* (Warsaw: Toshiah, 1902), *Shirim* (Odessa, 1908), *Kitvey Bialik Umivhar Tirgumav* (4 vols.; Berlin: Vaad Hayovel, 1923), *Kitvey Bialik* (4 vols.; Tel Aviv: Dvir, 1933; 2d ed., 1935), *Kol Kitvey Bialik*, Mavo mayet Y. Fichman (Tel Aviv: Dvir, 1939).

The poems translated in this volume were taken from *Kol Kitvey Bialik* (Tel Aviv: Dvir, 1939).

TCHERNICHOVSKY, SAUL (1875–1943)
Born in the Crimea, Russia. He was first taught Hebrew by his father and then by modern tutors until he was fifteen, He studied Russian at a village school and at the Gymnasium in Odessa, where he began to write poetry and translate into Hebrew. He studied at the universities of Heidelberg and Lausanne (1899–1906), became a doctor of medicine, and a practicing government physician in Kharkov, Petersburg, and Finland. In World War I he was a military surgeon with the Russian Red Cross. After 1922 he lived in Berlin; he visited Palestine in 1925, the United States in 1930, and then settled in Palestine in 1931. He continued to write and practice medicine all his life. He completed and edited the Hebrew medical dictionary commenced by Dr. A. Maze. In addition, he wrote a critical study of the Hebrew poet *Imanuel Haromi* (Tel Aviv, 1935). Among his translations are Homer's *Iliad* and the *Odyssey*, *Kalevala* (the Finnish epic), *Gilgamesh* (the Babylonian epic), Anacreon's *Poems*, Plato's *Symposium* and *Phaedrus*, Sophocles' *Oedipus Rex*, Moliere's *Le Malade Imaginaire*, Shakespeare's *Twelfth Night* and *Macbeth*, Goethe's *Reineke Fuchs*, and Longfellow's *Hiawatha*. He was a member of the Hebrew Language Committee and of the Executive Council of the Hebrew University. The city of Tel Aviv established a prize in his honor for translation into Hebrew. His own poems have been translated into English, French, German, Italian, and Russian.

Poetic works: *Hezyonot Umanginot* (Warsaw: Toshiah, 1899), with more poems under same title published in 1902; *Machberet Hasonnetot* and *Sefer Ha'idilyot* (Berlin, 1922); *Shirim Hadashim* (Leipzig, 1924); *Kitvey Shaul Tchernichovsky* (10 vols.; Berlin and New York, 1929–1934); *Kol Shirey Tchernichovsky* (Tel Aviv: Schocken, 1937); *Shirim* (Jerusalem: Yovel, 1943); *Shirim* (Tel Aviv: Schocken, 1951).

The poems translated in this volume were taken from *Shirim* (Tel Aviv: Schocken, 1951).

COHEN, YAKOV (1881–1959)
Born in Russia, he grew up in Poland and was educated at a school
conducted by a modern Hebrew teacher. He received a Ph.D. in
philosophy from the University of Bern. In 1910 he became
director of the Organization for Hebrew Language and Culture,
Berlin. He was supervisor of Hebrew gymnasiums in Poland and
lecturer in Hebrew Literature at the Institute of Jewish Studies,
Warsaw, from 1924 to 1934, when he left to settle in Palestine.
Besides lyric poetry, he wrote verse dramas and short stories, and
received the Bialik Prize for his verse drama. He translated
Goethe's *Iphigenia auf Tauris, Torquato Tasso,* and the first part of
Faust, for which he received the Tchernichovsky Prize. He was
editor of the journal *Hatkufah* and of the belles-lettres section of
Knesset, and a member of the Hebrew Language Committee.
  Poetic works: *Shirim* (1903, 1905, 1913, 1925, 1930); *Neurim
Unedudim* and *Bayn Haharavot* from *Ketuvim* (10 vols.; Tel Aviv:
Vaad Hayovel, 1938); *Tzion Baazikim* (Tel Aviv, 1941).
  The poem translated in this volume was taken from A. Barash,
ed., *Mivhar Hashiruh Huivrit Hahadasha* (Jerusalem: Schocken,
1948).

FICHMAN, YAKOV (1881–1958)
Born in Bessarabia, he received a traditional Hebrew education
and graduated from the Teachers' Institute of Grodno. In 1901 he
worked with Bialik in Odessa and later with Frishman on the
Hatsofeh, where his first poetry and critical essays on European
literature appeared. He joined the editorial staff of *Moriah* in 1909.
In 1925 he went to settle in Palestine, where he edited *Moledet,
Ma'barot,* and *Hashiloach.* His extensive essays on modern
literature made him a leading critic of this early period. His
textbooks for the study of Hebrew literature had an important
influence on Hebrew education. For many years he edited *Moznaim*
and was a member of the Hebrew Language Committee. His
translations include Hebbel's *Herod and Miriamne* and the poetry
of Heine and Goethe. His literary essays and critical works include
Bevaot (1919); *Bialik Haiyov Umaasov* (1933); *Anshe Besorah*
(1938); *Sofrim Behaiyahem* (1942); *Shirat Bialik* (Jerusalem:
Mosad Bialik, 1946), for which he received the Usishkin Prize;
Amat Habinyan (Jerusalem: Mosad Bialik, 1951), on the Odessa
group of Hebrew writers — Mendle, Achad Haam, Bialik,
Tchernichovsky; and *Ruchot Menagnot* (Jerusalem: Mosad Bialik,

1952), on Hebrew writers in Poland — Peretz, Frishman, Sokolow, Berditchewsky, *et al.*

Poetic works: *Givolim* (1911); *Yemei Shemesh* (1934); *Tzelalim Al Sadot* (1935); *Peat Sadeh* (1943), for which he received the Bialik Prize; *Aviv Beshomron* (1943); *Demuyot Kedumim* (Jerusalem: Mosad Bialik, 1948).

The poems translated in this volume were taken from A. Barash, ed., *Mivhar Hashirah Haivrit Hahadasha* (Jerusalem: Schocken, 1948).

SHIMONI, DAVID (1886–1957)

Born in Russia. At seventeen his first poems began to appear in the Hebrew journals. In 1909 he went to Palestine, where he worked as a guard and as a laborer in the agricultural communities of Rehovot and Petach Tikvah. He returned to Europe in 1910 to complete his education, receiving his Ph.D. in Philosophy and Semitic languages from the University of Wurzburg. In 1920 he returned to Palestine and devoted himself to literature. He received the Bialik Prize in 1936 and was a member of the Hebrew Language Committee. He made translations from the works of Tolstoi, Pushkin, Lermontov, and Heine.

Poetic works: *Yeshimon* (1911), *Saar Udemama* (1912), *Ketuvim* (*Shirim, Idyliot, Poemot, Shirim Upoemot*) (4 vols.; Tel Aviv: Dvir, 1925–1933), *Resisay Laiylah* (1940), *Mihtav Leay Sham* (1944), *Shirim* (Tel Aviv: Dvir, 1944).

The poems translated in this volume were taken from *Shirim* (Tel Aviv: Dvir, 1944).

SCHNEOUR, ZALMAN (1887–1959)

Born in Russia to a distinguished Hassidic family, he ran away to Odessa at the age of fifteen to study and pursue a literary career. He worked in Warsaw for the publishing house Toshiah, and was secretary to the eminent prose writers Frishman and Peretz; Bialik also encouraged him in his writing. From 1906 to 1908 he studied in Switzerland and in Paris. Thereafter he traveled about Europe and North Africa, and was interned as an enemy alien in Germany during World War I. He lived in Paris after the war, and during World War II he went to New York. In 1951 he settled in Israel, receiving the Bialik Prize in the same year. With Bialik and Tchernichovsky he was a major poet of the early period of modern Hebrew poetry. His novels written in Yiddish have been translated into French, English, and Hebrew: *Noah Pandre, Uncle Zama*, and *Men of Shklov*. A complete edition of Schneour's works was issued in 1958 by Dvir, Tel Aviv; it includes his novels, essays, reminiscences, and poetry.

Poetic works: *Im Shekiat Hahama* (Warsaw: Toshiah, 1907), *Shirim Ufoemot* (Warsaw: Toshiah, 1914), *Vilnah* (Berlin and New York, 1920-1923), *Hezyonot* (1924), *Gesharim* (1928), *Pirkey Yaar* (1933).

The poems translated in this volume were taken from *Shirim* (2 vols.; Tel Aviv: Dvir, 1958).

HAMEIRI, AVIGDOR (1890 — —)
Born in Hungary, he studied at the Rabbinical Seminary in Budapest. He was an officer in the Hungarian Army during World War I and was taken prisoner of war in Russia. He lived in Odessa until 1921, when he went to Palestine. There he edited literary journals and wrote poetry, essays, and short stories. In 1927 he founded the first Hebrew theater of satire. He received the Bialik Prize in 1935.

Poetic works: *Mayshiray Avigdor Feurstein* (Budapest, 1911), *Sefer Hashirim* (Jerusalem: Am Hasefer, 1932), *Hamoked Haran* (Tel Aviv: Dvir, 1944), *Halomot Bet Raban* (Jerusalem: Massada, 1946).

The poems translated in this volume were taken from *Hamoked Haran* (Tel Aviv: Dvir, 1944).

KARNI, YEHUDA (1884-1948)
Born in Russia, he was secretary for the Russian Zionist movement and editor of the literary journal *Olam* (Odessa). He went to Palestine in 1921, where he became editor of the daily newspaper *Haaretz*. He was awarded the Bialik Prize in 1945.

Poetic works: *Shearim* (Tel Aviv, 1923), *Bish'araich Moledet* (Tel Aviv, 1935), *Yerushalayim* (Tel Aviv, 1944), *Shir Vadema* (Tel Aviv, 1944).

The poems translated in this volume were taken from *Yerushalayim* (Tel Aviv, 1944).

BLUWSTEIN, RAHEL (1890-1931)
Born in Russia, she studied at a Hebrew public school in Poltava and was graduated from a Russian gymnasium. She left her studies at Kiev Art School in 1909 and went to Palestine, where she

was an agricultural worker in Rehovot and in the cooperative colony of Kinneret. In 1913 she studied agronomy in Toulouse, France. Forced to return to Russia by the outbreak of World War I, she taught in a school for refugee children. In 1919 she returned to Palestine, but lingering tuberculosis soon prevented physical work. She spent the last ten years of her life in and out of hospitals in Tel Aviv. She is buried in Kinneret.

Poetic works: *Safiah* (1927), *Mineged* (1930), *Nevo* (1932), *Shirat Rahel* (Tel Aviv: Davar, 1949).

The poems translated in this volume were taken from *Shirat Rahel* (Tel Aviv: Davar, 1949).

GREENBERG, URI TZVI (1894 — —)
Born in Galicia to a family of distinguished Hassidic rabbis, he received a traditional Hebrew education and served in the Austrian Army during World War I. He edited the *Albatross*, a journal of Yiddish expressionist poetry. In 1924 he joined the extreme nationalist group within the Zionist movement and wrote only in Hebrew. In that year he went to Palestine and worked in the labor corps, reclaiming land infested with malaria. He settled in Tel Aviv and devoted himself to poetry. He received the Bialik Prize for poetry in 1948 and was a member of the first Knesset (Parliament).

Poetic Works: *Eima Gedola Veyareah* (1925), *Hagavrut Ha'ola* (1926), *Anacreon al Kotev Ha'itzavon* (1928), *Hazon Ahad Haligyonot* (1928), *Kelapei Tish'im Vetish'a* (1928), *Kelev Bayit* (1929), *Sefer Hakitrug Veha'emunah* (1937), *Rehovot Hanahar* (Tel Aviv, Jerusalem: Schocken, 1951).

The poems translated in this volume were taken from *Anacreon Al Kotev Ha'itzavon* ("By the Waters of the Sava," "A Penny for You," and "In the Covenant's Radiance"), *Sefer Hakitrug Veha'emunah* ("At Your Feet, Jerusalem"), and *Rehovot Hanahar* ("We Were Not Likened to Dogs among the Gentiles" and "Lord! You Saved Me from Ur-Germany as I Fled").

LAMDAN, YITZHAK (1900–1955)
Born in Volhynia, Russia, to a Hassidic family, he received a traditional Hebrew education. Separated from his parents by World War I, he wandered with his older brother. In 1917 he joined the Russian Army under Kerensky. He went to Palestine in 1920 and worked as a laborer building roads and as a farmhand.

His first volume of poetry, the epic *Massadah*, was reissued in seven editions. For eighteen years he edited *Gilyonot*, the monthly journal which was noted for new poetry, prose, and criticism, and was particularly hospitable to young, unknown writers. He received the Brenner Prize in 1947.

Poetic works: *Massadah* (1927), *Baritmah Hameṣhuleshet* (1930), *Misefer Hayamim* (1940), *Mahanayim* (1944), *Bemaaleh Akrabim* (1945).

The poems translated in this volume were taken from *Massadah* ("In the Khamsin") and *Bemaaleh Akrabim* ("Israel").

HALKIN, SHIMON (1898 — —)
Born in Lithuania to a family of noted Hassidic rabbis, he received a traditional Hebrew education. He went to America in 1914 with his family and studied at Columbia and New York University, where he received his Ph.D. He then went to Palestine to teach and write. From 1939 to 1949 he held academic posts in the United States, teaching Hebrew literature. In 1949 he was appointed to the faculty of the Hebrew University and subsequently became head of the Department of Hebrew Literature. In 1954 he was Visiting Professor at the University of California, Los Angeles, where he inaugurated the Department of Hebrew. He wrote two novels, *Yehial Hahagri* and *Ad Mashber*. Among his translations are Shakespeare's *Merchant of Venice* and *King John*, Maeterlinck's *Blue Bird,* and Whitman's *Leaves of Grass,* for which he received the Tchernichovsky Prize. His works of criticism are *Araiy Vekeva* (Tel Aviv: Schocken, 1942) and *Modern Hebrew Literature: Trends and Values* (Tel Aviv: Schocken, 1950).

Poetic works: *Beyamim Shishah Velaylot Sheva* (1929), *Baruch Ben Neriah* (1934), *Al Ha'iy* (Jerusalem: Mosad Bialik, 1946).

The poems translated in this volume were taken from *Al Ha'iy* (Jerusalem: Mosad Bialik, 1946).

BAT-MIRIAM, YOCHEVED (1901 — —)
Born in Russia to a Hassidic family, she received a modern education in Russian and Hebrew. She began to publish in Hebrew journals by 1923. In 1929 she settled in Palestine where she taught and was active in literary circles.

Poetic works: *Mayrahok* (1932), *Eretz Yisrael* (1939), *Reayon* (1940), *Dmuyot Meofek* (1942), *Shirim Leghetto* (1943).

The poems translated in this volume were taken from A. Barash, ed., *Mivhar Hashirah Haivrit Hahadasha* (Jerusalem: Schocken, 1948).

SHLONSKY, AVRAHAM (1900 ——)
Born in Russia to a family of noted Hassidic rabbis, he was sent to Palestine when he was thirteen to study at the Gymnasia Hertzelia in Tel Aviv. At the outbreak of World War I he was obliged to finish his studies in Russia. There he became a member of Hehalutz, preparing for immigration to Palestine by agricultural training. Arriving in Palestine in 1921, he was a member of the labor corps and worked on road construction and on the land in the valley of Jezrael. Subsequently, he studied comparative literature in Paris, and on returning to Palestine he became the center of the Yachdav, a literary group that was working for new forms in Hebrew poetry. In 1926 he founded *Ketuvim*, a literary weekly, and later he edited *Turim* and *Ittim*. He was literary editor of *Al Hamishmar* (a daily newspaper of the socialist left) and editor of *Sifriyat Poalim* (Workers' Book Guild). Since 1951 he has edited *Orlogin*, a literary quarterly. He was awarded the Tchernichovsky Prize. He has translated more than seventy-three books and plays, thirty of which were performed on the Hebrew stage. Consequently, his writing was a major influence on the changing contemporary idiom of the language. His translations include Shakespeare's *King Lear* and *Hamlet*, Pushkin's *Eugene Onegin*, Gogol's *Revizor*, Sholokhov's *Virgin Soil* and *Quiet Flows the Don*, Moliere's *Tartuffe*, and poems of Bloch and Mayakovsky.

Poetic works: *Dvai* (1924), *Le'abba Imma* (1926), *Bagalgal* (1927), *B'eleh Hayamim* (1929), *Avnei Bohu* (1934), *Shirei Hamappolet vehapiyus* (1938), *Shirei Hayamim* (1946), *Al Milleit* (1947), and *Shirim* (2 vols.; Merhaviah: Sifriyat Poalim, 1954).

The poems translated in this volume were taken from *Shirim* (2 vols.; Merhaviah: Sifriyat Poalim, 1954).

SHALOM, S. (1904 ——)
Born in Galicia to a family of distinguished Hassidic rabbis, he fled to Vienna with his family at the outbreak of World War I. In 1922 the family went to Palestine, where he was graduated from the Teacher's College, Mizrahi, Jerusalem. He joined the founders of Kfar Hassidim and was one of the first teachers in that settlement. Later, he taught at Rosh Pinah in the upper Galilee. He studied at the University of Erlangen from 1929 to 1931. Afterward he

lived in Jerusalem until 1939, teaching Hebrew literature. He now lives in Haifa where he is an honorary citizen and is chairman of the Hebrew Writers Association. In 1941 he received the Bialik Prize. In 1951 he visited the United States. He received the Tchernichovksy Prize for the translation of Shakespeare's *Sonnets*. His volumes of short stories are *Yoman Bagalil, Aliyat Hahassidim,* and *Bemetah Hagavoah.*

Poetic works: *Belev Haolam* (1927), *Peleh Gma* (1934), *Sefer Hashirim Vehasonnetot* (1940), *On Ben Pelleh* (1942). *Panim el Panim* (1941), *Olam Belehavot* (1944), *Shabat Haolam* (1945), *Elan Bahut* (1946), *Shirim* (Tel Aviv: Yavneh, 1952).

The poems translated in this volume were taken from *Shirim* (Tel Aviv: Yavneh, 1952).

ALTERMAN, NATAN (1910 ——)
Born in Poland, his father was a Hebrew educator who spoke Hebrew to his son. He went to Palestine in 1924 and was graduated from the Gymnasia Hertzelia in Tel Aviv. He studied agronomy at the University of Nancy, France. From 1931 he was a member of the experimental literary group Yachdav and participated in *Turim*, the weekly edited by Shlonsky. In 1944 he became known for his column of verse satire, *"Hatur Hasheviyi"* (political and social criticism), which appeared weekly in *Davar* (the moderate socialist newspaper). His serious poetry shaped spoken Hebrew, bringing to it elements of an imagist idiom which evoked the appreciation of the Israeli youth. Among his translations are Racine's *Phedre*, and Shakespeare's *Othello* and *Merry Wives of Windsor*. His two new plays, *Kinneret-Kinneret* and *Pundak Haruhot*, were performed in Tel Aviv in 1961–1963. He received the Ruppin Prize.

Poetic works: *Kohavim Bahutz* (Tel Aviv: Mahberet L'Sifrut, 1938), *Simhat Aniyyim* (Tel Aviv: Mahberet L'Sifrut, 1944), *Makot Mitzraim* (Tel Aviv: Mahberet L'Sifrut, 1947), *Ir Hayonah* (Tel Aviv: Mahberet L'Sifrut, 1957).

The poems translated in this volume were taken from *Kohavim Bahutz* (1938) ("Memento of Roads," "Red Ridinghood," "Beyond Melody," and "Moon"), *Simhat Aniyyim* (1944) ("The Joy of the Poor"), and *Ir Hayonah* (1957) ("The Abandoned" and "The Maid") — all published by Mahberet L'Sifrut, Tel Aviv.

GOLDBERG, LEAH (1911 ——)
Born in Lithuania, she was graduated from the Hebrew Gymnasium

of Kovna and received her doctorate degree after studing philosophy and Semitic languages at the universities of Berlin and Bonn. She went to Palestine in 1935 and joined the Yachdav literary group with Shlonsky and Alterman, working with Shlonsky as translator and editor. She lectured on the history of the theater for the Habima dramatic school and was a drama and literary critic for various newspapers and journals. Her play *Mistress of the Mansion* was produced on the Hebrew stage. In 1954 she joined the faculty of the Hebrew University to lecture on comparative literature. She received the Ruppin Prize. Among her translations are Shakespeare's *As You Like It*, Ibsen's *Peer Gynt*, and Tolstoi's *War and Peace*. She collaborated with Shlonsky on an anthology of Russian poetry, and made translations from Rilke, Hofmannsthal, Verlaine, and Petrarch. She has also written poems and short stories for children.

Poetic works: *Tabaot Ashan* (1935), *Mihtav Minsiah Medumah* (1937), *Shibolet Yerokat Haayin* (1940), *Mibeti Hayashan* (1942), *Al Hapriha* (Tel Aviv: Sifriyat Poalim, 1948), *Barak Baboker* (Tel Aviv: Sifriyat Poalim, 1955).

The poems translated in this volume were taken from *Al Hapriha* (Tel Aviv: Sifriyat Poalim, 1948).

GILBOA, AMIR (1917 ——)
Born in Russia, he was graduated from a Hebrew gymnasium and prepared to go to Palestine by taking agricultural training with Hehalutz. He went to Palestine in 1937 and worked in quarries, at road building, and in agricultural settlements. Since 1941 he has lived in Tel Aviv. In 1942 he served in the British Army, and in 1948 he fought in the Israeli Army. Since the War he has worked in a publishing house. In 1961 he received the Shlonsky Prize for poetry.

Poetic works: *Laot* (Tel Aviv, 1942), *Sheva Reshuiot* (Merhaviah: Sifriyat Poalim, 1949), *Shirim Baboker, Baboker* (Tel Aviv: Hakibbutz Hameuhad, 1953).

The poems translated in this volume were taken from *Shirim Baboker, Baboker* (Tel Aviv: Hakibbutz Hameuhad, 1953).

ROKEAH, DAVID (1916 ——)
Born in Poland, he completed his university studies in electrical engineering there. He now lives in Tel Aviv although his work often takes him to Europe. He has visited almost all the countries

of Western Europe, and translations of his poetry have appeared
in European and American journals. A bilingual edition of his
poems published by Surkamp Verlag, Frankfurt, appeared in
September, 1963.

Poetic works: *Begesher Hayeud* (Tel Aviv, 1939), *Yamim Ashenim*
(Jerusalem, 1941), *Moadey Erga* (Jerusalem: Hotzaat Sifre Tarshish,
1954), *Arar Aley Shaham* (Jerusalem: Hotzaat Shpitzer, 1958).

The poems translated in this volume were taken from *Moadev
Erga* ("Zealots of Yearning," "Whirlwind," "Hands Full of Sun,"
and "Solar Years") and *Arar Aley Shaham* ("Negev," "Jerusalem,"
and "Open-Eyed Angel").

GURI, HAYYIM (1921 — —)
Born in Tel Aviv, he was graduated from Bet Hinuh and the
Caduri School of Agriculture. In 1947 he was sent to Central
Europe on a mission by the Haganah; in 1948 he served as a
captain in the Palmach (commando unit) of the Israeli Army.
After the War he studied Hebrew literature at the Hebrew
University, and in 1953 he attended the Sorbonne in Paris. He
lives in Jerusalem where he works as a journalist. In 1958 he was
sent to France and Algeria, and in 1962 to France and England.
He has translated French plays for the Hebrew stage.

Poetic works: *Pirhey Esh* (Tel Aviv, 1949), *Ad Alot Hashahar*
(Tel Aviv, 1959), *Shirey Hotam* (Tel Aviv: Hakibbutz Hameuhad,
1953), *Shoshanat Haruhot* (Tel Aviv: Hakibbutz Hameuhad, 1961).

The poems translated in this volume were taken from *Shirey
Hotam* (1953) ("The Silent Words" and "Requiescat") and
Shoshanat Haruhot (1961) ("His Mother," "Pictures of the Jews,"
"Odysseus," and "Piyyut for Rosh Hashana"), both published by
Hakibbutz Hameuhad, Tel Aviv.

AMIHAI, YEHUDA (1924 — —)
Born in Wurzburg, Germany, he went to Palestine in 1936 and was
graduated from Bet Sefer Maaleh in Jerusalem. From 1942 to 1946
he served in the British Army, and in 1954 in the Palmach of the
Israeli Army. After the War he completed his studies at the Hebrew
University and now lives in Jerusalem where he teaches Hebrew
literature and Bible in the secondary schools. He received the
Shlonsky Prize for poetry. The Schocken Press has published his
short stories and brought out his first novel in 1963.

Poetic works: *Achshav Ubeyamim H'aherim* (Tel Aviv: Hakibbutz

Hameuhad, 1955) and *Bemerhak Shtay Tikvot* (Tel Aviv: Hakibbutz Hameuhad, 1958).

The poems translated in this volume were taken from *Bemerhak Shtay Tikvot* (Tel Aviv: Hakibbutz Hameuhad, 1958).

HUSS, AVRAHAM (1924 — —)
Born in Poland, he went to Israel in 1932, attended school in Jerusalem, and received a M.Sc. in physics from the Hebrew University. He fought in the Israeli Army in 1948. After the War he did graduate studies at Imperial College, London, and received a Ph.D. in meteorology at the Hebrew University. His poetry and critical reviews appeared in literary journals in Israel. Translations of his poetry have appeared in American and European journals. In 1959 he was research associate at the University of California and is now a lecturer in meteorology at the Hebrew University.

The poems translated in this volume were taken from *Molad,* 1951.

GALAI, BENYAMIN (1921 — —)
Born in Russia, he went to Israel in 1928 and was graduated from the Gymnasia Hertzelia in Tel Aviv. During World War II he served in the British Air Force in North Africa, and in 1948 with the Israeli Army. He works as a public-relations consultant for the municipality of Haifa.

Poetic works: *Im Haruah* (1946), *Armonim* (1950), *Shivah Shelishit* (1954), *Al Hof Harahamim* (1958).

The poems translated in this volume were taken from *Dor Baaretz, antologiah shel sifrut Yisraelit* (Merhaviah: Sifriyat Poalim, 1958).

RIVNER, TUVIA (1924 — —)
Born in Czechoslovakia, he went to Israel as a child and completed his schooling there. He fought in the Israeli Army in 1948. He was with his wife when she was killed while riding in a bus that was ambushed. He has remarried and now lives with his family in Kibbutz Merhaviah, where he is a teacher and a librarian. He has published critical reviews as well as poetry.

Poetic works: *Haesh Asher Baeven* (Merhaviah: Sifriyat Poalim, 1959) and *Shirim Limtzo Et* (Merhaviah: Sifriyat Poalim, 1961).

The poems translated in this volume were taken from *Haesh Asher Baeven* (Merhaviah: Sifriyat Poalim, 1959).

HILLEL, OMER [OMER, HILLEL] (1926 ——)
Born in Kibbutz Mishmar Haemek, he finished his secondary
education there. During the War in 1948 he served in the Palmach
of the Israeli Army. After the War he studied for two years at the
Ecole Nationale d'Horticulture, Versailles. He lives in Tel Aviv,
where he is a landscape architect.
Poetic works: *Eretz Tzaharayim* (Tel Aviv: Kibbutz Hameuhad,
1950) and *Eretz Tzaharayim* (Tel Aviv: Kibbutz Hameuhad, 1957).
The poem translated in this volume was taken from *Eretz
Tzaharayim* (Tel Aviv: Kibbutz Hameuhad, 1957).

CARMI, T. (1925 ——)
Born in New York City, the son of a Hebrew teacher, he lived in
Palestine from 1931 to 1934. After graduating from Yeshivah
University in New York, he did postgraduate work at Columbia
University and later at the Hebrew University in Jerusalem. In
1946 he worked in France, in the orphanages for refugee children.
He settled in Israel in 1947 and was in the Air Force during the
War for Independence. He works as a translator and editor. His
translations of contemporary dramas by Bertold Brecht, Christo-
pher Fry, Edward Albee, Brendan Behan, and John Osborne have
appeared on the Israeli stage. He has also translated from the
poetry of Wallace Stevens. He received the Shlonsky Prize for
poetry.
Poetic works: *Moum v'halom* (Merhaviah: Mahberet L'Sifrut,
1951), *Eyn Prahim Shehorim* (Merhaviah: Mahberet L'Sifrut, 1953),
Sheleg B'yerushalayim (Merhaviah: Mahberet L'Sifrut, 1955),
Hayam Ha'ahron (Tel Aviv: Mahberet L'Sifrut, 1958), *Nahash
Hanehoshet* (Tel Aviv: Mahberet L'Sifrut, 1962). An English
translation of his *Selected Poems* was published in 1963 (New
York, St. Martin's Press; Andre Deutsch, London).
The poems translated in this volume were taken from *Eyn
Prahim Shehorim* (Merhaviah, 1953) ("René's Songs") and *Hayam
Ha'ahron* (Tel Aviv, 1958) ("She Sleeps"), both published by
Mahberet L'Sifrut.

TRAININ, AVNER (1928 ——)
Born in Tel Aviv, he was educated in Jerusalem and received a
Ph.D. in chemistry at the Hebrew University. In 1958–59 he was
a research associate at Cambridge University. He is a lecturer in
chemistry at the Hebrew University and has written a textbook

on physical chemistry. His poetry and short stories have appeared in Hebrew journals.

Poetic works: *Ayzovay Kir* (Merhaviah: Sifriyat Poalim, 1957).

The poems translated in this volume were taken from *Ayzovay Kir* (Merhaviah: Sifriyat Poalim, 1957).

MAR, YEHIEL (1921 ——)
Born in Poland, he came to Palestine in 1937 with Youth Aliyah. He was educated in the secondary schools of the kibbutz and was a member of Kibbutz Zeraim until 1943. In 1948 he was in the Israeli Army. Since that time he has lived in Tel Aviv.

Poetic works: *Melev Vanof* (Merhaviah: Sifriyat Poalim, 1951), *Kavim B'maagal* (Merhaviah: Sifriyat Poalim, 1957), *Mlo Hofnayim Ruah* (Merhaviah: Sifriyat Poalim, 1962).

The poem translated in this volume was taken from *Mlo Hofnayim Ruah* (Merhaviah: Sifriyat Poalim, 1962).